BLACK AWAKENING
IN
CAPITALIST AMERICA

BLACK AWAKENING
IN
CAPITALIST AMERICA

An Analytic History

ROBERT L. ALLEN

Africa World Press, Inc.

P.O. Box 1892
Trenton, New Jersey 08607

Africa World Press, Inc.
P.O. Box 1892
Trenton, New Jersey 08607

First Printing AWP edition 1990

Cover design by Ife Nii Owoo

Library of Congress Catalog Card Number: 90-80153

ISBN: 0-86543-172-8   Cloth
       0-86543-157-4   Paper

For black students and youth,
who must shoulder a burden
others have let fall

ACKNOWLEDGMENTS

Most books are the products of efforts by many different people. This one is no exception. Space does not permit me to note all of those who in some way aided in the preparation of this volume, but I would like to thank Pam Allen, Julius Lester, Conrad Lynn, Marty Olsen and Penny Schoner for their thoughtful criticisms and kind words of encouragement. I am especially indebted to Bill Mandel, who evaluated and criticized the manuscript with professorial diligence, offering many valuable insights in the process. Whatever worth there is in this book must be credited in large part to these friends. Whatever weaknesses remain are my responsibility alone.

A word of thanks also to the staff of the *Guardian* for permission to use material that appeared in somewhat different form in the pages of that publication.

R.L.A.

CONTENTS

BLACK AWAKENING
IN
CAPITALIST AMERICA

I. INTRODUCTION

The course of a social revolution is never direct, never a straight line proceeding smoothly from precipitating social oppression to the desired social liberation. The path of revolution is much more complex. It is marked by sudden starts and equally sudden reverses; tangential victories and peripheral defeats; upsets, detours, delays, and occasional unobstructed headlong dashes. It may culminate in complete victory, crushing defeat, or deadening stalemate. It may enjoy partial success but then be distorted by unforeseen circumstances. The final outcome is not predicted automatically by the initial conditions. The revolutionaries must contend not only with conscious reactionaries and counterrevolutionaries, but also with subtle social dynamics which act to stop or divert the revolution.

The black revolt is no exception to this process. Black America is an oppressed nation, a semicolony of the United States, and the black revolt is emerging as a form of national liberation struggle. But whether this struggle can be characterized primarily as a rebellion for reforms or a revolution aimed at altering basic social forms, even so basic a question as this cannot be given an unequivocal answer. Rebellion and revolution are interrelated but they are not identical, and no amount of militant posturing can alter this reality. It must be asked: Are black militant leaders simply opposed to the present colonial administration of the ghetto, or do they seek the destruction of the entire edifice of colonialism, including that subtle variant known as neocolonialism? The answer, as remarked, is not immediately clear. The reason for this lack of clarity lies partly in the fact that militant black leaders themselves are divided and in disagreement about what they are seeking. All speak of revolution. But revolution has become a cheap word in modern America. It is necessary to probe beyond oratory and rhetoric if one wishes to determine the substance and meaning of the black revolt. Initially, about all that can be said with certainty is that aggressive black anger, the distilled essence of four hundred years of torment and struggle, has burst upon the American scene. It is almost as though the scales of history, unbalanced by the spilled blood of countless black martyrs and heroes, were finally being set right by urban rebellions which were directly comparable to colonial insurrections.

The fact of black America as a semicolony, or what has been termed *domestic colonialism,* lies at the heart of this study. It is at one and the same time the most profound conclusion to be drawn from a survey of the black experience in America, and also the basic premise upon which an interpretation of black history can be constructed.

Many, blacks as well as whites, will object to the use of the term domestic colonialism to describe what they prefer to call the "race problem." Some object because they contend that the solution to the "race problem" is to be achieved by extending American democracy to include black people. Racial conflict would vanish as blacks are integrated into the American political and economic mainstreams and assimilated into American culture. Of course there will be problems, say these critics, but in the long run this is the only feasible solution.

Black militants (and many not so militant blacks) respond to this objection by asking what is meant by "in the long run." Black people have been on the run in this land for four centuries. Even after their so-called emancipation, blacks had to run several times as fast as whites just to maintain their status as impoverished and perennially exploited residents of the United States. These critics, say the militants, can cling to the myth of evolutionary change because they refuse to admit that for the oppressed victims of the United States, both at home and abroad, American democracy is nothing more than a sham, a false face which acts to hide the murder, brutality, exploitation, and naked force upon which the socioeconomic system of American capitalism is predicated. The critics deny the voices of protesters who, throughout the political history of this country, have indicted the masquerade of American democracy. They ignore a Robert Purvis, a black abolitionist, who more than one hundred years ago vented his contempt for "your piebald and rotten Democracy, that talks loudly about equal rights, and at the same time tramples one-sixth of the population of the country in the dust, and declares that they have 'no rights which a white man is bound to respect.' "[1]

But certainly things have changed since those words were spoken? Not so if one takes seriously the cries of outrage emanating from the supposed beneficiaries of change. Ernest W. Chambers, a black barber from Omaha, Nebraska, gave eloquent testimony to the illusory nature of "racial progress" when he told President Johnson's Riot Commission: "We have marched, we have cried, we have prayed, we have voted, we have petitioned, we have been good little boys and girls. We have gone out to Vietnam as doves and come back as hawks. We have done every possible thing to make this white man recognize us as human beings. And he refuses."[2] The consequence of this refusal was a black revolt which threatens to grow into a full-blown revolution.

The argument for democratization of the American social system assumes that there is still room in the political economy for black people. But this overlooks, for instance, the fact that black unemployment normally is double the rate for whites, and in some categories it runs at several times the white jobless rate. The jobs which black workers do hold are largely the unskilled and semiskilled jobs which are hardest hit by automation. Government-spon-

[1] Floyd B. Barbour (ed.), *The Black Power Revolt* (Boston: Porter Sargent, 1968), p. 49.
[2] *Ebony*, April 1968, p. 29.

sored retraining schemes are at best stopgap measures of limited value. Retraining programs are frequently unrealistic in terms of jobs actually available; people are trained in skills already obsolete. Realization of this fact led one female retrainee to exclaim: "We are being trained for the unemployed." Integration thus fails, not because of bad intentions or even a failure of will, but because the social structure simply cannot accommodate those at the bottom of the economic ladder. Some individuals are allowed to climb out of deprivation, but black people as a whole face the prospect of continued enforced impoverishment. Increasing numbers will be forced out of the economy altogether.

Blacks tend to blame whites as a whole for this situation, but not all American whites are blind to the implications of their country's history. Here and there a Truman Nelson will speak out in defense of the "right of revolution." Referring to the bitter lessons of the Reconstruction and post-Reconstruction eras, Nelson wrote:

> It is no answer to this argument of the right of revolution [as expressed, for example, in the U. S. Declaration of Independence] to say that if an unconstitutional act be passed, the mischief can be remedied by a repeal of it, and that this remedy can be brought about by a full discussion and the exercise of one's voting rights. The black men in the South discovered, generations ago, that if an unconstitutional and oppressive act is binding until invalidated by repeal, the government in the meantime will disarm them, plunge them into ignorance, suppress their freedom of assembly, stop them from casting a ballot and easily put it beyond their power to reform their government through the exercise of the rights of repeal.
> A government can assume as much authority to disarm the people, to prevent them from voting, and to perpetuate rule by a clique as they have for any other unconstitutional act. So that if the first, and comparatively mild, unconstitutional and oppressive act cannot

be resisted by force, then the last act necessary for the imposition of a total tyranny may not be. . . .

In sum, if there is no right of revolution there is no other right our officials have to respect.[3]

Nelson's analysis is essentially right. And implicit in it are the conclusions drawn by black revolutionaries: that the American oppressive system in its totality is "unconstitutional"; that this same system long ago decided and still maintains that oppressed blacks indeed have "no rights which a white man is bound to respect"; that the right of revolution is not something safely ensconced in the documents of Western history but is indelibly inscribed in the hearts and souls of all men.

But if all these conclusions are valid, then a violent conflict is in the offing. Peaceful coexistence is impossible if the contradictions are too great. It is precisely this possibility, nay, probability, of conflict, and fear of its consequences, which motivate some to discount any talk of domestic colonialism and imperialism. For if it is admitted that blacks comprise an oppressed nation, then it must also be admitted that as blacks press for liberation a violent and anti-colonial struggle becomes increasingly likely. Imperialist powers are not wont to relinquish gracefully and peacefully their proprietary claims over their colonial subjects. Hence to take seriously the concept of domestic colonialism is to require a revolutionary realignment on the part of those blacks and whites who support the liberation struggle. This is not an easy thing to do. It is not easy because of the depth of commitment required. It is not easy because more than a willingness to engage in revolutionary action is asked; another prime requisite is a willingness to study and to sort out the implications and repercussions of the revolutionary act. This means that the revolutionary must not only be armed with the weapons of his trade, but armed also with sufficient knowledge and political understanding to put those weapons to best use.

3 Truman Nelson, *The Right of Revolution* (Boston: Beacon Press, 1968), pp. 37–38.

6 BLACK AWAKENING IN CAPITALIST AMERICA

Of utmost importance for the revolutionary is a cogent analysis of the situation in which he finds himself. Many black writers and spokesmen have tried to define and analyze domestic colonialism. Back in 1962, social critic Harold Cruse wrote: "From the beginning, the American Negro has existed as a colonial being. His enslavement coincided with the colonial expansion of European powers and was nothing more or less than a condition of domestic colonialism. Instead of the United States establishing a colonial empire in Africa, it brought the colonial system home and installed it in the Southern states. When the Civil War broke up the slave system and the Negro was emancipated, he gained only partial freedom. Emancipation elevated him only to the position of a semi-dependent man, not to that of an equal or independent being. . . . The only factor which differentiates the Negro's status from that of a pure colonial status is that his position is maintained in the 'home' country in close proximity to the dominant racial group.⁴

Malcolm X sought to relate the black freedom movement to the general and anticolonial revolt taking place throughout the world. After his assassination, this ideological work was continued by SNCC (and later by the Black Panthers), which viewed black people as an internal colony of the United States. At a meeting of Latin American revolutionaries in Cuba in 1967, Stokely Carmichael elaborated upon this theme:

> We greet you as comrades because it becomes increasingly clear to us each day that we share with you a common struggle; we have a common enemy. Our enemy is white Western imperialist society. Our struggle is to overthrow this system which feeds itself and expands itself through the economic and cultural exploitation of nonwhite, non-Western peoples—the THIRD WORLD.

Black people in the United States are a part of this Third World, Carmichael said, and he continued:

⁴ Harold Cruse, *Rebellion or Revolution?* (New York: William Morrow & Co., 1968), pp. 76–77.

Our people are a colony within the United States; you
are colonies outside the United States. It is more than
a figure of speech to say that the black communities in
America are the victims of white imperialism and
colonial exploitation. This is in practical economic and
political terms true.

There are over thirty million of us in the United
States. For the most part we live in sharply defined areas
in the rural black belt areas and shantytowns of the
South, and more and more in the slums of the northern
and western industrial cities. It is estimated that in another five to ten years, two-thirds of our thirty million
will be in the ghettos—in the heart of the cities. Joining
us are the hundreds and thousands of Puerto Rican,
Mexican-American and American Indian populations.
The American city is, in essence, populated by people of
the Third World, while the white middle class flee the
cities to the suburbs.

In these cities we do not control our resources. We
do not control the land, the houses or the stores. These
are owned by whites who live outside the community.
These are very real colonies, as their capital and cheap
labor are exploited by those who live outside the cities.
White power makes the laws and enforces those laws
with guns and nightsticks in the hands of white racist
policemen and black mercenaries.

The capitalist system gave birth to these black en-
claves and formally articulated the terms of their
colonial and dependent status as was done, for example,
by the apartheid government of Azania [South Africa],
which the U.S. keeps alive by its support.[5]

Perhaps the best starting point for an analysis of domestic
colonialism was provided by J. H. O'Dell, an editor of
Freedomways magazine:

. . . Generally speaking, the popular notion about
colonialism is one of an overseas army and an overseas
establishment set up by the colonial power thousands

[5] The text of this speech was published as a mimeographed
pamphlet by the Third World Information Service, 35 Johnson
Avenue, Thornhill, Ontario, Canada.

of miles away from its home base. Thus, the idea of colonialism becomes identical with an overseas territory and strange, unfamiliar people living on that territory. However, this picture of colonialism is a rigid one and does not allow for its many varieties. A people may be colonized on the very territory in which they have lived for generations *or* they may be forcibly uprooted by the colonial power from their traditional territory and colonized in a new territorial environment so that the very environment itself is "alien" to them. *In defining the colonial problem it is the role of the institutional mechanisms of colonial domination which are decisive.* Territory is merely the stage upon which these historically developed mechanisms of super-exploitation are organized into a system of oppression. [Emphasis in original.][6]

O'Dell's central point is that colonialism consists of a particular kind of institutional or social system, and this system does not necessarily have to be tied to a specific disposition of territory. It can take a variety of forms, of which domestic colonialism in this country is one.

From this thesis, a working definition and analysis of domestic colonialism can proceed. Broadly speaking, colonialism can be defined as the direct and over-all subordination of one people, nation, or country to another with state power in the hands of the dominating power. Politically, colonialism means the direct administration of the subordinate group by persons drawn from the dominant power. Thus, in the classic African situation, European officials controlled the parliaments and governments of the colonies. Although there may have been some token representation of the indigenous population, effective power was in the hands of the European settlers. This political control was buttressed by a legal system designed to serve the interests of the white settlers. Europeans sat on the courts and operated the prisons, and white-controlled legislative bodies made laws, which carefully discriminated between

[6] *Freedomways,* Vol. 7, No. 1.

settlers and natives application. Under this legal system there was no such thing as a native winning a case against a white man. Finally, this whole political and legal edifice was protected and maintained by colonial armies composed of white and native mercenaries or members of the indigenous population who had been press-ganged into service. These colonial armies were charged with enforcing undemocratic colonial laws and generally keeping the natives in a state of subjugation.

If the status of the black population in the United States before World War II is examined, a situation strikingly similar to this colonial model is immediately evident. Even after emancipation, in states where blacks constituted clear voting majorities, political power was usurped by whites. (The brief Reconstruction era was the only period when blacks held some measure of political power roughly commensurate with their numbers.) This was done openly and blatantly without even the courtesy of a shame-faced renunciation of the principles of democracy—principles upon which this country was supposedly founded.

Legally, black people were always at the mercy of whites. The Constitution decreed that slaves were not whole human beings, and a separate system of laws was relied upon in meting out "justice" to any unfortunate slave who provoked the ire of his master.

Each slave state had a slave code which was designed to keep slaves ignorant and in awe of white power. Slaves were forbidden to assemble in groups of more than five or seven away from their home plantation. They were forbidden to leave plantations without passes and they could not blow horns, beat drums or read books. Slave preachers were proscribed and hemmed in by restrictions; and slaves were forbidden to hold religious meetings without white witnesses. Other provisions forbade slaves to raise their hands against whites and gave every white person police power over every Negro, free or slave.[7]

[7] Lerone Bennett, Jr., *Before the Mayflower* (Chicago: Johnson Publishing Co., 1964), p. 93.

After Reconstruction these slave laws were in effect reinstituted in the form of the infamous Black Codes and segregation statutes. Under these codes "It was a crime . . . for black people to be idle. . . . In some states, any white person could arrest any black person. In other states, minor officials could arrest black vagrants and 'refractory and rebellious Negroes' and force them to work on roads, levees, and other public work without pay. . . . Special provisions in other states forbade or limited the black man's right to own firearms."[8] Right up through modern times laws such as these were vigorously enforced against blacks even though the "laws" may not have been formally inscribed in any codebook.

Behind the political and legal framework of domestic colonialism stood the police power of the state, the state militia, and the U. S. Army. As if this were not enough, an informal colonial army was created by the Ku Klux Klan and other "white citizens" groups. It was the armed terrorism of these groups that helped in successfully undermining Reconstruction. And anyone who has lived in a "modern" black ghetto knows, it is no mere figure of speech when the predominantly white police forces which patrol these communities are referred to as a "colonial army of occupation."

Colonialism is not, however, a system of domination and oppression which exists simply for its own sake. There are very specific factors which account for the creation and continuation of colonialism. "Colonialism enabled the imperialist powers to rob the colonial peoples in a variety of ways. They were able to secure cheap land, cheap labour, and cheap resources. They were free to impose a system of low-priced payments to peasant producers of export crops, to establish a monopoly-controlled market for the import of the manufactured goods of the colony-owning power (the goods often being manufactured from

[8] Bennett, *Black Power U.S.A.* (Chicago: Johnson Publishing Co., 1967), pp. 50–51.

the raw materials of the colony itself), and secure a source of extra profit through investment."[9] Certainly not all of these specific factors were operative under the American form of domestic colonialism, but general economic motivation was of utmost importance. The colonial subjects were transported from their native land and brought to the "mother country" herself. There they became a source of cheap labor for a rapidly expanding economy. In large measure the foundation of American capitalism was built upon the backs of black slaves and black workers. As with other colonial peoples, the colonized blacks were prevented from developing a strong bourgeois middle class which could engage in widespread economic activity and compete with the white masters. Instead, the blacks were restricted to providing unskilled labor in the production of raw materials (e.g., cotton) for "export" to northern mills and foreign consumers.

But colonialism does make for some class divisions within the ranks of the colonized. In fact, colonial rule is predicated upon an alliance between the occupying power and indigenous forces of conservatism and tradition. This reactionary alliance was made in order to minimize the chances that the colonial power would have to resort to brute force in preserving its domination. This was an early version of modern "pacification" techniques. Thus, the colonial power played tribes off against each other and used traditional tribal chiefs as puppets and fronts for the colonial administration. In return, the rajahs, princes, sheikhs, and chiefs who collaborated with the colonial powers were rewarded with favors and impressive-sounding but usually meaningless posts. Hence, although colonialism is defined as direct rule of one group by another, it does nonetheless involve a measure of collaboration between the colonists and certain strata of the indigenous population.

Under American domestic colonialism, since the African

[9] Jack Woddis, *An Introduction to Neo-Colonialism* (New York: International Publishers, 1967), p. 16.

social structure was completely demolished, the beginnings of class divisions had to be created among the slaves. The most important such division was between "house niggers" and "field niggers." The former were the personal servants of the masters. They were accorded slightly better treatment than the field hands and frequently collaborated and consorted with the white rulers. Vestiges of this early social division still can be found in black communities today.

Another important collaborator and force of conservatism was the black preacher. The black minister remains today an important, if not the most important, social force in most black communities. This is because historically the black preacher was the first member of the black professional class, the black elite. He frequently had, no matter how small, some degree of education; he enjoyed a semi-independent economic status, and he had access to God-given truths which were denied to ordinary blacks. Consequently, he was highly respected and looked upon by the black community as its natural leader.

While it must be said that the black church has performed an essential function in maintaining social cohesion in black communities through decades of travail and suffering, it cannot be denied that the black preacher is often identified as an "Uncle Tom," a collaborator. He is seen as a traitor to the best interests of his people. This is not a role which the black minister consciously assumed. Like the modern black middle class, he is torn with conflicting loyalties, sometimes drawn to his own people, sometimes drawn to the "foreign" rulers. The minister, in accepting Christianity, also in some degree identified with the major moral values and institutions of white society. Consequently it was relatively easy for him to work with whites, even though this sometimes amounted to a betrayal of blacks.

In general the black community experiences little difficulty in seeing white so-called morality for the hypocrisy and cant that it is. Yet the black middle class, of which the black preacher is only the most conspicuous part, as the artificially created stepchildren of white society, acts as though it is driven to uphold that society's values and attitudes—even when whites fail to do so themselves.[10]

Colonialism is more than simply a system of political oppression and economic exploitation. It also fosters the breakup of the "native" culture. Family life and community links are disrupted, and traditional cultural forms fall into disuse. Under domestic colonialism this process is even more destructive. Slave families were completely shattered and cultural continuity almost totally disrupted. The blacks who were kidnapped and dragooned to these shores were not only stripped of most of their cultural heritage, they soon lost the knowledge of their native African languages. They were forced to speak in the tongue of the masters and to adapt to the masters' culture. In short, blacks were the victims of a pervasive cultural imperialism which destroyed all but faint remnants (chiefly in music) of the old African forms.

(2)

Despite the analysis just made, there will still be those who object to the application of a framework of domestic colonialism to the internal structure of the United States. Their chief argument is that black people more and more are being granted the same political rights as those accorded to whites. The passage of a host of civil rights laws and their enforcement, even though less than vigorous, clearly supports this conclusion, it can be argued.

It must be admitted that there is some merit to this argument. Certainly the situation of black people has changed in recent years. However, whether this can be counted as anything more than a mixed blessing is the subject matter to be investigated in this book. To be more explicit, it is the

[10] It was this peculiar compulsion to which E. Franklin Frazier addressed himself in his classic study, *Black Bourgeoisie*.

central thesis of this study that black America is now being transformed from a colonial nation into a neocolonial nation; a nation nonetheless subject to the will and domination of white America. In other words, black America is undergoing a process akin to that experienced by many colonial countries. The leaders of these countries believed that they were being granted equality and self-determination, but this has proved not to be the case.

Under neocolonialism an emerging country is granted formal political independence but in fact it remains a victim of an indirect and subtle form of domination by political, economic, social, or military means. Economic domination usually is the most important factor, and from it flow in a logical sequence other forms of control. This is because an important aim of neocolonialism is "to retain essentially the same economic relationship between imperialism and the developing countries as has existed up until now."[11]

An especially instructive example in the methods of neocolonialism is provided in the case of Ghana. Ghana became an independent country in 1957 and projected throughout the progressive world the hope that all of Africa might soon be composed of free nations pursuing an independent, self-determined course to economic development. Kwame Nkrumah, the new nation's leader, was known as an outstanding opponent of colonialism and a champion of African unity. But in 1966 Nkrumah was overthrown in a bloodless coup and the face of neocolonialism—a neocolonialism which had been active in Ghana since independence—was exposed.

Briefly, Ghana achieved formal independence, but the government's belief that foreign financial and economic institutions could provide the vehicle for economic development resulted in Ghana's being subservient to foreign capital. Ultimately a coup was prompted by the contradictions stemming from this situation.

11 Woddis, p. 87.

Until 1961 governmental passivity and reliance on foreign economic institutions was Ghana's economic development strategy. For example, cocoa is Ghana's chief export product. The owners of Ghanaian cocoa farms are Ghanaian. However, the prices paid to cocoa producers and the export of cocoa were controlled by the British-dominated Cocoa Marketing Board. The CMB was set up in 1948 ostensibly to protect the cocoa farmer from the uncertainties of the world cocoa market and to provide a reserve fund which could be used to develop the country's economy. In actual operation, the CMB served as a convenient way for Britain to drain off Ghana's "surplus" capital. This capital was then used to enhance Britain's economic standing.

Imports from Great Britain into Ghana were controlled by the United Africa Company, a firm which was active in several African countries and which accumulated yearly net profits higher than the tax revenues of most of them. The UAC, because of its interest in maintaining its market for foreign imports, adopted a tacit policy of containing or taking over for itself any independent manufacturing operations which threatened to get under way in Ghana. Consequently, the UAC played a prominent role in preventing the development of a genuine and strong native, capitalist class. Rather, Ghanaian capitalists were kept dependent on foreign capital and foreign economic institutions. This entrenchment of huge amounts of foreign, merchant capital, coupled with the fact that foreign-owned banks largely controlled the availability of domestic investment capital, assured that Ghana could not be economically independent.

In 1961 Ghana sought to break free of the grip of neo-colonialism. An increasing balance of payments deficit, dwindling financial reserves, and failure to attract new foreign investment capital forced the Ghanaian government to search for a new development strategy. The government adopted a new Seven-Year Plan which held out socialism as a goal. However, by socialism the ruling Convention People's Party meant merely "a set of techniques and institutions which enable rapid economic progress and economic independence in the face of a colonial heritage."[12] It did not mean the restructuring of property relations and the reorganization of the whole mode of production which is normally identified with socialism.

In any event, the change came too late. Ghana's economic condition had deteriorated dangerously, and a new military-bureaucratic elite was preparing to replace the old political elite of the CPP. This new elite believed that by consciously acting in favor of the old colonial power (instead of "flirting" with socialism), and by proclaiming its intention to govern in the name of austerity and efficiency, it could resolve the economic problems with which Ghana was afflicted. But in reality this new elite was simply pursuing in revised form the old policies which the CPP advocated until 1961. And Ghana remains a victim of neocolonialism.

One further point deserves comment. Neocolonialism is a form of indirect rule, which means that there must be an agency in the indigenous population through which this rule is exercised. Fitch and Oppenheimer in their study of Ghana noted that:

> The colonial governments yield administrative powers to the "natives" only when vital British interests are reasonably secure. These natives must show themselves willing and able to serve as post-colonial sergeants-of-the-guard over British property: rubber in Malaya, land in Kenya, oil in Aden, bauxite in British Guiana. When no cooperative stratum has yet emerged, "independence" is delayed. Meanwhile, elements hostile to British interests are liquidated, shoved aside or co-opted.
>
> The problem for the British in colonial Africa has been to shape a native ruling class strong enough to

[12] Bob Fitch and Mary Oppenheimer, *Ghana: End of an Illusion* (New York: Monthly Review Press, 1966), p. 109.

protect British interests, but still weak enough to be dominated.[13]

The Nkrumahan political elite served for a time as just such a "native ruling class," even though the members of this elite were militant nationalists. When Nkrumah awoke to this reality and attempted to reverse himself, he was soon ousted from office.

(3)

In the United States today a program of *domestic neo-colonialism* is rapidly advancing. It was designed to counter the potentially revolutionary thrust of the recent black rebellions in major cities across the country. This program was formulated by America's corporate elite—the major owners, managers, and directors of the giant corporations, banks, and foundations which increasingly dominate the economy and society as a whole[14]—because they believe that the urban revolts pose a serious threat to economic and social stability. Led by such organizations as the Ford Foundation, the Urban Coalition, and National Alliance of Businessmen, the corporatists are attempting with considerable success to co-opt[15] the black power movement.

[13] Fitch and Oppenheimer, p. 12.
[14] For an insightful recent study of corporate domination of American society, see *Who Rules America?* by G. William Domhoff (Englewood Cliffs, New Jersey: Prentice-Hall, 1967). Domhoff concludes in this carefully documented study that an identifiable "governing class," based upon the national corporate economy and the institutions nourished by that economy, exercises effective control over the national government and indeed the whole of American society.
[15] That is, to assimilate militant leaders and militant rhetoric while subtly transforming the militants' program for social change into a program which in essence buttresses the status quo.
  Domhoff's conclusion is supported by an investigation of the American economy. In 1967, the most recent year for which complete figures were available, there were over one and a half million corporations active in the economy. Yet, of this

Their strategy is to equate black power with black capitalism.

In this task the white corporate elite has found an ally in the black bourgeoisie, the new, militant black middle

---

corporate multitude, a mere five hundred, the top industrial companies, accounted for nearly 45 percent ($340 billion) of the total Gross National Product for that year. Economist A. A. Berle has estimated that the 150 largest corporations produce half the country's manufactured goods, and that about two-thirds of the economically productive assets of the United States are owned by not more than five hundred companies. Markets for whole industries are each dominated by fewer than five corporations: aircraft engines, automobiles, cigarettes, computers, copper, heavy electrical equipment, iron, rubber, structural steel, etc. All of this places enormous economic power in the hands of a small number of semiautonomous firms. These firms in turn are controlled by largely self-perpetuating and interlocked managerial groups consisting in all of a few thousand managers and directors—the core of the corporate elite.

The fantastic economic power of these autonomous corporations has direct repercussions in the nation's political and social life. In fact, the corporations are a primary force shaping American society. Andrew Hacker, writing in *The Corporation Takeover* (New York: Harper & Row, 1964), remarked that "A *single* corporation can draw up an investment program calling for the expenditure of several billions of dollars on new plants and products. A decision such as this *may well determine the quality of life for a substantial segment of society:* Men and materials will move across continents; old communities will decay and new ones will prosper; tastes and habits will alter; new skills will be demanded, and the education of a nation will adjust itself accordingly; even government will fall into line, providing public services that corporate developments make necessary." (Emphasis added; p. 10.)

Multiply this by five hundred, and the magnitude of corporate power is immediately evident. More and more, a relative handful of firms dominate the society, yet they are not subject to the sort of democratic checks and balances which are (formally, at least) imposed on the government. These firms can decisively affect the fate of American society, but they are not controlled by that society. Consequently, bringing corporate power under social control should be a major problem listed on the public agenda.

class which became a significant social force following World War II. The members of this class consist of black professionals, technicians, executives, professors, government workers, etc., who got their new jobs and new status in the past two decades.[16] They were made militant by the civil rights movement; yet many of them have come to oppose integrationism because they have seen its failures. Like the black masses, they denounced the old black elite of Tomming preachers, teachers, and businessmen-politicians. The new black elite seeks to overthrow and take the place of this old elite. To do this it has forged an informal alliance with the corporate forces which run white (and black) America.

The new black elite announced that it supported black power. Undoubtedly, many of its members were sincere in this declaration, but the fact is that they spoke for themselves as a class, not for the vast majority of black people who are not middle class. In effect, this new elite told the power structure: "Give us a piece of the action and we will run the black communities and keep them quiet for you." Recognizing that the old "Negro leaders" had become irrelevant in this new age of black militancy and black revolt, the white corporatists accepted this implicit invitation and encouraged the development of "constructive" black power. They endorsed the new black elite as their tacit agents in the black community, and black self-determination has come to mean control of the black community by a "native" elite which is beholden to the white power structure.

Thus, while it is true that blacks have been granted formal political equality, the prospect is—barring any radical

[16] In size this new black middle class is still quite small, although it has grown rapidly. A rough estimate of its dimensions can be gathered from the fact that in 1966 about one-eighth of all black families had annual incomes of $10,000 or more. In that same year, however, more than 70 per cent of black families received incomes of less than $7,000, and about half of these reported incomes below the poverty level.

changes—that black America will continue to be a semi-colony of white America, although the colonial relationship will take a new form.

But this is getting into the substance of the study. To understand the meaning of this process and how it has come about, it is necessary to recall the events of a certain summer day when a new phrase was thrust into the popular American vocabulary.

II. THE SOCIAL CONTEXT
OF BLACK POWER

In the summer of 1966 two events occurred which were to have momentous impact on the black liberation movement. Superficially they appeared unrelated, but both were responses to the oppression of black people in the United States and, in the dialectic of history, they were to become deeply intertwined. The setting for the first event was a hot summer day in Mississippi. James Meredith, the first black man to graduate from the University of Mississippi, had been making his famous "march against fear" through his home state. Joining the march were FBI men, newspaper reporters and photographers, assorted well-wishers, and Stokely Carmichael. It was June.

Carmichael was then new to his post as chairman of the Student Nonviolent Coordinating Committee, but he was no stranger to Mississippi. Mississippi was an especially hated symbol of black oppression. Carmichael was intimately acquainted with the economic deprivation and political disenfranchisement which still, despite so-called civil rights legislation, were the central facts of life for the black residents of that state. He knew of Mississippi violence—the violence which struck down Meredith just shortly after his bold journey began. He knew that demonstrations and marches had not, and could not, substantially alter these facts. He and other SNCC staff members had been searching for some other more efficacious and direct means for attacking a monolithic exploitative edifice which seemed impregnable and without moral compunction. They thought they had found a solution in the idea

of black political power. Willie Ricks, another SNCC
staffer on the Meredith march, reduced this concept to two
words: black power. The two words were forcefully ex-
pressive and could be used to make a lively chant, as
Carmichael and Ricks soon showed.

The news media pounced upon this new slogan. They
treated it as a hot item and flashed the chant across the
country, much to the consternation of a nervous American
public. At that time nobody outside of a handful of people
in SNCC could give a rational explanation of what black
power meant. But many black people who heard the new
expression grasped its essence easily. It related directly to
their experience, their lack of power. On the other hand,
the mass mind of white America was gripped with fear
and horror at the thought that blackness and power could
be conjoined.

The second event of concern to us in that summer was
much less dramatic, although of equal importance, and its
implications were not to become the subject of hysterical
debates. In fact, except among insiders who knew better,
if was almost a routine occasion. Certainly an address by
McGeorge Bundy, president of the multi-million-dollar
Ford Foundation, to the annual banquet of the National
Urban League in Philadelphia could not be construed as
headline-making news. Bundy told the Urban Leaguers
that the Ford Foundation, the biggest foundation in the
country, had decided to help in the task of achieving "full
domestic equality for all American Negroes." This announcement came as no immediate surprise to Bundy's
hearers. For some time the foundation had been involved in
efforts to upgrade black higher education, and it had given
money to Urban League projects in the field of housing. It was, therefore, logical to think that in time the foundation might expand these efforts.

What the Urban League delegates and the American
public did not know was that the gigantic Ford Foundation,
which already had fashioned for itself a vanguard role in
the neocolonial penetration of the Third World, was on

the eve of attempting a similar penetration of the black militant movement. This was the hidden relationship between black power chants in Mississippi and the August meeting in the City of Brotherly Love. Both events represented responses, although with totally different objectives, to the crisis that trapped the black population and to the by then obvious fact that the formal gains won by the civil rights movement had not solved the problem of oppression of the black nation.

(2)

The interrelation of the Ford Foundation and black power cannot be understood without first recalling the social context in which the black freedom movement found itself in the summer of 1966. The main ingredients of this context were: The civil rights phase of the black liberation struggle was drawing to a stalemated conclusion, and, in its wake, followed the urban revolts, sparked by stagnating conditions in the ghettos; new leaders, such as Robert Williams and Malcolm X, who were the cutting edge of an embryonic nationalist movement, had been destroyed before they could organize an effective and continuing cadre of followers; and, finally, the Vietnam war and other developments in the Third World were having an increasing impact on black militant thinking in the United States.

To begin, the traditional southern-based nonviolent civil rights movement had largely ground to a halt and was in its death throes. Innumerable demonstrations and marches in countless cities had drawn thousands upon thousands of black people into hopeful activity. They let themselves be brutalized, beaten, jailed, and killed, following the admonitions of moralizing leaders who told them to "love your enemy" and "turn the other cheek." All of this suffering must surely culminate in freedom some day, the leaders said.

By the summer of 1963, after years of intense struggle

and many deaths, it seemed that some dramatic new step must be taken to bring the longed-for freedom a little closer. Grass-roots leaders talked about marching on Washington and shutting that city down until blacks were granted full equality. But this militant sentiment was quickly co-opted by the Kennedy Administration and the liberal-labor coalition in the Democratic party, which has long claimed the black vote as its inalienable possession. Thus, the March on Washington, which drew over 250,000 participants, became a summer picnic held in the honor of John Kennedy and his civil rights bill, which blacks were led to believe was the answer to their prayers.

But not all was sweetness and light on that noteworthy day. There was dissent and grumbling in the wings. John Lewis, then chairman of SNCC, had written a militant speech not in keeping with the harmonious feelings scheduled to be put on public display in the capital. The speech was censored by march organizers. The uncensored version read in part:

> In good conscience, we cannot support the Administration's civil rights bill, for it is too little, and too late. There's not one thing in the bill that will protect our people from police brutality. . . . What is in the bill that will protect the homeless and starving people of this nation? What is there in this bill to insure the equality of a maid who earns $5.00 a week in the home of a family whose income is $100,000 a year?[1]

Lewis was asking pertinent questions, but these were "outside" the sphere of civil rights and, therefore, were not appropriate areas for federal intervention.

The Civil Rights Law that was eventually passed in 1964 required, at least on paper, the ending of racial discrimination in voting procedures, certain areas of public accommodation and public facilities, and some places of employment. It also provided for public school desegregation. The

[1] Joanne Grant (ed.), *Black Protest* (Greenwich, Connecticut: Fawcett Publications, Inc., 1968), p. 375.

catch, in this and in the 1965 Voting Rights Act, was in enforcement. Blacks who believed that their civil rights had been infringed upon were required to go through lengthy and elaborate procedures to secure redress. Even so, enforcement was slow, sporadic, and largely ineffective. Federal registrars were sent in, occasionally. Some of the worst areas they never reached. The net result of this procrastination was that black people and their leaders were educated to the fact that legislation means nothing without effective enforcement. And enforcement, particularly when legislation flies in the face of social convention or established interests, depends on power. The federal government had the power, but it needed the support of the southern reactionaries who chaired major committees in the Senate and House. Hence, civil rights laws became merely more testimony to the truism that American democracy is subservient to the economic and political interests of those who hold power.

The experience of the Mississippi Freedom Democratic party in 1964 provided more confirmation of this fact. Voter registration drives were a central concern of SNCC from 1961 to 1965. At that time SNCC activists thought that voting strength could be used effectively to pressure the national Democratic party—a party that claimed to be the friend of black people. Thus SNCC decided that by creating a parallel political structure in the form of the MFDP, they could then challenge and defeat the racist Mississippi Democratic party at the national convention in Atlantic City. By pledging their unwavering loyalty to the national slate, which the "regular" delegation did not, the MFDP dissidents believed they could secure the ouster of the racist state delegation and, thereby, record a victory for the democratic process. But the national party, seeking support in the South, decided to employ the vicious weapon of racism once again and rebuffed the challengers.[2] This

[2] The fact that four years later the challengers were seated at the Chicago convention was more indicative of the growing militance of the Afro-American movement than suggestive of

was another bitter but enlightening lesson for the black movement.

The civil rights movement failed not only because of these setbacks but also because even the small victories it won benefited mainly the black middle class, not the bulk of the black poor. Thus blacks who were "qualified" could get jobs. If there were no jobs in industry, there were frequently openings in the anti-poverty programs for those with suitable credentials. After desegregation laws were passed, more affluent blacks could dine at downtown restaurants or take in shows at previously segregated theaters. Those who had the money and the stomach for a fight could even buy homes in formerly all-white suburbs. In its heyday the integrationist civil rights movement cast an aura which encompassed nearly the whole of the black population, but the black bourgeoisie was the primary beneficiary of that movement.

Hence, in 1966, despite eleven years of intense civil rights activity and the new anti-poverty programs, the median income of a black family was only 58 percent of the income of an average white family, and black unemployment still ran twice as high as white unemployment, despite the war-induced prosperity which the country was enjoying. In some categories, conditions were considerably worse. Unemployment among black teen-agers ran at 26 percent. In the Hough area of Cleveland, which experienced a rebellion in 1966 and again in 1968, black unemployment in 1965 ran at 14 percent, only two percentage points below what it was in 1960. Another important indicator, the black subemployment rate, which reflects part-time work, discouraged workers and low-paid

---

any change of heart on the part of national Democrats. In 1964 the MFDP was itself a militant movement, but by 1968, national Democrats viewed the seating of a then comparatively moderate MFDP as a means of discrediting black militants and of proffering to black people the frail hope that electoral politics—under the protective wing of the Democratic party—was still a viable means for effecting social change.

workers, was 33 percent in 1966 in the "worst" areas of nine major cities.

The quality of education, despite some gains in the number of years of formal schooling attained, remained low. Thus black students tested out at substantially lower levels than white youths: up to three years' difference in "level of achievement" among twelfth-graders. Residential segregation proved to be the toughest nut for the integrationist movement to crack. In 1966 a survey of twelve cities in which special censuses were taken revealed *increased* rates of segregation in eight of them.

Perhaps the most significant indication of the middle-class nature of the civil rights movement was the fact that it did absolutely nothing to alleviate the grim plight of the poorest segments of the black population. As late as 1968, a group of six doctors found evidence of widespread and long-standing malnutrition and starvation in the rural South. The situation in the cities was little better. A joint 1967 report by the U. S. Bureau of Labor Statistics and the Bureau of the Census outlining the social and economic condition of blacks in this country concluded that "perhaps the most distressing evidence presented in this report indicates that conditions are stagnant or deteriorating in the poorest areas." In U.S. cities of one million population or more, the percentage of nonwhite families living in "poverty areas" between 1960 and 1966 remained constant at 34 percent. In New York and Chicago, however, the percentage increased. In Cleveland's Hough district, median family income declined over this same period. In the Watts district of Los Angeles also conditions did not improve.

It is in these figures that one sees clearly the genesis of urban rebellion. For poor blacks, North and South, the civil rights movement accomplished virtually nothing besides raising false hopes. The promised salvation was not forthcoming. An explosion was inevitable.

The explosion began in 1964 with the Harlem rebellion and fourteen other urban revolts. City after city was shaken as the conflagration spread across the country in subsequent "long hot summers." The rebellions were almost entirely spontaneous and unorganized eruptions, but they had an underlying drive, a basic logic: Most of the attacks and looting were directed against the property of white merchants who exploit the black community. This was the pattern in Harlem and a year later in the Los Angeles revolt. Black people were in a sense "reclaiming" the merchandise which had been stolen from them in the form of underpaid labor and exploitative prices.

By their actions the black "rioters"—who by no means were an insignificant minority—were vigorously repudiating the civil rights Negro leaders. They were calling for new leadership willing to confront head-on the problems arising from oppression and powerlessness, and who could speak to the needs of the majority of the black masses.

But such a militant new leadership, if it arose, would represent a direct threat to the established order, and, therefore, it would be suppressed and destroyed by any means the authorities thought necessary. Nonviolent demonstrations, while presenting a *moral challenge* to unjust practices, did not constitute a *threat* to the established distribution of power. It was clear who had the power and who didn't. If, however, blacks started arming, even if only for purposes of self-defense, then this was another matter altogether. For an unjust social system can exist only by maintaining a monopoly on available force. If those who oppose the unjust system are able to break that monopoly, then they are that much closer to destroying the system. So a Robert Williams, who in the late 1950s organized a chapter of the National Rifle Association among blacks in Monroe, North Carolina, could not be lightly dismissed.

Williams, in his capacity as chairman of the Union County chapter of the NAACP, had become personally acquainted with the workings of southern justice. He knew that the courts were in open and blatant alliance with reactionary governments and racist businessmen. "This court," Williams bitterly remarked to a reporter, "has proved that Negroes cannot receive justice from the courts. They must convict their attackers on the spot. They must meet violence with violence." For this statement he was suspended from the NAACP.

Williams was smeared by the mass media, and liberal whites who supported and encouraged the nonviolent movement turned their backs on him. Isolated and maligned, Williams reluctantly decided that he should not stand in the way of a movement which then seemed to be making progress despite its passive tactics in the face of police brutality. Williams stood aside as seventeen Freedom Riders came into Monroe to picket the county courthouse. The six-day protest by the handful of nonviolent demonstrators attracted a huge mob of racist whites who cursed and spat on the pickets. Tension mounted and finally the crowd ripped into the defenseless protestors as the police watched with smiles on their faces. Some of Williams' armed men came to the scene and rescued some of the demonstrators.

But Williams was caught in a dilemma. The protestors had unwittingly drawn into town thousands of angry racists, many of them armed. He and his rifle squad were greatly outnumbered and outgunned. To make matters worse, a middle-aged white couple, supposedly on a sightseeing trip, wandered into the ghetto. They were taken from their car and, in the confusion, threats were made against their lives and a futile attempt was made to use them as hostages in order to get the remaining demonstrators out of jail. Rumors flew throughout the countryside that insane blacks had kidnapped a white couple and were torturing them. Police planes began circling overhead and state police, local police, and deputized residents started massing for a bloody charge into the black community.

A decision had to be made. The odds were too great. The white couple was released unharmed, and Williams' group voted that he and his family should leave to avert a slaughter. Williams and his family escaped, first to Canada and then to Cuba, where they were given political asylum.

Williams lived in Cuba for three years and then went to China, where he now resides. Meanwhile, federal kidnapping charges were filed against him, making it impossible for him to return with impunity.

In Williams' case the authorities sought to suppress a militant and potentially dangerous (to them) movement by destroying its leadership. A few years later a variation of this technique, political assassination, would be used in an effort to destroy the young movement which had sprung up around Malcolm X.

Malcolm, the ideological father of the black power movement and one man to whom Harlem's angry masses looked for new leadership, was killed just fifty weeks after he officially broke with the Nation of Islam—the Black Muslims. During that last year of his life Malcolm made two trips to Africa and the Middle East which seriously influenced his thinking. He began carefully to re-evaluate the social and political ideas which he had accepted while in the Muslims. He set up the Organization of Afro-American Unity—patterned after the Organization of African Unity—which he hoped would implement his new ideas and launch a decisive attack on the problems confronting blacks in America. Assassins' bullets cut down this new beginning before it bore fruit.

Malcolm had become a follower of Elijah Muhammad, "Messenger of Allah," while serving a ten-year prison term for armed robbery. Before that he had lived in the underworlds of Harlem and Boston's Roxbury district. He was probably attracted to the Muslims by their open denunciation of the "white devils" as oppressors of the black race and Muslim campaigns for self-help and moral uplift among converts—factors which brought many ex-convicts into the Nation. Released from prison in 1952, Malcolm's keen mind and penchant for oratory soon thrust him into the top Muslim leadership. In 1954, he was appointed minister of Temple No. 7 in Harlem. He became the first "national minister" in 1963. Malcolm traveled over the country evangelizing, and establishing new temples, while adroitly sparring with critics. He was quick-witted, with a biting sense of humor, and he knew how to handle an audience—black, white, or mixed.

Malcolm was an activist, and this was at the root of his split with Muhammad. In the 1960s the Muslims were increasingly charged by black militants with talking tough but never doing anything. The freedom movement was gaining momentum, and it was no longer enough simply to denounce "white devils." The Muslims abstained from any form of political or social activism, and Malcolm was beginning to have his doubts about the wisdom of this policy. In his autobiography, he admitted that, while still in the Nation, he began to think the Muslims could be a "greater force in the American black man's over-all struggle—if we engaged in more *action*."[3]

But such ideas clashed with the aims of Muhammad and his lieutenants. Malcolm was suspended from the Muslims in December 1963, allegedly for his highly publicized "chickens coming home to roost" remark about President Kennedy's assassination. It soon became clear, however, that the suspension was to be of indefinite duration and that he was no longer welcome among Muslims. The following March, Malcolm announced that he was breaking completely with Muhammad. He said that he was willing to plunge into the civil rights struggle around the country because every local campaign "can only heighten the political consciousness of the Negroes. . . ."[4]

Carefully reshaping his thinking, shifting Muslim dogma and dropping unacceptable tenets while incorporating new ideas picked up from his wide experiences with non-Muslims, Malcolm started constructing his political ideology. He realized the need for unity among black people if they were effectively to attack racism and exploitation in America. He called himself a disciple of black nationalism,

[3] *The Autobiography of Malcolm X* (New York: Grove Press, 1965), p. 293.
[4] Quoted in George Breitman, *The Last Year of Malcolm X* (New York: Merit Publishers, 1967), p. 19.

which he carefully defined as the effort of blacks to organize a movement of their own to fight for freedom,
justice, and equality. The kernel of black nationalism, he
said, was the idea that black people should control the
economy, politics, and social institutions of their own
communities. Thus he identified black nationalism with
the general concept of self-determination.

After the split Malcolm no longer endorsed utopian
separatism: the doctrine that blacks should return to Africa
or devote their efforts to setting up a black state in the
United States. He still rejected integrationism, as either
phony tokenism or an attempt to assimilate blacks into a
decadent white society. Unlike the Muslims, who attributed the cause of black oppression to the evil of the white
race, Malcolm realized that it was in the structure of society to which one could trace, not only the roots of black
people's misery, but also the genesis of white racism itself.
In a speech in May 1964, Malcolm argued:

> The system in this country cannot produce freedom
> for an Afro-American. It is impossible for this system,
> this economic system, this political system, this social
> system, this system, period. It's impossible for this sys-
> tem, as it stands, to produce freedom right now for the
> black man in this country.[5]

In answer to a question from the audience he said, "It's
impossible for a white person to believe in capitalism and
not believe in racism. You can't have capitalism without
racism. And if you find someone and you happen to get
that person into a conversation and they have a philosophy
that makes you sure they don't have this racism in their
outlook, usually they're socialists or their political philosophy is socialism." He thus carefully and consciously
avoided falling into the defeatist trap of attributing racism
to "human nature."

Although he advocated self-determination for blacks,
Malcolm understood that this could never be achieved

[5] Breitman, *The Last Year of Malcolm X*, p. 33.

within the framework of an exploitative, capitalist system. Again, unlike other black nationalists, Malcolm realized that it was in the interests of militant blacks to work for change throughout American society. For it is only if the total society is changed, that the possibility of genuine self-determination for blacks can be realized. Black control of black communities will not mean freedom from oppression so long as the black communities themselves are still part of or subservient to an outside society which is exploitative.

Malcolm did not live long enough to elaborate fully a program of action. He did advocate that blacks engage in bloc voting, although he noted that sometimes, as in 1964, there was not much choice between a Republican wolf and a Democratic fox. In its statement of aims, the Organization of Afro-American Unity stated that it would "organize the Afro-American community block by block to make the community aware of its power and potential; we will start immediately a voter-registration drive to make every unregistered voter in the Afro-American community an independent voter; we propose to support and/or organize political clubs, to run independent candidates for office, and to support any Afro-American already in office who answers to and is responsible to the Afro-American community."[6] In the economic sphere the OAAU merely pledged that it would "wage an unrelenting struggle" against economic exploitation of all forms.

Malcolm realized that the system he opposed was based ultimately upon force, and that the dynamic of radical social change in America was moving inexorably toward a violent confrontation. In a speech in New York on April 8, 1964, Malcolm described the process he saw unfolding:

So today, when the black man starts reaching out for what America says are his rights, the black man feels that he is within his rights—when he becomes the victim

[6] Breitman, *The Last Year of Malcolm X,* p. 109.

of brutality by those who are depriving him of his rights —to do whatever is necessary to protect himself. An example of this was taking place last night at this same time in Cleveland, where the police were putting water hoses on our people there and also throwing tear gas at them—and they met a hail of stones, a hail of rocks, a hail of bricks. A couple of weeks ago in Jacksonville, Florida, a young teen-age Negro was throwing Molotov cocktails.

Well, Negroes didn't do this ten years ago. But what you should learn from this is that they are waking up. It was stones yesterday, Molotov cocktails today; it will be hand grenades tomorrow and whatever else is available the next day. . . . There are 22 million African-Americans who are ready to fight for independence right here. . . . I don't mean any nonviolent fight, or turn-the-other-cheek fight. Those days are over. Those days are gone.[7]

As though he wanted to be certain that his audience (which was mostly white) had not misunderstood, Malcolm added that the black revolt was being transformed into "a real black revolution."

Revolutions are never fought by turning the other cheek. Revolutions are never based upon love-your-enemy and pray-for-those-who-spitefully-use-you. And revolutions are never waged singing "We Shall Overcome." Revolutions are based upon bloodshed.[8]

Thus Malcolm saw the black revolt metamorphosing into a violent revolution. But strangely, at the end of this speech, he seemed to retreat from the position he had taken throughout his talk. "America," he said, "is the first country on this earth that can actually have a bloodless revolution." Why did he think this was so? "Because the Negro in this country holds the balance of power, and if the Negro in this country were given what the Con-

[7] George Breitman (ed.), *Malcolm X Speaks* (New York: Grove Press, Inc., 1965), p. 49.
[8] Breitman, p. 50.

stitution says he is supposed to have, the added power of the Negro in this country would sweep all of the racists and the segregationists out of office. It would change the entire political structure of the country."[9]

This was clearly inconsistent with the major thrust of his speech. Malcolm had no faith in the efficacy of political reform. Only a few moments earlier he had pointed out that the black man "can see where every maneuver that America has made, supposedly to solve [the race] problem, has been nothing but political trickery and treachery of the worst order." Malcolm apparently held ambivalent attitudes on the question of violence. He advocated self-defense; yet he knew that no revolution was made using the tactics of self-defense. He knew that the black revolt held the potential of turning into a revolution and that revolutions involve aggressive violence; yet he could conclude that America might be the first country to experience a bloodless revolution.

This ambivalence probably stemmed from misgivings Malcolm had about potential allies. He knew that for the black revolution to succeed it needed revolutionary allies, and he saw two possible sources of such allies: militant whites in the United States and the people of the newly emerging nations—the former colonies of Africa and Asia, and the oppressed people of Latin America. But he had grave doubts about so-called white radicals. He thought that many of them could not seriously identify with a struggle the aim of which was to undermine and destroy the basic premises and institutions of their own society. The remainder, he thought, would probably be co-opted: "You can cuss out colonialism, imperialism, and all other kinds of 'ism,' but it's hard for you to cuss that dollarism. When they drop those dollars on you, your soul goes."[10] As far as white workers were concerned, he had no faith at all that they could be anything but reactionary and racist.

[9] Breitman, *Malcolm X Speaks*, p. 57.
[10] Breitman, *The Last Year of Malcolm X*, p. 32.

With beliefs such as these, it would be natural for Malcolm to hesitate to advocate that blacks undertake anything more than self-defense. His major concern, wisely, was to prevent genocide, not encourage it. He knew that in a revolutionary situation only the presence of revolutionary forces outside the black communities could prevent mass slaughter of the black population. He saw no such forces in evidence, and therefore was forced to equivocate, torn between the seemingly conflicting needs of racial survival and social revolution.

In spite of his reservations about white radicals and militants, Malcolm still regarded them as potential allies. He believed that some whites were genuinely fed up with the system, and he thought that some type of alliance might occur if they could establish proper communication with black militants. "Proper communication," to Malcolm's mind, definitely was not the kind of black-white alliances that had existed in the past in which the black component was usually only an appendage to white-controlled organization.

In any case, such an alliance was for the moment only a secondary consideration; the first was the creation of black unity. Militant blacks, he said, had to consolidate their own forces, work out their own program and strategy, and build a strong movement before there could be any meaningful move toward an alliance with whites. The immediate goal of white militants, Malcolm thought, should be to build a viable movement within white communities. Any linkup that might then occur would be between equals.

It was in Africa in the last year of his life that he saw the best and most numerous allies of American blacks. He was implacably opposed to the thesis that since black people are only a minority in this country, they should accept the leadership of white liberals. Malcolm argued that black people should identify with the majority of the world's oppressed and downtrodden peoples and elevate the black freedom struggle to the level of an international struggle for human rights.

Malcolm believed that the people of Africa, Asia, and Latin America were victims of "the international power structure," that U.S. neocolonialism was the main weapon of this power structure, but that the colonial revolt had shown the enemy to be invincible no longer. International capitalism, he believed, was slowly being beaten back and replaced with various kinds of socialisms. At an OAAU rally in Harlem on December 20, 1964, less than a month after his last return from Africa, Malcolm said:

> Almost every one of the countries that has gotten independence has devised some kind of socialistic system, and this is no accident. This is another reason why I say that you and I here in America—who are looking for a job, who are looking for better housing, looking for a better education—before you start trying to be incorporated, or integrated, or disintegrated, into this capitalistic system, should look over there and find out what are the people who have gotten their freedom adopting to provide themselves with better housing and better education and better food and better clothing.
>
> None of them are adopting the capitalistic system because they realize they can't. You can't operate a capitalistic system unless you are vulturistic; you have to have someone else's blood to suck to be a capitalist. You show me a capitalist, I'll show you a bloodsucker. . . .[11]

That capitalism, in its colonial quest, bred racism was self-evident to Malcolm. In his view this partly accounted for the presence of racism in a supposedly egalitarian America. That same America had profited greatly from the colonial slave trade and now she stood as the "last bulwark of capitalism."

Urging that U.S. blacks "internationalize" their fight for freedom, Malcolm contended that black people, as victims of domestic colonialism, should view their struggle in terms of the worldwide anticolonial revolt; and he took concrete steps to make this more than mere rhetoric. He

[11] Breitman, *The Last Year of Malcolm X*, pp. 35–36.

formulated a plan for linking the domestic freedom movement to the international anticolonial revolt. "The civil
rights struggle," he reasoned in his April address in New
York, "involves the black man taking his case to the
white man's court. But when [the black man] fights it at
the human-rights level, it is a different situation. It opens
the door to take Uncle Sam to the world court. Uncle Sam
should be taken to court and made to tell why the black
man is not free in a so-called free society. Uncle Sam
should be taken into the UN and charged with violating
the UN charter of human rights."[12] At another point
Malcolm drew an analogy to give clarity to his argument:
"If South Africa is guilty of violating the human rights
of Africans then America is guilty of worse violations of
the rights of twenty-two million Africans on the American
continent. And if South African racism is not a domestic
issue, then American racism also is not a domestic issue."

On his last trip to Africa, in July 1964, Malcolm began
marshaling support for his plan to bring the American
racial problem before the United Nations under the human
rights provision of its Charter.[13] He was admitted as an
observer to the Cairo conference of the OAU, where he
made an impassioned plea for the African nations to
arraign the United States before the UN. He also made
personal visits to individual heads of African states. Malcolm's activities in Africa caused deep concern in Washington. The New York *Times* reported that State De-

[12] This was not the first time blacks had sought to arraign the
U.S. before the United Nations. Nearly two decades ago the
Civil Rights Congress under the leadership of attorney William
L. Patterson presented a petition to the UN charging the U.S.
government with committing the crime of genocide against the
black race. The petition contained 135 pages of damning evidence implicating the entire governmental structure of the U.S.
in the systematic oppression, maiming and murder of black
men, women and children.
[13] Malcolm's hopes for implementing this plan might also have
played a part in his ambivalent feelings concerning the necessity for a violent revolution.

partment officials said that if "Malcolm succeeded in convincing just one African government to bring up the charge at the United Nations, the United States government would be faced with a touchy problem." The newspaper report said the United States would find itself in the same category as South Africa in a debate before the world body.

Throughout his travels in Africa, Malcolm was followed. On July 23, 1964, the day before he was to address the OAU conference, his food was poisoned at his hotel in Cairo, and he was seriously ill. On his return to the United States, Malcolm became a familiar figure at the UN. By the fall of 1964 his plan to indict the U. S. Government was in high gear, and Malcolm was becoming an increasingly serious threat to U.S. overseas interests. It was reported that the State Department attributed to Malcolm's activities a good part of the strong stand taken by African states against U.S. intervention in the Congo. As long as Malcolm remained in Muhammad's Nation of Islam, he was of no concern to the power structure. Freed of Muslim restraints, Malcolm threatened to bring the impact of the world revolution right into this country.

He did not live to see his plan come to fruition. On the morning of February 13, 1965, his home was fire-bombed— by professionals. He and his family barely escaped injury. Malcolm at first blamed the Muslims, but he soon suspected that other parties were at work. As he said, he knew intimately the Muslims' capabilities and limitations. The following Sunday the "other parties" were more successful. Malcolm was shot to death at a meeting in New York.[14]

The assassination threw Harlem into a panic. Many feared that a bloodbath would follow in which Malcolm's supporters and Muslims would gun each other down on the streets. As it turned out, the Muslim Temple in Harlem

[14] Malcolm's fears that he might be assassinated for political reasons were not the result of paranoia. See, for example, Eric Norden's article in the February 1967 issue of *The Realist*.

was fire-bombed but no one was killed. The more sophisticated were not afraid of such a mindless orgy of murder. They saw instead in Malcolm's death a continuation of a calculated pattern which began with the forced exile of Robert Williams, led to the jailing of Bill Epton, militant leader of the Harlem chapter of the Progressive Labor party, on "criminal anarchy" charges for his role in the Harlem rebellion, and now climaxed in the removal of yet another militant black leader: It was this continuing decimation of militant black leadership that posed the real danger, not a bloodbath triggered by warring blacks.

Malcolm X died, but not his ideas. One of the most important of these was how the struggle of blacks in this country was bound up with the outcome of revolutionary struggles in the Third World. This message was especially timely because it was at the end of 1964 and beginning of 1965 that the United States started its massive buildup in Vietnam, and Malcolm was one of the first black leaders to stand in opposition. He did so not because he was a pacifist or morally outraged. He opposed the war out of a sense of solidarity with the Vietnamese liberation fighters. Malcolm had great admiration for the courage of the Vietnamese guerrillas: "Little rice farmers, peasants, with a rifle—up against all the highly-mechanized weapons of warfare— jets, napalm, battleships, everything else, and they can't put those rice farmers back where they want them. Somebody's waking up." Implicit in Malcolm's admiration was his recognition of a principle which is fundamental to guerrilla struggles everywhere: namely, that the revolutionary spirit of the people is more effective than the enemy's technology.

Vietnam, one of three countries composing what used to be called Indochina (Vietnam, Cambodia, Laos), had been under French colonial rule since the latter part of the nineteenth century. But Vietnamese nationalism was irrepressible. Major nationalist uprisings occurred in 1916 and 1930. It was also in the latter year that Ho Chi Minh formed the Indochina Communist Party.

It is interesting to note that Ho, who visited this country
while serving as mess boy aboard a ship more than fifty
years ago, had a long-standing concern for black people.
As early as 1924 he wrote an article for a French publication denouncing lynching in the United States. That
article opened with the paragraph:

> It is well known that the black race is the most op-
> pressed and most exploited of the human family. It is
> well known that the spread of capitalism and the dis-
> covery of the New World had as an immediate result
> the rebirth of slavery which was, for centuries, a scourge
> for the Negroes and a bitter disgrace for mankind. What
> everyone does not perhaps know, is that after sixty-five
> years of so-called emancipation, American Negroes still
> endure atrocious moral and material sufferings, of which
> the most cruel and horrible is the custom of lynching.[15]

He also wrote an article for the same publication in
which he exposed and attacked the Ku Klux Klan. These
writings reveal that Ho, while an ardent Vietnamese pa-
triot and militant nationalist, was from the outset a revolutionary internationalist who understood the need for
solidarity among all oppressed peoples. In a later polemic
against French colonialism, Ho pointed out that the treatment of all "natives" is the same, be they Vietnamese or
Afro-Americans:

> Before 1914, they were only dirty Negroes and dirty
> Annamese [Vietnamese], at the best only good for pull-
> ing rickshaws and receiving blows from our administra-
> tors. With the declaration of the joyful new war [World
> War I], they became the "dear children" and "brave
> friends" of our paternal and tender administrators and
> of our governors—more or less general. They [the na-
> tives] were all at once promoted to the supreme rank of
> "defenders of law and liberty." This sudden honor cost
> them rather dear, however, for in order to defend that
> law and that liberty of which they themselves are de-

[15] Bernard B. Fall, *Ho Chi Minh on Revolution* (New York:
New American Library, 1967), p. 51.

prived, they had suddenly to leave their rice fields or their sheep, their children and their wives, in order to cross oceans and go and rot on the battlefields of Europe.[16]

During World War II Vietnam fell under Japanese domination. The Vietnamese patriots fought the Japanese as they had the French. With the withdrawal of the Japanese in 1945, Ho Chi Minh formally announced the formation of an independent, provisional government and proclaimed the Democratic Republic of Vietnam. Interestingly, the Vietnamese document proclaiming Vietnam's independence from France was modeled after the American Declaration of Independence. But independence was not yet secured. After the war the French returned and attempted to reimpose colonial rule. A long and bitter struggle ensued which culminated with the French suing for peace in 1954.

Under the Geneva Agreements it was decided that Vietnam, Cambodia, and Laos were to become independent countries. To facilitate the French withdrawal Vietnam was to be *temporarily* partitioned at the seventeenth parallel. Vietminh (guerrilla) forces were to withdraw north of this "provisional military demarcation line" and the French were to withdraw to the South before completely leaving the country. This partition was purely a matter of military expediency, and it was never intended to become a political boundary between two distinct countries. The Agreements also banned the introduction of more troops into Vietnam and promised that elections would be held throughout the country by July 20, 1956, after which, Vietnam was to be reunified. The United States did not sign the Geneva documents, but instead declared that it would refrain from the threat or use of force to disturb the Agreements.

But this American promise of nonintervention proved to be worthless. Within two years the U. S. Government

16 Fall, p. 73.

helped set up the dictatorial Ngo Dinh Diem regime in
the South. The elections were abrogated on the grounds
that "conditions in Communist North Vietnam made
free elections impossible." Diem instead imposed a vio-
lently repressive government on the South Vietnamese, and
although there was much propaganda about "land reform," action was not forthcoming. The harshness of the
Diem regime sparked uprisings in 1957. By the following
year Vietnamese indigenous to the South had begun organizing guerrilla operations against Diem. In December 1960,
the National Liberation Front was organized with its stated
goal of seeking to "overthrow the camouflaged colonial
regime of the American imperialists and the dictatorial
power of Ngo Dinh Diem, servant of the Americans, and
institute a government of national democratic union."
Within four years the NLF had brought the Diem regime
to the brink of collapse. American economic and military
aid was poured into the country. More "advisers" were
sent, but all to no avail. By the end of 1964 the situation
had reached crisis proportions. In January 1965, 30 percent of new recruits in the South Vietnamese army de-
serted. Everywhere Vietnamese students and Buddhist
monks were calling for negotiations and an end to the
fighting.

It was at this juncture that the Johnson Administration
decided on open military intervention (a euphemism for
aggression), including bombing of the North. The U. S.
Government had determined that at all costs it could not
allow South Vietnam to become a socialist country, American propaganda about "self-determination" and "freedom
of choice" to the contrary notwithstanding. There were two
basic and interrelated reasons for this. First, the United
States had entered the conflict to "stop communism—that
is, to enforce its interpretation of President Kennedy's
agreement to drop the policy of overthrowing Castro as
the price for withdrawal of Soviet missiles from Cuba in
1962. This interpretation was that a permanent delimitation
of the world into communist and capitalist spheres had

thus been arrived at. Second, U.S. officials wanted to insure that the rich natural resources of Southeast Asia remained available for exploitation by the "free world." According to an oft-quoted statement made in 1953 by President Eisenhower:

> If we lost Indochina and the Malay peninsula, the tin and tungsten we so greatly value from that area would cease coming. . . .
> Finally, if we lost all that, how would the free world hold the rich empire of Indonesia?—the prodigious supplies of rubber and rice—the areas of Thailand and East Pakistan?
> So when the United States votes $400,000,000 to help [the French in] that war, we are not voting a giveaway program. We are voting for the cheapest way we can to prevent the occurrence of something that would be of a most terrible significance to the U.S.A., our security, our power and ability to get certain things we need from the riches of the Indonesian territory and from Southeast Asia.

The conclusion to be drawn from such evidence as this is that the Vietnam war, far from being a mistake or an aberration, was the logical consequence of American imperialism. Its expressions in policy stem not from the personal whims of individual leaders, although personality does play a part, but from the necessities of the American socioeconomic system and its political manifestations.

The American escalation of the war prompted protest activity in this country. In the spring of 1965, twenty-five thousand antiwar demonstrators marched in Washington. As opposition to the war mounted, Martin Luther King urged President Johnson to issue "unconditional and unambiguous" pleas for peace talks. King's statement raised the question of a possible alliance between the civil rights movement and the antiwar movement. Robert Browne, an Afro-American college professor and activist in the antiwar movement, summarized in late 1965 the reasons favoring such an alliance:

(1) the recognition that the civil rights movement represents the moral conscience of America and therefore naturally belongs in the vanguard of the Vietnam protest, felt now to be the number one moral issue confronting American society.

(2) the argument that the billions of dollars being diverted to the Vietnam war represents funds which might otherwise be available for giving substance to the programs necessary for raising the Negro to a level of real equality in American life.

(3) the belief that the civil rights objectives are unachievable under the present organization of American society and therefore must necessarily be fought for as part of a large effort to remake American society, including its foreign policy.

(4) the view that the Vietnam war is intimately involved in American racist attitudes generally, and therefore falls naturally within the range of American Negroes' direct sphere of interest.[17]

Within the context of the moderate civil rights movement which still existed at that time, these were advanced arguments. The latter two arguments particularly were soon to be sharpened and used by black militants in their attacks on government policy.

On January 6, 1966, SNCC issued a statement opposing the Vietnam war and in essence supporting draft resistance. According to SNCC staffer Fred Meely in an unpublished report, the origins of this statement can be traced to a SNCC Executive Committee meeting in April 1965, during which chairman John Lewis urged the organization to take a formal stand against the war. The first big antiwar march—backed primarily by Students for a Democratic Society—was to take place on April 17, and the Executive Committee voted to support the SDS march. At a full staff meeting in November of that year, SNCC discussed at length the question of taking a public stand on the war, the draft, and the relation of the war to the plight of Afro-Americans. It was decided to have a state-

[17] *Freedomways*, Vol. 5, No. 4.

ment drafted and circulated to the staff for approval and
to hold workshops on these issues at SNCC's projects. The
statement was prepared and submitted for staff comment
in December.

On January 4, 1966, SNCC worker Sammy Younge, Jr.,
was murdered in Tuskegee, Alabama, when he sought to
use the "white" restroom at a gas station. This incident
precipitated the antiwar statement. "Samuel Younge was
murdered because U.S. law is not being enforced. Vietnamese are being murdered because the United States
is pursuing an aggressive policy in violation of international
law. The U.S. is no respecter of persons or law when such
persons or laws run counter to its needs and desires." The
statement continued:

> We are in sympathy with and support the men in this
> country who are unwilling to respond to the military
> draft which would compel them to contribute their lives
> to U.S. aggression in the name of the "freedom" we
> find so false in this country.

It suggested that the "building [of] democratic forms
within the country" was a valid, if not legal, alternative to
the draft. It would be a few months yet before SNCC took
an all-out draft resistance stand and began to develop a national antidraft program.

(3)

In summary, then, this is the social and political climate
in which Stokely Carmichael found himself in the summer
of 1966. Carmichael attempted to pick up the threads of
Malcolm X's thought and apply them to this social context.
But he was uncertain as to how to move. He was torn
between reformism and revolution. He could not decide at
that time whether he was a black rebel or a black revolutionary. His ambivalences were indicative of the uncertainties which permeated the black militant movement, and

they were a prophecy of the open split which was soon to develop between rebels-for-reform and revolutionaries.

Carmichael's class background was not unlike that of other SNCC members. Born in Trinidad, Carmichael came to this country at the age of eleven with his family and settled in New York City. After attending the elite Bronx High School of Science, Carmichael received a bachelor's degree from Howard University in 1964. While at Howard he was active in the student government as well as a local civil rights organization called the Non-violent Action Group. Thus, before joining SNCC, the up-and-coming young man was being primed for the black middle class. This was true of most SNCC activists in 1966. Although they may have come from poor or working-class families, the young students themselves were headed for middle-class status. Their whole college experience was designed to inculcate them with the values of the black bourgeoisie, including its terrible ambivalences and self-hatred. As E. Franklin Frazier and others have noted, the black bourgeoisie is divided between conflicting compulsions to identify with blacks or with the white middle class. Depending on circumstances, it vacillates between these two contradictory identities. The fact that most of SNCC's staff come out of such a background makes it easier to comprehend and account for the ideological twists and turns taken by the organization. These ideological waverings were reflective of the insecurity and equivocation of the black middle class, which SNCC in a sense represented.

In a widely read article published in the September 22, 1968 issue of the *New York Review of Books,* Carmichael struggled with the problem of power: how to attack and weaken oppressive white power and create in its stead the liberating force of black power. Most of what Carmichael wrote then was not new. It was based upon the nationalist tradition which extended from Martin R. Delaney through Malcolm X. Actually, it must be admitted that Carmichael's early statements did not go as far as the militant internationalism and anticapitalism of Malcolm X or the revolutionary violence then being advocated by Robert Williams from exile in China. But where Malcolm and Williams were stopped before they could organize a mass following, Carmichael was not. A young and charismatic leader, his ideas served as a catalyst for the intellectual development of black rebels and revolutionaries alike. Where Malcolm X had battered himself against a wall of hostility and indifference, the SNCC leader was successful in injecting the issue of self-determination into a black freedom movement which had appeared stalemated. The urban rebellions legitimized and gave prominence to this issue and made it a matter for serious discussion and planning among both black militants and the white power structure. Both were probing the strengths and weaknesses of the idea of black self-determination.

Starting with the "basic fact that black Americans have two problems: they are poor and they are black," Carmichael wrote that SNCC, "almost from its beginning," sought to develop a program aimed at winning political power for impoverished southern blacks. He did not foresee, however, that the growing militancy of the black middle class would lead that class also to demand political power. But political for the black bourgeoisie, the black elite, is not the same as political power for the black poor, the bulk of the black population. It is quite possible for this elite group to achieve a measure of political *and* economic power within the American capitalist system, but this does not necessarily imply any change for the black majority. Just as the civil rights movement made important gains for the middle class but left the poor largely untouched, there is no intrinsic reason to think a bourgeois black power movement will not follow a similar course. This is the central issue which later was to split the black power movement into moderate and militant factions, with the Congress of Racial Equality being a leading organization among the former while SNCC and the Black Panthers took the lead among the militants.

Furthermore, Carmichael almost certainly did not expect then that white corporate leaders would court and pander to the political and economic aspirations of the black bourgeoisie as a way of countering the revolutionary thrust of the militants. Just as early opponents of the Vietnam war thought of that conflict as a mistake inadvertently made by the U. S. Government, so did black power advocates in 1966 view black oppression as a curable malady which was basically foreign to the American social system. Certainly the more sophisticated war opponents and black militants talked about things being wrong with the system, but what they had in mind were *deficiencies* in the social structure. They were not yet thinking, as Carmichael later would, that perhaps the system in its totality must be redesigned. Instead, the antiwar people thought that the deficiency could be remedied by electing peace candidates to Congress who would end the war. The black power militants identified the deficiency as general lack of black participation in the political process.

As a result of this orientation, it was not surprising that black power emerged initially as an effort to reform the social system. At that time black militants were sophisticated enough to know that integration was not satisfactory because it did not change political relations and consequently could not affect the oppression suffered by most blacks. Hence it was logical to conclude that only the political integration of black people *as a group* into American society could offer any real hope. Therefore Carmichael defined black power as group integration into the political process. "In such areas as Lowndes [County, Alabama], where black men have a majority, they will attempt to use it to exercise control. This is what they seek: control. Where Negroes lack a majority, black power means proper representation and sharing of control. It means the creation of power bases from which black people can work to change statewide or nationwide patterns of oppression through pressure from strength—instead of weakness. Politically, black power means what it has always meant to

SNCC: the coming together of black people to elect representatives and *to force those representatives to speak
to their needs."*

A year later Carmichael would use virtually the same
definition of black power in the book which he co-authored
on the subject. In it, however, he made it explicit that he
thought of black power as only another form of traditional
ethnic group politics. "The concept of Black Power rests
on a fundamental premise: *Before a group can enter the
open society, it must first close ranks.* By this we mean that
group solidarity is necessary before a group can operate
effectively from a bargaining position of strength in a
pluralistic society."[18]

This belief that black people are much like other ethnic
groups in America lies at the heart of the reformist tendency in black nationalism. In his book, *The Crisis of the
Negro Intellectual,* Harold Cruse argues that if America
could only be forced to face the fact that competing ethnic
groups are its basic social reality, then a kind of "democratic cultural pluralism" could be established resulting in
genuine black equality. Nathan Wright, chairman of the
1967 Newark Black Power Conference, expressed a similar
view in his book, *Black Power and Urban Unrest.* Wright
urged black people to band together as a group to seek
entry into the American mainstream. For example, he
called for organized efforts by blacks "to seek executive
positions in corporations, bishoprics, deanships of cathe-
drals, superintendencies of schools, and high-management
positions in banks, stores, investment houses, legal firms,
civic and government agencies and factories."[19] Wright's
version of black power is aimed at benefiting the black
middle class. This bourgeois approach also characterized
CORE's brand of black nationalism.

[18] Stokely Carmichael and Charles V. Hamilton, *Black Power:
The Politics of Liberation in America* (New York: Random
House, 1967), p. 44.
[19] Nathan Wright, Jr., *Black Power and Urban Unrest* (New
York: Hawthorn, 1967), p. 43.

What this approach overlooks is the fact that black people are *not* like other ethnic groups in American society. To begin with, blacks came to these shores, not as immigrants seeking a better life, but as slaves intended for use as forced laborers. The racist ideology erected to justify slavery served after the Civil War to keep blacks oppressed and subservient, even though it was in the economic interests of white industrialists to hire black workers. But these businessmen, infected by their own racist dogma, preferred to import foreign labor. With the advent of the civil rights movement, the monolithic structure of racism began to show cracks, but by then it was already too late. Black people were to enjoy the unfortunate distinction of being among the first surplus products of an advanced American technology and economic system. Thus accelerated technological innovation in a decreasingly competitive and increasingly monopolist economy combined with racism have acted in concert to phase black people out of American society.

It would have made sense at the close of the Civil War to plan for the assimilation of black people as a group into the American mainstream. Racism made this impossible. Now, as racism begins to crumble, the requirements of an advanced technological economy increasingly exclude black workers from the active labor force. Hence racism, the stepchild of slavery, prevented black people from following in the footsteps of other ethnic groups.

Today, even if racism were vanquished, blacks would find their situation basically unaltered because almost always they do not possess the skills valued by the economy. Even under ideal circumstances, this lack of skills would require a generation to correct.

Finally, as city governments are increasingly integrated with state and federal agencies, and municipal political machines are disbanded, an important mechanism for ethnic group advancement is shut off to blacks. For it is city hall which has been a traditional stepping-stone to economic security and political power for European ethnic groups. The current move to rationalize city government and integrate it into the larger national structure is one of the prime requirements for the smooth functioning of a complex and advanced society. A consequence of this process is that city politics can no longer be a free-for-all scramble responsive to the ethnic group (or groups) which can muster the most votes. Instead, the city government itself becomes a mechanism for the realization of national priorities—and this necessarily tends to eliminate a major channel for the anticipated advancement of black people as an ethnic group.[20]

Economically, Carmichael in his *New York Review* article called for a cooperative effort among black people. "When we urge that black money go into black pockets, we mean the communal pocket. We want to see money go back into the community and used to benefit it. We want to see the cooperative concept applied in business and banking." This concept was later incorporated into the CORE program.

Economic cooperatives, frequently advocated in the past, were to be the salvation of the black community. But this economic program assumes that the economy is still open to new enterprises, be they individual or collective. This assumption is unrealistic in an era when small businesses are failing at a high rate and large-scale commercial enterprises, because of the virtual monopoly of gigantic corporations, are extremely difficult to launch. The Small Business Administration reports that not more than 3 percent of all U.S. business concerns are owned by non-whites. A flagrant example of this economic imbalance is seen in Washington, D.C., where about two-thirds of the

[20] There are vastly more blacks employed in government today than ever before, but this is not reflective of a net increase in political power for the group, since almost all of these positions are lower-level jobs which have no political weight.

population is black, but only some two thousand out of twenty-eight thousand businesses are owned by blacks, and their volume is only an infinitesimal fraction of the whole. This situation is not likely to change to any significant degree. The failure rate on special small business loans, many of which are granted to black businessmen, is about double the rate of regular loans.

More importantly, even if a cooperative economic venture were successfully initiated, its managers, in order to keep it afloat, would have to be responsive to the demands and constraints imposed by the over-all competitive economic system rather than to the needs of the surrounding black community. For example, a retail food cooperative would find itself in direct competition with huge supermarket chains, which control not only retail outlets, but also farms and ranches, processing and packaging plants, advertising agencies, and transportation and distribution facilities. Without this kind of horizontal and vertical monopoly, a cooperative business would encounter insurmountable obstacles that would make large-volume, price-competitive and efficient operation virtually unachievable. On the other hand, the establishing of a large-scale cooperative monopoly would be extraordinarily difficult because of the heavy financing required and the adamant opposition of firms already solidly entrenched in the industry. Hence a black retail cooperative would very likely find itself forced to charge higher prices or to operate at a loss.

Even if the cooperative somehow managed to survive these difficulties, benefits to the community from such a marginal undertaking would be minimal at best. The major beneficiaries from the cooperative would be the administrators and managers hired to operate it. After all, their salaries must be met before there can be any price reductions or dividend payments. Consequently, black capitalism, even on a cooperative basis, would function primarily to the advantage of middle-class blacks who have management skills—the class least in need of such benefits because it is increasingly favored by American society at large.

The need for "psychological equality" and "black consciousness" was also stressed in Carmichael's 1966 article. "Only black people can convey the revolutionary idea that black people are able to do things themselves. Only they can help create in the community an aroused and continuing black consciousness that will provide the basis for political strength." This thought would later be taken to its logical extreme by cultural nationalist Ron Karenga: "The revolution being fought now is a revolution to win the minds of our people." Karenga would argue that the black revolt could not proceed until the cultural revolution had been won. "We must free ourselves culturally before we succeed politically." The cultural nationalist would replace the hope of black revolution with a curious mystique encompassing black culture and art and reactionary African social forms. "To go back to tradition is the first step forward," wrote Karenga. In essence the cultural nationalists asked nothing more than that black people be accorded recognition as a distinct cultural group. If it meant pacifying rebellious ghettos, white America was only too happy to grant this minor concession.

The question of potential allies is perhaps one of the most difficult problems facing black militants. Carmichael struggled with the problem but without much success. He was looking for a numerically significant section of the white population which might become an ally of blacks. He thought that poor whites might play this role. "We hope to see, eventually, a coalition between poor blacks and poor whites." Yet, a few lines later, he stated: "Poor whites everywhere are becoming more hostile—not less—partly because they see the nation's attention focussed on black poverty and nobody coming to them." Carmichael suggested that middle-class young whites assume the task of organizing poor whites, but he didn't seem to have much confidence in the successful outcome of this project. Perhaps he realized that poor whites were as much trapped by their own racism as blacks were trapped by white racism. He certainly recognized this fact in the case of white industrial workers—long the hope of the white left—who, seeing their own security threatened, can now be counted among the most vicious racists in the country.

When the young white activists failed to "civilize" the white community, they were roundly castigated and attacked by black militants for not being serious radicals. But this easy criticism missed the point. If black survival really is at stake, as black militants are fond of asserting, then black radicals must assume primary responsibility for seeing to it that hostile whites are neutralized and friendly whites are won over to an effective joint struggle. This is not to say that black organizers should begin flooding into white suburbs. Obviously not. It is to say, however, that it is ridiculous to contend that racism and exploitation are the white man's problems. For if racism and exploitation are allowed to continue, it will be the black community as a whole, not sympathetic middle-class white students, which will be the greatest loser. It is thus politically irresponsible to lament that no domestic allies are in sight. The black radical, if *he* is serious, must take it upon himself to search out, and if necessary create, allies for the black liberation struggle.

The original formulation of black power as expressed by Carmichael contained not only the seeds of militant black reformism but also the genesis of revolutionary black nationalism.

Any social order maintains itself through the exercise of power, whether directly or indirectly. In particular, the groups or classes within a society which enjoy a privileged status as a result of the functioning of the social system seek to preserve that system in a stable equilibrium. They do this by accumulating and using power. Power is based ultimately on (1) the availability of force, and (2) the existence of pervasive social attitudes or social mythologies, accepted by all segments of the society, that justify the actual use of force against external or internal threats. Whether a threat exists and how it is defined is normally determined by those who hold power. In a theocracy, for example, force may be available in the form of a holy army, and the loyalty of the army is assured by a religious mythology which is accepted and internalized by soldiers and commanders alike.

In the United States force is available to the ruling structure in the form of police and army. These forces may be deployed in the name of "freedom," "law and order," or "the American way." This rhetoric is based partly on popular ideas about the nature of American society and partly on the social mythology of "private property rights," the defense of which is the most socially important ultimate—though not always immediate—justification for the use of force. Nearly all Americans believe, because they have been taught from childhood to believe, that those who are designated as "owners" have an inherent and inalienable right to use in any manner they alone see fit that which is termed "property."[21]

The social consequences of this belief are enormous. Thus the disposition of property, such as industrial plants, corporations, banks, retail and wholesale consumer enterprises, etc., which decisively affects the lives of millions of people and which derives its value and meaning from its *social nature* is left in the hands of private individuals or small groups whose overriding concern is the profits accruing from this property rather than its social utility. Profits

[21] The term "property" as used here does not refer to personal or family belongings such as clothing, a house, or an automobile. Rather, it refers to *social* property; that is, property (e.g., a supermarket) the use of which *requires* the active economic involvement of larger social groupings (e.g., employees, customers).

in turn create wealthy owning and managerial classes, and an economic dictatorship of these classes is subtly imposed on the whole society. The result is the partial nullification of political democracy.

That political democracy in the U.S. has not been totally destroyed is evident in the passage of reform measures and laws aimed at curbing the power of various economic interests. But at the state and national levels particularly, the country's legislative machinery has allied itself—through the apparatus of the Democratic and Republican parties— with one wing or another of the economic establishment. As this establishment is not yet monolithic there is room within its ranks for considerable dissension, conflict and change. Consequently, it is open to some outside pressure for reform, but it is not open to an attack on its own position of power nor will it knowingly tolerate an effective challenge to the social fiction on which that power is predicated.

The socially shared belief in the sacrosanct qualities of private property is a fundamental premise of the ideology of capitalism. To the extent that the general American population accepts the mythology of private property—that is, the notion that private individuals should be the sole determinants of the disposition of what is in reality social property—it will continue to defend the privileges and prerogatives of those classes which benefit most from this mythology. The reason for this is that the educational system implants and reinforces the belief that this social myth can operate to the *individual* advantage of any given person if only he works hard enough or displays sufficient cunning. Hence many an American, even if sophisticated enough to recognize the injustices of the social system, will nevertheless vigorously defend it because of the insistent hope that some day he or his children will achieve a full measure of security and comfort within that system.

This discussion raises several questions. Is the capital-

istic competitive game fixed? If so, why? Are there alternative methods of ordering social relations within a society? As far as black people are concerned, there can be
little doubt that the game is fixed. Blacks for the last
hundred years have been "free" to beat their way to the
top. Many have tried, but in relative terms, black people
today are just about exactly where they were at the close of
the Civil War; namely, at the bottom of the heap. In 1966
Carmichael knew that the game was fixed, but he was not
yet ready to deal with the question of whether it was the
nature of the capitalist game to be fixed. That is, he was
not at that point an anticapitalist. To take such a position
would require more time and thought.

The American social mythology of private property and
the government's monopoly on force were both implicitly
challenged in the 1966 article. This challenge was made
explicit by the urban rebellions which have occurred since
1964. Carmichael raised the question of whether a country
"where property is valued above all" could be the setting
for a humanistic society. He recognized that it was this
ideology which justified the use of force against black
people—be they called "uppity niggers," "rioters," or just
plain "criminals." That being the case, one could only
conclude, as Carmichael did, that the black man "may
also need a gun and SNCC reaffirms the right of black men
everywhere to defend themselves when threatened or attacked."

Carmichael couched these implicitly revolutionary
thoughts in cautious language. Since 1966, however, it has
become ever more clear that the black revolt will be accompanied by violence because those who propagate the
mythology of property rights will not allow peaceful
change. It is precisely this social fiction of property rights,
and the system of force and exploitation which it justifies,
which stand as the prime enemies of black people. It is in
this sense that the looting which accompanied urban rebellions was a rudimental revolutionary act. Looting con-

stitutes a direct assault upon the edifice of private property. As sociologists Russell Dynes and E. L. Quarantelli have noted: "The looting that has occurred in recent racial outbreaks is a bid for the redistribution of property."[22] This statement expresses the objective social implication of an act whose immediate motive may be any number of personal or subjective factors. The question this poses for black militants is: Can such a redistribution be effected within the present social framework? Black rebels, advocates of bourgeois nationalism, think this is altogether possible. Black revolutionaries think not; they are increasingly anticapitalist.

Carmichael identified the black communities as exploited colonies of the United States. He added: "For a century, this nation has been like an octopus of exploitation, its tentacles stretching from Mississippi and Harlem to South America, the Middle East, southern Africa, and Vietnam; the form of exploitation varies from area to area, but the essential result has been the same—a powerful few have been maintained and enriched at the expense of the poor and voiceless colored masses."

This identification of the black struggle with anticolonial movements in the Third World had revolutionary implications. At the psychological level it shattered the sense of isolation felt by many black militants. They could view themselves as part of a worldwide revolution. "Black Power is not an isolated phenomenon," wrote Julius Lester, a former SNCC field secretary. "It is only another manifestation of what is transpiring in Latin America, Asia, and Africa. People are reclaiming their lives on those three continents and blacks in America are reclaiming theirs. These liberation movements are not saying give us a share; they are saying we want it all! The existence of the present system in the United States depends upon the United States taking all. This system is threatened more and more each day by the refusal of those in the Third World to

[22] *Transaction,* May 1968.

be exploited. They are colonial people outside the United States; blacks are a colonial people within. Thus, we have a common enemy. As the Black Power movement becomes more politically conscious, the spiritual coalition that exists between blacks in America and the Third World will become more evident."[23]

At the ideological level, Carmichael's thesis gave militant black intellectuals a powerful analytical tool. Black writer Lawrence P. Neal touched upon this when he pointed out that the colonial model "breaks down the ideological walls which have contained the struggle thus far. It supplies the black theorist and activist with a new set of political alternatives."[24]

If black people formed a dispersed semicolony within this country, superficially unlike other colonies, but sharing certain features with them, then a "new set of political alternatives" might exist in the form of a black national liberation struggle. National liberation stands in sharp contrast to the strategy of integration; and it represents a distinct advance over traditional black nationalism, which frequently drifts toward escapist solutions as a consequence of its unconscious defeatisms. In the years following World War II, national liberation movements flourished throughout the Third World. To the extent that the domestic colonial view of black America is valid, its theories and experiences can be of invaluable aid to the black liberation movement.

A Third World intellectual, who was to have tremendous impact on the thinking of black militants, was Frantz Fanon. Born in Martinique, Fanon was a black psychiatrist, who had studied medicine in France. During the French-Algerian War, he was assigned to a hospital in Algeria. However, he soon found his sympathies inclining toward the rebels. He subsequently joined the revolution

[23] Julius Lester, *Look Out, Whitey!* (New York: Dial Press, 1968), p. 138.
[24] Floyd B. Barbour (ed.), *The Black Power Revolt* (Boston: Porter Sargent, 1968), p. 141.

and served as a doctor, propagandist, and diplomat of the Algerian FLN. As such he was an articulate spokesman for the Algerian revolution. But he did not live to see the climax of that revolution. In 1961, it was discovered that he was suffering from cancer, and within a few months, at the age of thirty-six, he was dead.

Fanon produced a number of works dealing with the problems of national liberation. One of the most important of these was *The Wretched of the Earth,* which has since become required reading for black revolutionaries. It would be well at this point to recall part of Fanon's argument because it is especially relevant to the present stage of the black liberation movement.

Fanon first noted that the colonial world is divided in two. A dividing line is established between the natives and the colonists. This boundary is maintained by the police, who also have responsibility for enforcing colonial law within the native quarter. The natives are pacified and subjugated by brute force. This force dehumanizes the native. The colonists treat him as nothing better than an animal; he has no personality or humanity. He is simply an object to be used at the pleasure of the colonists. This is seen especially in the violence with which Western values are imposed on the native, and the native, in freeing himself, must ultimately reject them.

> The violence with which the supremacy of white values is affirmed and the aggressiveness which has permeated the victory of these values over the ways of life and of thought of the native mean that, in revenge, the native laughs in mockery when Western values are mentioned in front of him. In the colonial context the settler only ends his work of breaking in the native when the latter admits loudly and intelligibly the supremacy of the white man's values. In the period of decolonisation, the colonised masses mock at these very values, insult them and vomit them up.[25]

[25] Frantz Fanon, *The Wretched of the Earth* (New York: Grove Press, 1963), p. 35.

The prime message which the colonial rulers bring to the native is that he must submit completely to the newly established status quo. "The first thing which the native learns is to stay in his place, and not to go beyond certain limits. This is why the dreams of the native are always of muscular prowess; his dreams are of action and of aggression. . . ."[26]

"The colonised man will first manifest this aggressiveness which has been deposited in his bones against his own people. This is the period when the niggers beat each other up. . . ."[27] The native is forced to accept a status quo which he hates. In his anger he becomes irrational and turns against his family and friends.

Where individuals are concerned, a positive negation of common sense is evident. While the settler or the policeman has the right the live-long day to strike the native, to insult him and to make him crawl to them, you will see the native reaching for his knife at the slightest hostile or aggressive glance cast on him by another native; for the last resort of the native is to defend his personality vis-à-vis his brother.[28]

If the native does not express such pent-up aggression against his own people, then he sublimates it and it finds outlet in religious mysticism or art forms. The native is possessed by spirits and demons, or he exhausts himself "in dances which are more or less ecstatic."

But colonial forms do not endure indefinitely. The colonial power by its own actions helps to create classes among the natives which are capable of initiating an anti-colonial struggle: the Westernized intellectuals and the native commercial elite. These are the classes that frequently begin nationalist agitation and organize nationalist political parties. They array themselves in opposition to

26 Ibid., p. 41.
27 Ibid., p. 42.
28 Ibid., p. 43.

the traditional tribal chiefs who have cooperated with and sold out their people to the colonial power. But because they are themselves elites, standing on the backs of the native masses, the intellectual and native business classes alone are incapable of transforming the nationalist struggle into a revolutionary struggle aimed at liberating all of the native population. These classes vacillate, sometimes threatening to do violence to the colonial rulers, sometimes seeking to strike compromises which are advantageous to themselves. Thus Fanon wrote: "The native intellectual has clothed his aggressiveness in his barely veiled desire to assimilate himself to the colonial world. He has used his aggressiveness to serve his own individual interests."[29]

> Thus there is very easily brought into being a kind of class of affranchised slaves, or slaves who are individually free. What the intellectual demands is the right to multiply the emancipated, and the opportunity to organise a genuine class of emancipated citizens. On the other hand, the mass of the people have no intention of standing by and watching individuals increase their chances of success. What they demand is not the settler's position of status, but the settler's place. The immense majority of natives want the settler's farm. For them, there is no question of entering into competition with the settler. They want to take his place.
>
> The peasantry is systematically disregarded for the most part by the propaganda put out by the nationalist parties. And it is clear that in the colonial countries the peasants alone are revolutionary, for they have nothing to lose and everything to gain. The starving peasant, outside the class system, is the first among the exploited to discover that only violence pays. For him there is no compromise, no possible coming to terms; colonisation and decolonisation are simply questions of relative strength. The exploited man sees that his liberation implies the use of all means, and that of force first and foremost.[30]

[29] *Ibid.*, p. 48.
[30] *Ibid.*

Once the native masses begin picking up weapons, then the colonists become loudest in their pleas for nonviolence. They assert that nonviolence is the only way to achieve social change, and they invite the native elites into their offices to discuss the situation. The colonial rulers are particularly fearful because "blown-up bridges, ravaged farms, repressions and fighting harshly disrupt the economy." The native politicians unintentionally contribute to this unrest: "The politicians who make speeches and who write in the nationalist newspapers make the people dream dreams. They avoid the actual overthrowing of the state, but in fact they introduce into their readers' or hearers' consciousness the terrible ferment of subversion."[31]

When the native masses make their move and begin burning and destroying, then it must be admitted by all concerned that the colonial society is in deep crisis. "The authorities . . . take some spectacular measures. They arrest one or two leaders, they organize military parades and maneuvers, and air force displays." But these displays of force only serve to reinforce native aggressiveness. "The repressions, far from calling a halt to the forward rush of national consciousness, urge it on." The nationalist politicians are surprised by the insurrections; they are overtaken by events. But the nationalist leaders move quickly to take advantage of the situation. They make militant statements and claim to be speaking in the name of the rebelling native masses. They contend that if sweeping reforms are made, then order can be restored. They may even demand an end to colonialism. The colonial power welcomes this opportunity to deal with "reasonable" spokesmen. The colonists offer the nationalist leaders a share in power over the colony. They may even grant political independence to the colony, if pressure is great enough, and support those nationalist leaders who pledge that they will restore order and protect the economic

[31] *Ibid.,* p. 54.

interests of the colonists. In short, the imperialists' objective is for colonialism to be transformed into neocolonialism, and the nationalist native elites to cooperate with their former enemies in subduing and controlling the rebellious colony. The revolution, they hope, will be subverted and the native masses will thereby find themselves under the yoke of a new ruling class. The main difference is that where once foreign rulers oppressed the *entire* nation, now a minority of the nation exploits and oppresses its unpropertied majority.

Fanon presented this analysis more than six years ago, but it accurately describes the juncture at which the black liberation movement finds itself today.

(4)

At its 1966 national convention meeting in Baltimore, Maryland, the Congress of Racial Equality endorsed black power. A unanimously adopted resolution said in part:

Black Power is effective control and self-determination by men of color in their own areas.

Power is total control of the economic, political, educational, and social life of our community from the top to the bottom.

The exercise of power at the local level is simply what all other groups in American society have done to acquire their share of total American life.

The summer of 1966 was an important turning point for CORE, as it was for SNCC. Until then, CORE had been an integrationist organization relying on the tactics of nonviolent, direct action to achieve its goals. Founded by James Farmer in 1942 as an offshoot of the Quaker-pacifist Fellowship of Reconciliation, CORE immediately set out on an activist course. It organized the first sit-ins in Chicago in 1942, and it sent the first "freedom riders" through the South in April 1947.

Over the years the organization's membership grew from the initial handful of black and white activists. Like SNCC, CORE was a middle-class organization. It differed from SNCC in that SNCC members, being younger, were not yet committed to middle-class jobs or middle-class life styles. It was, therefore, easier for SNCC members to identify with the impoverished black majority. CORE differed from the NAACP in that the latter is wealthier, better established, and more solidly bourgeois. The NAACP aims at reforming certain aspects of a system whose assumptions it shares. It carries out these reformist efforts through the socially accepted channels of the ballot box, court cases, and legislative lobbying. CORE, on the other hand, while being a more militant and less affluent organization than the NAACP, still does not reject the basic ideological assumptions of American society, although it may question them. CORE employed less orthodox and more militant methods of reform. It used direct-action techniques in an effort to bring pressure on institutions it sought to change. As some observers have noted: "At a given point, after pressure from outside the system has been successful, it is possible for the less privileged reformist group to be allowed to work inside the system."[32]

CORE was eclipsed by William L. Patterson's Civil Rights Congress until 1951, then by Martin Luther King's campaigns in the middle 1950s and the student sit-ins which began in 1960. It was not until it organized the renowned "freedom rides" to Alabama and Mississippi in 1961 that CORE was catapulted into national prominence. As a result of these activities, the organization's membership began to change. In 1963, black members for the first time accounted for more than half of CORE's total membership. CORE was attracting to its ranks militant, middle-class blacks who were disillusioned with the NAACP. The following year, the Brooklyn chapter announced that it would organize a "stall-in" on the opening

[32] Fitch and Oppenheimer, *Ghana*, p. 27.

day of the New York World's Fair to protest discrimination in hiring practices at the fairgrounds. This was indicative of the organization's new militancy and the shifting of its focus to the urban North. This announcement touched off a heated controversy both within and outside of CORE.

Another sign of CORE's shifting center of gravity occurred in November 1964. Clarence Funnye, then chairman of the Manhattan chapter, announced that his group would abandon demonstrations in favor of long-range economic and social programs in Harlem. The organization still had integration as its goal, but it was trying to address itself to the needs of northern blacks, for whom de facto segregation and the lack of adequate housing and jobs were more serious problems than the kind of de jure discrimination which had characterized the South. A further sign was the interest expressed by the downtown New York chapter in organizing an independent political party. The chapter chairman asserted that this was necessary because existing local political organizations were incapable of bringing about needed improvements. Meanwhile, Brooklyn CORE was then involved in organizing rent strikes.

At its 1965 convention—the theme of which was "Black Ghetto: The Awakening Giant"—CORE rescinded its constitutional ban on partisan political activity. The new emphasis within the organization was summarized and in effect given official sanction by National Director James Farmer:

> The major war now confronting us is aimed at harnessing the awesome political potential of the black community in order to effect basic social and economic changes for all Americans, to alter meaningfully the lives of the Black Americans . . . and to bring about a real equality of free men.[33]

[33] Francis L. Broderick and August Meier (eds.), *Negro Protest Thought in the Twentieth Century* (New York: Bobbs-Merrill, 1965), p. 422.

The government could not do this job, Farmer asserted, because of its built-in resistance to fundamental change. "We can rely upon none but ourselves as a catalyst in the development of the potential power of the black community in its own behalf and in behalf of the nation."

It is clear that the objectives we seek—in the wiping out of poverty and unemployment, elimination of bad housing, city planning for integration in housing and schools, quality education—are political objectives depending upon responses we can exact from political machinery. We can no longer rely on pressuring and cajoling political units toward desired actions. We must be in a position of power, a position to change those political units when they are not responsive.[34]

Farmer contended that what was needed was "independent political action through indigenous political organizations" modeled after the MFDP. "Such ghetto-oriented political movements must avoid, at all costs," he said, "becoming an adjunct to, or a tool of, any political party, bloc, or machine. They must be controlled by the interests of the black ghetto alone."[35]

Another significant development at the 1965 convention was the introduction of a resolution opposing United States involvement in the Vietnam war. The resolution was tabled, however, on a plea from Farmer.

The man who chaired this convention was Floyd Mc-Kissick, then national chairman. The following year, in March, McKissick was named to replace Farmer as na-

[34] Ibid., p. 425.
[35] In 1968 Farmer himself ran unsuccessfully for Congress as the Liberal Party and Republican Party candidate in the newly created Twelfth Congressional District in Brooklyn. This was hardly an exercise in the kind of "independent politics" which he advocated in 1965. Rather it represented an alliance between him and the liberal wing of the power structure, and led him ultimately into the Nixon Administration.

tional director. McKissick was born in Asheville, North Carolina, in 1922. He graduated from Morehouse College in Atlanta, one of the great training institutions for the black bourgeoisie, and then went on to the University of North Carolina Law School where he took a law degree. McKissick mixed civil rights activity with his legal career, and, beginning in 1960, he became one of the leaders of the sit-in movement in North Carolina.

The black power resolution passed by CORE in 1966 seemingly eliminated racial integration as the group's goal and instead replaced it with the goal of "racial co-existence through black power." But what is this "racial co-existence" if it is not simply another form of group assimilation? CORE had substituted militant-sounding group integration for the now discredited goal of individual integration. The difference was in degree, not in kind.

The resolution also contained the sentence: "It is significant to note that historically the only times in the United States when great numbers of Black people have been mobilized has been around the concept of Nationalism, as in the case of Marcus Garvey and the Muslims." This is important to keep in mind, because at subsequent conventions, the organization would be racked by disputes between orthodox black nationalists and those who adhered to the new nationalist position advocated by Roy Innis. The traditional nationalists wanted CORE to come out in favor of a separate territory for black people, but Innis projected the idea of a black nation of city-states dispersed throughout the country. In 1968 this dispute would provoke a split in CORE's ranks.

On the question of violence, CORE tried to straddle the fence. The Baltimore meeting adopted a resolution urging "that CORE continue its adherence to the tactic of direct nonviolent action, that the concepts of nonviolence and self-defense are not contradictory, nonviolent meaning non-aggressive, but not precluding the natural, constitutional and inalienable right of self-defense."

CORE was reshaping itself. It was attempting to respond to and organize the new militancy which had infected certain parts of the black middle class, as a result of the rebellions initiated by the black masses. In so doing, CORE was to assume a role akin to that played by bourgeois-nationalist political elites in an underdeveloped country undergoing a transformation from colonialism to neo-colonialism.

(5)

By the time SNCC and CORE raised the cry of black power, the sophisticated, white establishment already had begun to sketch the general outlines of its response to the new, black militancy. It was not so much the specific slogan of black power that motivated this response; rather it was prompted by the same domestic conditions that underlay the rise of black militancy: The failure of the civil rights movement to alleviate the continuing impoverishment of the black communities and the consequent urban outbreaks.

The rebellions especially forced white reactionaries and liberals alike to conclude that direct white administration of the black ghettos, at least in some instances, was no longer operating satisfactorily. Some new form of administration was clearly called for if the ghettos were to be pacified and "law and order" restored. Of course there were some, mostly at the state and local government levels, who thought brutal repression to be the best answer. Traditional liberals, though, still hoped to find a panacea in government-sponsored social welfare programs. But a drastically new situation necessarily calls forth a drastically new response. The black rebellions, which threatened to set the torch to every major American city and seriously disrupt the functioning of the economy, represented just such a drastically new situation.

The beginnings of the new response could be glimpsed in Ford Foundation president McGeorge Bundy's August 2, 1966 address to the National Urban League's annual banquet in Philadelphia. "We believe," said Bundy, "that full equality for all American Negroes is now the most urgent domestic concern of this country. We believe that the Ford Foundation must play its full part in this field because it is dedicated by its charter to human welfare." Bundy told the Urban League meeting that in addition to the familiar fields of jobs, education, and housing, the Foundation thought that the areas of leadership, research, communication, and justice were also important concerns for the black movement. He suggested that "stronger leadership" was needed because "it is easier to understand and work for the recognition of basic civil rights than it is to understand and work for the improvements in skills and schools, in real opportunity, and in the quality of life itself, which are the next business of us all." In other words, as the civil rights movement faded away a new breed of black and white leader was required to negotiate "the road from right to reality."

In the area of research, Bundy threw out several questions which he said needed answers: "What kinds of better schools will help most to turn the tide of hope upward in the ghettos? What patterns of cooperation—among whites and Negroes—business, labor, and government—can bring new levels of investment to both the city center and the southern rural slum? What really are the roots of prejudice and how can we speed its early and widespread death?" The first two questions are especially significant because Bundy was later to become deeply embroiled in New York City's school decentralization dispute, and the Foundation would play a leading role in promoting private business investment in the ghetto. Anticipating this latter development, Bundy urged in his remarks that "strong-minded business leadership can put itself in the forefront of the effort to open doors for the Negro."

Significantly, Bundy also hinted that the political arena was to assume greater importance in the black struggle. "We know . . . that political influence brings political results," he told the group. He did not say, however, that the Foundation would soon play an indirect part in electing Carl Stokes as the first Negro mayor of Cleveland.

Communication is of utmost importance, Bundy stressed, because "the prospects for peaceful progress are best when men with different parts to play keep talking straight and clear, one to another. Nothing is more dangerous in such a time than for men to lose touch with each other." In this Bundy was absolutely right. He knew that the rebellions signaled a serious breakdown in communication between ghetto residents and municipal, state, and federal power structures. Thus communication, which in the lexicon of those who wield power is synonymous with control, had to be restored at any cost.

As for justice, Bundy simply said that it should be given top priority.

Finally, Bundy came to the heart of what he wanted to say. He told the Urban League group that there are certain interlocking institutions which bind blacks and whites together. One of the most important of these is the city, and "the quality of our cities is inescapably the business of all of us. Many whites recognize that no one can run the American city by black power alone," the reason being, he suggested at a later point, that urban black majorities would still be faced with white majorities in state houses and the U. S. Congress. But if the blacks burn the cities, then, he stated, it would be the white man's fault and, importantly, "the white man's companies will have to take the losses." White America is not so stupid as not to comprehend this elemental fact, Bundy assured the Urban Leaguers. Something would be done about the urban problem. "Massive help" would be given to the ghettos, and the Ford Foundation would take the lead in organizing the campaign.

Thus the Ford Foundation was on its way to becoming

the most important, though least publicized, organization manipulating the militant black movement. Housed in an ultramodern headquarters building on East Forty-third Street in New York, the Foundation is deeply involved in financing and influencing almost all major protest groups, including CORE, SCLC, the National Urban League, and the NAACP. Working directly or indirectly through these organizations, as well as other national and local groups, the Foundation hopes to channel and control the black liberation movement and forestall future urban revolts.

The Foundation catalogs its multitude of programs and grants under such headings as: public affairs, education, science and engineering, humanities and the arts, international training and research, economic development and administration, population, international affairs, and overseas development. The list reads like a selection from the courses offered by a modern liberal arts college. Race problems are listed as a subclass of public affairs.

Under the leadership of Bundy, former Special Assistant to the President for National Security Affairs—and in this capacity one of the chief architects of this country's aggression in Vietnam—the Ford Foundation in 1966 made an important decision to expand its activities in the black movement. Prior to that time, the organization had limited its activities among black Americans to philanthropic efforts in education and research projects, all aimed at incorporating more blacks into the middle-class mainstream. The 1966 decision, which was made in response to the black rebellions, was a logical extension of an earlier decision to vigorously enter the political arena.

Established in 1936 by Henry and Edsel Ford, the Foundation initially made grants largely to charitable and educational institutions in the state of Michigan. According to its charter, the purpose of the organization is "To receive and administer funds for scientific, educational and charitable purposes, all for the public welfare, and for no other purposes. . . ." Most of the Foundation's income has derived from its principal asset: Class A nonvoting stock in the Ford Motor Company.

In 1950, serving as an outlet for war profits, the Foundation expanded into a national organization, and its activities quickly spread throughout the United States and to some eighty foreign countries. In a special Board of Trustees' report prepared at that time, the Foundation announced its intention of becoming active in public affairs by "support[ing] activities designed to secure greater allegiance to the basic principles of freedom and democracy in the solution of the insistent problems of an ever changing society." This vague mandate, which at first meant little else than underwriting efforts to upgrade public administration, was gradually brought into sharper focus as the Foundation experimented with new programs.

In 1962, Dyke Brown, then a vice president with responsibility for public affairs programs, could write that the Foundation's interest had "shifted from management and public administration to policy and the political process." He added that these programs "tended to become increasingly action- rather than research-orientated," which meant that the Foundation had to be prepared to take certain "political risks." How an officer of a supposedly nonpolitical, nonpartisan philanthropic institution could justify such a statement can be understood by examining how the Foundation views its relationship to the major political parties and the government. Simply stated, the Foundation sees itself as a mediator which enlightens Democrats and Republicans as to their common interests, and the reasons why they should cooperate.

For example, the Foundation has sponsored many "nonpartisan" conferences of state legislators and officials with the purpose of stressing "nonpolitical" consideration of common problems. Such bipartisan activities insure the smooth functioning of state and local political machinery by reducing superfluous tensions and other sources of

political conflict which might upset the national structure
and operation of U.S. corporate society.

One specific role of the private foundations *vis-à-vis* the
government was made explicit by Henry T. Heald, Bundy's
predecessor as president of the Ford Foundation, in a
speech given at Columbia University in 1965. "In this country, privately supported institutions may serve the public
need as fully as publicly supported ones," Heald said.
"More often than not they work side by side in serving
the same need." What accounts for the growth of this
"dual system of public and private decision in community
and national affairs"? Heald continued,

> For one thing, privately supported organizations en-
> hance the public welfare by their relatively broad free-
> dom to innovate. They can readily try out new ideas and
> practices. They can adopt improved techniques and
> standards that may become models for other institutions
> in their fields, both public and private.[36]

In short, Heald argued that, through their activities,
private foundations could serve as a kind of advance
guard, paving the way for later government activity, not
only in the usual fields of education and scientific research,
but also in the area of "social welfare." Hence, the private
foundation can act as an instrument of social innovation
and control in areas which the government has not yet
penetrated, or in areas where direct government intervention would draw criticism.

An example of the former is the federal anti-poverty
program. Well in advance of federal efforts in this field,
the Foundation made grants for comprehensive anti-poverty
projects in Boston, New Haven, Oakland, Philadelphia,
Washington, D.C., and North Carolina.

Over the years, then, the Foundation's objectives shifted
as it assumed a more aggressive role in American society

[36] "American Foundations and the Common Welfare," by
Henry T. Heald (Ford Foundation pamphlet SR/9).

and the American empire abroad. No longer simply a charitable organization in a strict sense, the Foundation has become a major social institution, dedicated to preserving social stability and encouraging economic development of neocolonial nature, both in the United States and in those parts of the world which the U. S. Government and business interests consider to be of strategic importance.

Stability and capitalist development are essential to the tranquil internal growth and external expansion of the American empire. Instability and underdevelopment, whether at home or abroad, breed violence and revolution. It is for this reason that by the end of 1966 the Foundation had committed seventy-two million dollars to research in population control in the United States, Britain, Europe, Israel, Australia, Asia, and Latin America. It is for this reason that it devotes approximately one-fifth of its annual budget to training personnel and building economic institutions in underdeveloped countries. It is for this reason that a year after Bundy's Philadelphia speech, the Foundation was to grant a substantial sum to CORE—the money to be used for "peaceful and constructive efforts" in Cleveland's rebellious Hough district. And it is for this reason that in September 1968, it announced plans to invest an initial ten million dollars in the building of black capitalism.

To come to the point, the Ford Foundation had shaped itself into one of the most sophisticated instruments of American neocolonialism in "underdeveloped nations," whether abroad or within the borders of this country.

This is the general line of Foundation thinking which confronted Bundy as he stepped from his "little State Department" in the White House at the beginning of 1966. And he was ideally suited to further advancing these aims. From his years of working in the U.S. power structure, Bundy had nurtured a keen appreciation for the complexities involved in political manipulation and the seemingly contradictory policies which often must be pursued simultaneously in order to obtain a given end.

Bundy summarized his political outlook in an article entitled "The End of Either/Or," published in January 1967, in the magazine *Foreign Affairs*.[37] Bundy first asserted that foreign policy decisions are related to U.S. national interests, although he did not state who determines these interests or sets priorities. He then went on to criticize those who view foreign policy options in terms of simple extremes. "For twenty years, from 1940 to 1960, the standard pattern of discussion on foreign policy was that of either /or: Isolation or Intervention, Europe or Asia, Wallace or Byrnes, Marshall Plan or Bust, SEATO or Neutralism, the U.N. or Power Politics, and always, insistently, anti-Communism or accommodation with the Communists." The world is not so simple, Bundy wrote, and "with John F. Kennedy we enter a new age. Over and over he [Kennedy] insisted on the double assertion of policies which stood in surface contradiction with each other: resistance to tyranny and relentless pursuit of accommodation; reinforcement of defense and new leadership for disarmament; counter-insurgency and the Peace Corps; openings to the left, but no closed doors to the reasonable right; an Alliance for Progress and unremitting opposition to Castro; in sum, the olive branch and the arrows."[38]

Bundy learned that it is necessary to work both sides of the street in order to secure and expand the American empire. Hence he was a stanch supporter of Kennedy's and Johnson's war policies in Vietnam, while at the same time stressing the necessity of keeping channels open to the Soviet Union. Such a man was perfectly suited to work with black groups, including black power advocates, while at the same time local governments were arming and preparing to use force to suppress the black communities. The seeming contradiction here, to use Bundy's word, was only a "surface" manifestation.

[37] Vol. 45, No. 2.
[38] Bundy, p. 192.

(6)

While the bright young men of the Ford Foundation were calmly assessing the black revolt, the nation's public spokesmen fanned the flames of hysteria. For them black power was an unfathomable evil. It smacked of "racism in reverse" and threatened violence. "We must reject calls for racism," warned Vice President Hubert Humphrey, "whether they come from a throat that is white or one that is black." Even before Carmichael mentioned black power, columnists Evans and Novack had launched the smear campaign in the Washington *Post* on May 25, 1966, by describing him as the voice of "the extreme black racists." Roy Wilkins, head of the NAACP, integrated the anti-Carmichael attack by stirring up fears of violence. "We of the NAACP," he solemnly announced, "will have none of this. It is the father of hatred and the mother of violence. Black power can mean in the end only black death."

The most sophisticated assault came from that archcritic, Bayard Rustin. Rustin was forced to admit that "progress" was an illusion; that black people were in worse economic shape, lived in worse slums, and attended more highly segregated schools then than in 1954. He admitted that civil rights laws were not being effectively enforced; yet he still contended:

> Southern Negroes, despite exhortations from SNCC to organize themselves into a Black Panther party [at the time, this was the popular name of the Lowndes County Freedom Organization], are going to stay in the Democratic Party—to them it is the party of progress, the New Deal, the New Frontier, and the Great Society— and they are right to stay.[39]

For Rustin it was inconceivable that blacks could do anything outside of the liberal-labor coalition of the Demo-

[39] *Commentary*, September 1966.

cratic party, even though he was well aware of the decep-
tive nature of the progress which this coalition loudly
claimed to have made on behalf of black people. For him
black power was a threat not because it portended "racism"
or "violence," but because it further undermined an already shaky coalition. "The winning of the right of Negroes to vote in the South insures the eventual transformation of the Democratic Party. . . . The Negro vote will
eliminate the Dixiecrats from the party and from Congress," Rustin intoned in a subtle effort to entice black
militants back into the reformist fold. In a word, he could
not part with his own illusions about "a liberal-labor-civil
rights coalition which would work to make the Democratic
Party truly responsive to the aspirations of the poor. . . ."
Over the succeeding years, these words were to acquire
an increasingly hollow ring.

(7)

In the fall of 1966, there occurred two other events that
were of serious import for the black liberation movement.
In September the first attempt in the North was made, not
altogether intentionally, to apply black power thinking to a
concrete situation. The New York City school system was
in another crisis. Harlem parents were demanding an effective voice in the running of a school—I.S. 201. The second
event occurred at the other end of the country with little
fanfare. The Black Panther party was founded in October
in Oakland, California.

For years black parents and community leaders had
been fighting for an integrated school system in New York.
To dramatize their complaint they organized an impressive
school boycott in the spring of 1964. But the impact of
the boycott was minimal. The Board of Education paid
lip service to the parents' demands, but then went on its
way in its usual lumbering fashion. The fall crisis was
precipitated by the construction of a "model school" in

central Harlem. When the site was originally selected in 1958, parents had warned the Board that the location guaranteed that the school would be segregated. The Board blandly replied that the proposed school would be so good that white parents would send their children to it.

When the new intermediate school was completed, it faced a pupil boycott. Some 80 percent of the expected students were black, and the overwhelming majority of the remainder were Puerto Rican. Clearly, the school was segregated, despite the school board's earlier assurances to the contrary. A negotiating team, representing the Harlem community, decided that if the school were not to be integrated, then there should be some formal mechanism for the black community to participate in setting up a curriculum and selecting personnel for the school. The hope was that such a mechanism would prevent I.S. 201 from becoming just like every other second-rate ghetto school.

At first the liberal teachers backed the black parents, but when it appeared that some of their own "professional" prerogatives would be challenged, they switched sides.

The negotiating team demanded two things. It sought the establishment of a special council controlled by parents and the community to run the school in joint control with the school board; and it wanted I.S. 201 to have a black principal. At that time only four of New York's 870 principals were black. The parents wanted a black principal at the school to provide a positive image for their children.

But a white principal, Stanley Lisser, had already been chosen by the school board superintendent, Bernard Donovan. From an individual point of view, Lisser probably was as technically qualified as any, but his appointment conflicted with a changing social consciousness in the black community. With an extremely tense situation on his hands, Donovan reversed himself and pressured Lisser into resigning. This provoked an immediate and angry response from the teachers. For them it was a clear-cut case of race being given priority over qualifications, and, in

the professional-bureaucratic world, giving preferential consideration to anything but "merit" is a grave heresy. The
very next day they picketed the Board of Education and
got Donovan to refuse Lisser's resignation. This reversal
was applauded as a victory by the United Federation of
Teachers, the teachers' union. The UFT president-elect,
Albert Shanker, said: "Had the Board prevailed, our
school system would have been destroyed." He warned
that "We must not permit extremism on the part of some
parents to create a teacher backlash aimed at erecting a
wall between the public and the schools."

News of the reversal and the union's elation were
greeted with great bitterness in Harlem, where some had
hoped for an alliance of parents and teachers against the
school board. The issue of "professionalism" shattered
these hopes.

A related issue drove in deeper the wedge between parents and teachers. Shanker had called for special facilities
for "disturbed children." Two or three such pupils can
totally disrupt a classroom. But the black parents viewed
this as an attempt to brand additional stigmas on their
children. To them, the so-called disruptive child was simply
a result of a demoralizing and dehumanizing school system. They argued that it was bad teachers and bad schools
which created "disturbed" children, not vice versa. For
them the answer lay in getting rid of poor teachers and
bringing the schools under community control, not in setting up special facilities for the "disruptive" pupils.

After weeks of indecision and foot-dragging on the I.S.
201 dispute, the school board, under pressure from Mayor
John Lindsay, promised to appoint a "task force" to investi-
gate the whole problem of ghetto schools and to make
recommendations for sweeping changes. The Board of
Education never set up such a "task force," but Mayor
Lindsay did—and it was headed up by none other than
McGeorge Bundy.

While this dispute was raging in New York, two black

students at Merritt College in Oakland—Huey P. Newton and Bobby Seale—were organizing the local black community and encouraging black people to arm themselves. Appropriating the symbol of the Lowndes County Freedom Organization, Newton and Seale called their new organization—the Black Panther Party for Self-Defense. Explaining the symbolism, Seale said: "It's not in the panther's nature to attack anyone first, but when he is attacked and backed into a corner, he will respond viciously and wipe out the aggressor." The "aggressor" in this case happens to be the police who patrol black communities.

Newton and Seale drew upon the experience of black people in Los Angeles. Following the 1965 Watts uprising, the black community there organized the Community Alert Patrol. CAP was funded in large part by federal money, and its function was to protect members of the black community from police harassment and brutality. Whenever police were observed stopping black people for "investigation and interrogation," CAP headquarters would be notified and a CAP patrol vehicle dispatched to the scene to observe and report on the conduct of the police officers. The CAP team would also inform the black person under detainment of his legal rights.

The Panther founders took the CAP idea one step further. To dramatize their determination to curb police mistreatment of blacks, the Panthers instituted armed patrols. This was perfectly legal, and the Panthers scrupulously avoided violating the law. Whenever police harassed ghetto residents, Panthers would arrive on the scene bearing rifles and shotguns. The Panthers also habitually carried with them law books from which they could quote the appropriate section of the legal code being violated by the police.

The patrols were successful. A noticeable decrease was observed in the number of incidents of police harassment of the ghetto population at large, but the police increasingly turned on the Panthers themselves. The success of the patrols and the fact that the Panthers were armed and obviously ready to "take care of business" made a deep impression on the black community, particularly among the youth and young adults. The organization grew steadily as new recruits—mostly from poor and working-class families—streamed in. Seale and Newton became chairman and minister of defense, respectively, of the young organization. Unlike SNCC and CORE, the Panthers were not a middle-class group. The majority of their rank-and-file members were recruited from the rebellious ghetto underclass. As one moves up into the leadership of the group, however, the incidence of middle-class members increases. In a sense, the Panther leadership represents an alliance between militant college students (or ex-students) and unlettered ghetto youths.

The Panthers are more than simply a self-defense or community patrol operation. They regard themselves as being in the vanguard of the black revolution. In an interview with this writer, Seale explained the party's political philosophy: "We tried to establish an organization that would articulate the basic desires and needs of the people and in turn try to organize black people into having some kind of power position so they can deal with the power structure. The party realizes that the white power structure's real power is its military force; is its police force. And we can see that our black communities are being occupied by policemen just like a foreign country might be occupied by foreign troops. Our politics comes from our hungry stomachs and our crushed heads and the vicious service revolver at a cop's side which is used to tear our flesh, and from the knowledge that black people are drafted to fight in wars, killing other colored people who've never done a damn thing to us. So how do we face these cops in the black community? We have to face them exactly how they come down on us. They come down with guns and force. We must organize ourselves and put a shotgun in every black man's home. Our political stand is that politics is war without bloodshed, and war is politics with bloodshed."[40]

The politics of the Black Panther party is expressed in its program. To "articulate the basic desires and needs" of black people, the Panthers in 1966 drafted a ten-point platform and program.

1. *We want freedom. We want power to determine the destiny of our black community.*

We believe that black people will not be free until we are able to determine our destiny.

2. *We want full employment for our people.*

We believe that the federal government is responsible and obligated to give every man employment or a guaranteed income. We believe that if the white American businessmen will not give full employment, then the means of production should be taken from the businessmen and placed in the community so that the people of the community can organize and employ all of its people and give a high standard of living.

3. *We want an end to the robbery by the white man of our black community.*

We believe that this racist government has robbed us and now we are demanding the overdue debt of forty acres and two mules. Forty acres and two mules was promised one hundred years ago as restitution for slave labor and mass murder of black people. We will accept the payment in currency which will be distributed to our many communities. The Germans are now aiding the Jews in Israel for the genocide of the Jewish people. The Germans murdered six million Jews. The American racist has taken part in the slaughter of over fifty million black people; therefore, we feel that this is a modest demand that we make.

4. *We want decent housing, fit for shelter of human beings.*

We believe that if the white landlords will not give decent housing to our black community, then the housing and the land should be made into cooperatives so that

[40] Excerpts from this interview were published in the *Guardian,* January 6, 1968.

our community, with government aid, can build and make decent housing for its people.

5. *We want education for our people that exposes the true nature of this decadent American society. We want education that teaches us our true history and role in the present-day society.*

We believe in an educational system that will give to our people a knowledge of self. If a man does not have knowledge of himself and his position in society and the world, then he has little chance to relate to anything else.

6. *We want all black men to be exempt from military service.*

We believe that black people should not be forced to fight in the military service to defend a racist government that does not protect us. We will not fight and kill other people of color in the world who, like black people, are being victimized by the white racist government of America. . . .

7. *We want an immediate end to police brutality and murder of black people.*

We believe we can end police brutality in our black community by organizing black self-defense groups that are dedicated to defending our black community from racist police oppression and brutality. The Second Amendment to the Constitution of the United States gives a right to bear arms. We therefore believe that all black people should arm themselves for self-defense.

8. *We want freedom for all black men held in federal, state, county, and city prisons and jails.*

We believe that all black people should be released from the many jails and prisons because they have not received a fair and impartial trial.

9. *We want all black people when brought to trial to be tried in a court by a jury of their peer group or people from their black communities, as defined by the Constitution of the United States.*

We believe that the courts should follow the United States Constitution so that black people will receive fair trials. The Fourteenth Amendment . . . gives a man a right to be tried by his peer group. A peer is a person from a similar economic, social, religious, geographical, environmental, historical, and racial background. To do this the court will be forced to select a jury from the black community from which the black defendant came. We have been, and are being tried by all-white juries that have no understanding of the "average reasoning man" of the black community.

10. *We want land, bread, housing, education, clothing, justice, and peace. And as our major political objective, a United Nations-supervised plebiscite to be held throughout the black colony in which only black colonial subjects will be allowed to participate, for the purpose of determining the will of black people as to their national destiny.*

When, in the course of human events, it becomes necessary for one people to dissolve the political bonds which have connected them with another, and to assume, among the powers of the earth, the separate and equal station to which the laws of nature and nature's God entitle them, a decent respect to the opinions of mankind requires that they should declare the causes which impel them to the separation.

We hold these truths to be self-evident, that all men are created equal; that they are endowed by their Creator with certain inalienable rights; that among these are life, liberty, and the pursuit of happiness; that, to secure these rights, governments are instituted among men, deriving their just powers from the consent of the governed; that, whenever any form of government becomes destructive of these ends, it is the right of the people to alter or to abolish it, and to institute a new government, laying its foundation on such principles, and organizing its powers in such form, as to them shall seem most likely to effect their safety and happiness. Prudence, indeed, will dictate that governments long established should not be changed for light and transient causes; and, accordingly, all experience hath shown, that mankind are more disposed to suffer, while evils are sufferable, than to right themselves by abolishing the forms to which they are accustomed. But, when a long train of abuses and usurpations, pursuing invariably the same object, evinces a design to reduce them under absolute despotism, it is their right, it is their duty, to throw off such government, and to provide new guards for their future security.

This program is of great significance because it represented the first concrete attempt to spell out the meaning of black power. It is a sweeping program, ranging from such mundane but fundamental matters as employment and education to broad issues of freedom and self-determination (with the preamble to the U. S. Declaration of Independence included as witness to the fact that the Black Panthers fall squarely within the stream of American revolutionary tradition).

In the winter of 1968 Seale announced four community programs that the Panthers were undertaking as part of their drive to implement the ten-point political program. These included free breakfasts for needy black children, a petition campaign for community control of police, and efforts to establish free health clinics in the black community and black liberation schools. Some have charged that these activities, and indeed the whole Panther program, are basically reformist. Replying to this, Seale remarked: "Some people are going to call these programs reformist but we're revolutionaries and what they call a reformist program is one thing when the capitalists put it up and it's another thing when the revolutionary camp puts it up. Revolutionaries must always go forth to answer the momentary desires and needs of the people, the poor and oppressed people, while waging the revolutionary struggle. It's very important because it strengthens the people's revolutionary camp while it weakens the camp of the capitalist power structure."[41]

Reforms are ends in themselves when implemented by the power structure, but when implemented by the ordinary working people of the black community, through an independent black political party, reforms can become one

[41] *The Movement,* March 1969.

means to the creation of a revolutionary new society. The critical question is who, or more specifically, what class *controls* the making of reforms, and for what *purpose?*

Both the Panthers and SNCC considered themselves to be revolutionary black nationalist organizations. Black nationalism is usually treated by the mass media as a sensational but peripheral phenomenon of no more than passing interest. Actually, nationalism is imbedded in the social fabric of black America, and this must be understood if the problems of the black liberation movement are to be fully appreciated.

III. BLACK NATIONALISM

Black power as a variant form of black nationalism has roots that reach deep into the history and social fabric of black America. Like an unsatisfied need or a nagging conscience, black nationalism is an insistent motif that wends its way through black history, particularly of the last 150 years. One writer has called nationalism the rejected strain, implying that assimilationism—the desire to be fully incorporated into the surrounding white society—is the dominant, and the only significant, sentiment among black people.

A glance at history suggests that it would be more correct to say that nationalism, and overt separatism, are ever-present undercurrents in the collective black psyche which constantly interact with the assimilationist tendency and, in times of crisis, rise to the surface to become major themes.

Both nationalism and assimilation spring from black people's wish to be an integral part of a jargon society. This, after all, is what is meant by saying that man is a social animal. Nationalism, however, is rooted in the Afro-American's experience of being forcibly excluded from and rejected by a society which is usually overtly, and always covertly, racist and exploitative. In periods of social crisis —that is, when repression and terror are rampant or hopes of progress have been dashed—the resulting suspicion that equal participation is impossible becomes a certainty. Nationalist leaders and intellectuals come to the fore and assert that not only is racial integration not possible, it is not even *desirable*. Such an eventuality, they contend, would destroy the group's distinctive culture and its sense of ethnic identity.

Thus in the decade prior to the Civil War, a period of increasing despair for blacks, emigration movements were in vogue. The Fugitive Slave Act was passed by Congress as part of the Compromise of 1850, and thousands of fugitive slaves were forced to flee to Canada if they were to secure their freedom. In 1854 the Kansas-Nebraska Act opened northern territory to slavery and, in the infamous Dred Scott decision of 1857, the U. S. Supreme Court sanctioned the notion that black people were not citizens. These were indeed grim years for the nearly 4½ million blacks then living in this country.

Many free blacks, such as Frederick Douglass, became active in the abolitionist movement, but others sought some other way out of an increasingly oppressive situation. Martin R. Delaney was one of the latter. In 1852 Delaney advocated that black people emigrate to the east coast of Africa to set up a nation of their own. "We are a nation within a nation," he argued, sounding a now familiar note, "as the Poles in Russia, the Hungarians in Austria; the Welsh, Irish, and Scotch in the British dominions."[1] Delaney called for a convention of the best black intellects —"a true representation of the intelligence and wisdom of the colored freemen"—to lay plans for his colonial expedition. A convention to thrash out the question of emigration was actually held in 1854. Three proposals were presented to this convention. In addition to Delaney's, there were proposals that blacks emigrate to Central America or to Haiti. Envoys were dispatched to these proposed areas of colonization to investigate conditions and sound out local governments.

The emigrationists were not without their critics. Many free blacks opposed the idea of emigration. Douglass, for example, expressed the fear that the emigration effort

---

[1] Herbert Aptheker (ed.), *A Documentary History of the Negro People in the United States,* Vol. I (New York: Citadel Press, 1951), pp. 327–28. It took an additional century, however, for black people's *consciousness* of their nationhood to become fairly widespread.

would encourage the best educated of the race to depart the country, leaving behind those least qualified to press forward with the emancipation struggle. But this was not the only reason that blacks were critical of colonization schemes.

One of the earliest colonization attempts was undertaken in 1815 by Paul Cuffee, a relatively wealthy New England black sailor. Cuffee arranged for a small group of black colonists to travel to Africa. This action is believed to have inspired the formation of the white-controlled American Colonization Society in 1816. By and large, however, blacks were hostile to the Society's colonization plans. Their opposition stemmed not so much from any lack of desire to separate from whites but rather because they strenuously objected to the racist reasoning whites used in justifying emigration. The Society, which counted a number of slaveholders among its founders, had as its express purpose the removal of free blacks to Africa on the grounds that they were a "dangerous and useless part of the community."[2] This slur incensed most free blacks and turned them irreversibly against any thought of colonizing Africa. Only a few wanted so desperately to escape the torture that was America that they would solicit aid even from racists. Abraham Camp, a free black from Illinois, wrote a letter in 1818 to the Society accepting its offer of aid in traveling to Africa, "or some other place." "We love this country and its liberties, if we could share an equal right in them," Camp wrote, "but our freedom is partial, and we have no hope that it will ever be otherwise here; therefore we had rather be gone. . . ."[3]

The Civil War and its aftermath put an end to talk of emigration. The Emancipation Proclamation formally ended slavery, and black people were officially granted citizenship. Hopes were high among blacks that equality and the good life were just over the horizon. Blacks sought

[2] *Ibid.*, p. 71.
[3] *Ibid.*, p. 72.

in every conceivable way to participate fully in the nation's life, to become just ordinary Americans. It truly seemed that Douglass's faith, the faith that white America could change and accommodate itself to blacks, was justified.

Black men were elected to serve in every southern legislature. South Carolina could even boast of a black majority in its legislative chambers. Some twenty blacks served in the U. S. House of Representatives, and the state of Mississippi sent two black senators to Washington. These were the years of Reconstruction, and even the Ku Klux Klan and its campaign of terrorism seemed for the moment insufficient to stem the rising tide of black hope.

But what the Klan and southern terrorists alone could not bring about, a tacit alliance of southern reactionaries with northern business interests and an uneasy northern white populace could indeed accomplish. Historian Lerone Bennett, Jr., has noted that

> Throughout this period, Northern reporters and Northern opinion-makers were shrewdly and effectively cultivated by Southerners who dangled the bait of profit, telling Northern industrialists that nothing stood between them and maximum exploitation of the rich resources of the South except "Negro governments."[4]

The northern industrialists, being businessmen, fell for the bait of promised profits and began clamoring for a "settlement" of the troubles which had developed in the South as a result of terrorist violence and the Depression of 1873. Meanwhile, nervous whites in the North, more concerned with maintaining domestic tranquillity than insuring justice for all, were nearly panicked into a stampede by the seemingly indecisive Hayes-Tilden presidential election of 1876 which brought with it the threat of a new civil war.

Hayes, a Republican, was bitterly opposed in the South, but it appeared that he had won a majority of the electoral

[4] Bennett, *Black Power U.S.A.* (Chicago: Johnson Publishing Co., 1967), p. 348.

votes. The southerners staged a filibuster, which disrupted the orderly counting of the electoral votes in the House of Representatives. An ominously threatening atmosphere developed as it became clear that inauguration day would come and pass without a President having been chosen. With pressure mounting from both industrialists and the general northern public, a "settlement" was reached in the form of the Hayes-Tilden compromise of 1877. Hayes promised the white Southerners "the right to control their own affairs in their own way." In return for an end to the filibuster, he also said he would withdraw the federal troops remaining in the South.

These federal troops had been practically the only thing standing between black people and their tormentors. True, there were some black militia units organized, but with the return of state power to the hands of white racists, these black men didn't stand much of a chance. The "settlement" was climaxed when the U. S. Supreme Court, in another infamous decision, declared the Civil Rights Act of 1875 unconstitutional. Southern states rewrote their constitutions to disenfranchise black people, and any blacks who still showed an interest in the ballot were terrorized and murdered by the Klan. Segregation replaced slavery as the accepted mode of black subjugation.

This was a bitter experience for blacks, who realized that as far as their supposed white friends were concerned, when self-interest conflicted with anti-slavery idealism, the latter proved dispensable.

Thousands of blacks were lynched in the South between 1880 and 1900. Hundreds of thousands of others soon began the great northward trek in a vain search for some nonexistent promised land. They were met by hatred and violence little different from what they had known in the South. There were anti-black riots in New York in 1900; in Springfield, Ohio, in 1904; in Greensburg, Indiana, in 1906, and another massive riot in Springfield in 1908.

It was this crisis which thrust forward both Booker T. Washington and W. E. B. DuBois as spokesmen. These men were ideological antagonists and, while neither is usually regarded today as being a black nationalist, the thinking of both exhibited curiously nationalist undertones. Washington is frequently described as an Uncle Tom accommodationist while DuBois is thought of as the father of the civil rights protest movement. Both leaders were trying to force a viable response to the imposition of segregation and growing anti-black violence.

Social critic Harold Cruse has argued that "Washington actually laid the basic economic foundation and motivation for Negro Nationalism in America even though he, himself, was no militant Nationalist."[5] The reason for this, according to Cruse, is that Washington was "the Negro bourgeois prophet par excellence" and black nationalism "is usually bourgeois in its origins in its earliest inceptions." Washington advocated the uplifting of the black masses through industrial education and economic self-help projects. He founded Tuskegee Institute as a school to train black workers in agricultural and industrial vocations, and among his economic enterprises was the African Union Company, which he organized to promote trade between American blacks and the Gold Coast of Africa. At the turn of the century, to provide an institutional base for his idea that in the building of a black capitalist class lay the way to racial economic advancement, Washington founded the Negro Business League. Washington was willing to forgo black participation in politics and to accept segregation as the price to be paid for white financial support of his educational and economic efforts. But he thought that this was only a temporary concession and honestly believed that the black man who succeeded in business would be "treated with the highest respect by the members of the white race."

Unconsciously, Washington was playing a part analogous to the classic role assumed by a national bourgeoisie in an underdeveloped, colonial country. He was trying to create

[5] *Liberator*, August 1964.

a native (black) capitalist class and appealed to the latent nationalist sentiment of the native (black) masses in urging them to support this new class. At the Eleventh Annual Conference of the Negro Business League in 1910, Washington, in a keynote address, urged his hearers to leave "determined that each individual shall be a missionary in his community—a missionary in teaching the masses to get property, to be more thrifty, more economical, and resolve to establish an industrial enterprise wherever a possibility presents itself."[6] Washington believed that the masses would follow this course out of a sense of racial pride and solidarity (what would be called "black consciousness" today). Those who took his advice, however, probably did so for other reasons. Abram L. Harris, in his book *The Negro as Capitalist,* contends that, "Although ostensibly sponsored as the means of self-help or racial cooperation, as it was sometimes called, through which the masses were to be economically emancipated, Negro business enterprise was motivated primarily by the desire for private profit and looked toward the establishment of a Negro capitalist employer class."[7] Leaving aside the question of personal motivations, the projected social consequence of Washington's actions was to create an economic class among Negroes which could compete with white capitalists for the Negro market. This is exactly the same task assumed by a young national bourgeoisie in a colonial country. Since neither the embryonic black capitalist class, nor its colonial counterpart, have sufficient economic strength in their early years to offset the power of entrenched white business interests, they must whip up nationalist feeling among the masses if their struggle is to be successful. Calls to "support your own kind" become weapons in a fierce battle for economic hegemony. It is in this sense that Washington is to be viewed as a spokesman for bourgeois nationalism. The difficulty with Washing-

[6] Quoted in E. Franklin Frazier, *Black Bourgeoisie* (New York: Collier Books, 1957), p. 134.
[7] Quoted in Frazier, pp. 129–30.

ton's program was that he failed to see that American capitalism had by then left the stage of free competition and entered that of monopoly (in the industrial and corporate areas), with bank loans and credits, not a businessman's own small capital, determining his success. Blacks had no capital to speak of, and financiers, who after all are capable of recognizing a threat to their own interests, saw no reason to provide them any. As a result, black businesses down to the present day have been largely confined to small-scale marginal operations. There is no substantial black capitalist class, only a handful of black capitalists.

DuBois was an archcritic of Washington. He accused Washington of shifting the burden for black oppression from the nation as a whole to the shoulders of black people. He attacked Washington for counseling submission to oppression. DuBois helped organize the Niagara Movement in 1905 to counter the program of the Washingtonians. Following in the tradition of Frederick Douglass and basing themselves on the tenet that "Persistent manly agitation is the way to liberty," the black intellectuals who formed the Niagara Movement drafted a statement of principles calling for, among other things, male suffrage, full civil rights, economic opportunity, and education of black youths according to ability. These were the militants of the day, and they would brook no talk of the black man meekly accepting his assigned lowly place in the order of things. "We refuse to allow the impression to remain," they thundered, "that the Negro-American assents to inferiority, is submissive under oppression and apologetic before insults. Through helplessness we may submit, but the voice of protest of ten million Americans must never cease to assail the ears of their fellows, so long as America is unjust."[8] The order must be changed, protested the Niagara activists.

Unfortunately, the Niagara Movement seldom got beyond oratorical protest, and eventually it was absorbed into the newly formed National Association for the Ad-

[8] Aptheker, *Documentary History,* Vol. II, p. 902.

vancement of Colored People. The NAACP, established in 1910, soon became the major mass-based organization demanding Negro admission into the mainstream of American life.

But there was another aspect to DuBois' character during this period: his cultural nationalism. DuBois expressed an almost mystical faith in the dignity and innate sense of justice found in the souls of black folk. He felt that a strong cultural and psychological bond existed between American blacks and Africans, and he suggested that the communalism of the African clan might readily be transferred to black America. DuBois gave verbal form to his faith in a "Credo" written in 1904:

> Especially do I believe in the Negro Race; in the beauty of its genius, the sweetness of its soul, and its strength in that meekness which shall inherit this turbulent earth.
> I believe in pride of race and lineage itself; in pride of self so deep as to scorn injustice to other selves; in pride of lineage so great as to despise no man's father; in pride of race so chivalrous as neither to offer bastardy to the weak nor beg wedlock of the strong. . . .[9]

DuBois' fight for the word "Negro" as against small-n "negro" or "colored," was as militant and significant for its day as the recent fight for the word "black," now that "Negro" has come to represent the mentality of an NAACP very much changed from the time when DuBois was its guiding figure.

Soon DuBois developed an interest in Pan-Africanism, and he organized Pan-African Congresses in 1911, 1918, 1923, 1927, and 1945.[10] Pan-Africanism was anti-

[9] *Ibid.*, p. 899.
[10] William Z. Foster, *The Negro People in American History* (New York: International Publishers Company, Inc., 1954), p. 468. Foster contends that the importance of the Pan-African conference held during the peace talks after World War I was that "it emphasized the solidarity of American Negroes with the oppressed colonial peoples, and especially that it expressed the national sentiments of the American Negro people" (p. 435).

colonial, anti-imperialist in conception and purpose, and no mere cultural movement. DuBois and the African George Padmore are the acknowledged fathers of African nationalism, and DuBois could hardly be that without having been, in some measure, himself a black nationalist. DuBois' nationalism was so insistent that at times it completely overwhelmed his fervor for Marxism. For a short period, very early in his life, he had been influenced by Marxism, but in 1933 he wrote an article for *Crisis* magazine entitled "Marxism and the Negro Problem," in which he asserted that both the white capitalist and the white proletariat participate in the exploitation of black people. When it comes to racial oppression, DuBois the nationalist argued, whites are all the same. But within a very few years, the activity of some Marxists, specifically the Communist Party, for admission of blacks into unions, for food for the hungry in the Great Depression and against blatant expressions of racism as was seen in the Scottsboro case, began the process that closed with DuBois joining the Communist Party in the last decade of his life.

If the crisis theory being outlined here is correct in explaining outbursts of nationalist feeling, then the question arises why DuBois and Washington were not more overt black nationalists? In the case of DuBois, it was probably his early affinity for the Marxism of the Socialist party, with its color blindness, that held him back from becoming an outspoken black nationalist. Throughout his life DuBois seemed to be trying with limited success to reconcile nationalism with Marxism. As for Washington, his close ties with prominent white benefactors insured that he could not safely utter any militant statements and required that he couch his nationalism in very cautious terms. The thesis of Washington's 1895 Atlanta Exposition Address, for example, when stripped of its timorous formulations and apologies, can be boldly restated in terms which would satisfy even the most ardent nationalist. Without altering basic meaning, "Cast down your buckets where you are" can become "We must build an independent economy in the black community." Or, "In all things that are purely social we can be as separate as the fingers" could have been, "We have no desire for social intercourse with a cold and soulless race."[11]

An essential feature of black nationalism is that the nationalist makes a virtue of the fact of black separateness from the bulk of American society. The only difference in the formulations above is that one set of statements does so in a halfhearted manner and the other set asserts separateness as a positive good.

Incidentally, both Washington and DuBois are excellent examples of the ambivalence which afflicts middle-class black leaders. DuBois once wrote that "The Negro group has long been internally divided by dilemmas as to whether its striving upwards should be aimed at strengthening inner cultural and group bonds, both for intrinsic progress and for offensive power against caste; or whether it should seek escape wherever and however possible into the surrounding American culture."[12] The middle-class black leader, particularly in times of social stress, personifies this dilemma. This is because, as will be examined in later pages, the black middle class as a whole vacillates between the two approaches posited by DuBois.

Another major crisis for the Negro occurred at the time of World War I. When the war was declared, white leaders plied black people with promises of equality. President Woodrow Wilson assured blacks that "With thousands of your sons in the camps and in France, out of this conflict you must expect nothing less than the enjoyment of full citizenship rights—the same as are enjoyed by every other citizen."[13] More than 350,000 black men served in the

[11] This is no fanciful stretching of the imagination. A "militant" restatement of Washington's thesis was expressed by Nathan Wright in *Black Power and Urban Unrest*, p. 20.
[12] Quoted in E. U. Essien-Udom, *Black Nationalism* (New York: Dell, 1962), p. 43.
[13] Quoted in Herbert Aptheker, *Toward Negro Freedom* (New York: New Century Publishers, 1956), p. 114.

U. S. Armed Forces, and most of these were sent to France. But the promises proved to be empty. The Klan was reorganized in Georgia in 1915 and spread rapidly across the country. Within ten years it had an estimated membership of four million. In July of 1917 a white mob ran wild in East St. Louis, wrecking some three hundred homes of blacks and killing 125 black men, women, and children. In the first year after the war, seventy blacks were lynched. Many of these were black soldiers, some still wearing their uniforms. Black soldiers who had fought bravely in France, many of them winning citations for heroism, were not even permitted to march in the Paris Victory Parade of 1919.

During this same period, from 1915 to 1919, the black exodus from the South reached flood proportions. Some 750,000 black refugees migrated to the North searching for jobs and seeking to escape the legal and illegal barriers to progress which had been thrown up in the southern states.

It was in this setting that black nationalism again found expression, this time in the person of Marcus Garvey. Garvey took Washington's economic program, clothed it in militant nationalist rhetoric, and built an organization which in its heyday enjoyed the active support of millions of black people. Garvey, a Jamaican by birth, "identified the problem of American Negroes with the problem of colonialism in Africa. He believed that until Africa was liberated, there was no hope for black people anywhere."[14] He founded his Universal Negro Improvement Association in 1914 in Jamaica with the motto: "One God! One Aim! One Destiny!" But it was not until Garvey established his group in New York's Harlem in 1917 that it began to assume notable proportions. Within two months the UNIA had fifteen hundred members.

The African student of American black nationalism, E. U. Essien-Udom, outlined Garvey's beliefs:

[14] Essien-Udom, p. 48.

Garvey's ideology was both nationalist and racial. His nationalist objective was the redemption of Africa for "Africans abroad and at home." He advocated racial purity, racial integrity, and racial hegemony. He sought to organize Negroes in the United States into a vanguard for Africa's redemption from colonialism and hoped eventually to lead them back to Africa. The major instrument for the achievement of these objectives was economic cooperation through racial solidarity. He believed that if the Negroes were economically strong in the United States, they would be able to redeem Africa and establish a world wide confraternity of black people. Above all, he believed that the Negroes of the world, united together by the consciousness of race and nationality, could become a great and powerful people.[15]

Garvey believed that economic power through ownership of businesses could lay a solid foundation for eventual black salvation. He established the Black Star Steamship Company, the Negro Factory Corporation, and sent a commercial and industrial mission to Liberia. All of these undertakings turned out to be complete failures because of incompetence, mismanagement, and other difficulties.[16]

Garvey was a charismatic leader, and his movement had a certain theatrical quality and flamboyance which made it appealing to the black masses. Colorful parades, uniforms, and marching songs were distinctive traits of the UNIA. At an ostentatious convention in 1920, Garvey himself was named Provisional President of Africa and President-General and Administrator of the UNIA. A "provisional government" was formed, and Garvey conferred knighthood upon the members of his "High Executive Council."

In 1925, Garvey was convicted of using the mails to defraud. The sentence was commuted by President Calvin Coolidge in 1927, and Garvey was deported as an undesirable alien. He died in London in 1940. After Garvey

15 *Ibid.*, p. 50.
16 *Ibid.*, p. 51.

was deported, his movement split into factions and degenerated. Thousands of hopeful blacks lost the precious savings which they had invested in the UNIA.

Black bourgeois nationalism was in decline from 1930 through 1945. The Depression struck Negroes with disproportionate severity, but the New Deal, created partly in response to pressure from the left, eased the situation. Blacks were admitted to federal work projects and Civilian Conservation Corps camps.

It was during this period that the Communist Party succeeded in establishing itself for a time as the leading advocate of equal rights for black people. Politically, the Communists recognized the Negroes in the Black Belt to be a nation, and in the northern ghettos to be a national minority suffering special discrimination, unlike the older Socialist party, which regarded blacks simply as dark-skinned poor workers and farmers without special problems.[17] The Communists, however, did not press their program of self-determination of the Black Belt and instead concentrated on trade union work and antidiscrimination struggles. They organized the American Negro Labor Congress, while their interracial Trade Union Unity League fought "to wipe out discrimination against Negro workers

[17] In 1928 the Communist Party adopted a resolution which declared: "While continuing and intensifying the struggle under the slogan of full social and political equality for the Negroes, which must remain the central slogan of our Party for work among the masses, the Party must come out openly and unreservedly for the right of Negroes to self-determination in the Southern states, where the Negroes form a majority of the population. . . . The Negro question in the United States must be treated in its relation to the Negro question and struggles in other parts of the world. The Negro race everywhere is an oppressed race. Whether it is a minority (U.S.A., etc.), majority (South Africa), or inhabits a so-called independent state (Liberia, etc.), the Negroes are oppressed by imperialism. Thus, a common tie of interest is established for the revolutionary struggle of race and national liberation from imperialist domination of the Negroes in various parts of the world." (Foster, p. 461).

in the industries and in the unions," and demanded "equal pay for equal work, especially for Negroes. . . ."[18] In 1930 the ANLC was succeeded by the League of Struggle for Negro Rights, with Langston Hughes as president. On May 8, 1933, it led a march of thirty-five hundred to Washington to present President Roosevelt the "Bill of Civil Rights for the Negro People" which it had drafted.

In the South, the Communists organized the Sharecroppers Union in 1931 which attained six thousand members by 1934 in Alabama, Florida, Georgia, and the Carolinas. It defended farmers against foreclosures even to the use of guns. Five were killed in such encounters.

In March 1930, the Communist Party claimed a total of about fifteen hundred black members, but by 1938 this figure had risen to ten thousand, or 14 percent of total Party membership.[19] Adam Clayton Powell praised the Communists, and said that "Today there is no group in America, including the Christian Churches, that practices racial brotherhood one-tenth as much as the Communist Party."[20]

The Unemployed Councils founded by the Communists were the largest and most militant interracial organizations this country has known. A nineteen-year-old black Communist organizer, Angelo Herndon, led an interracial march for welfare in Atlanta, Georgia, in 1932. Sentenced to eighteen to twenty years on the chain gang for "attempting to incite to insurrection," he was freed by an immense national campaign which brought into the Communist movement his lawyer, Benjamin Davis, who later became, as a Communist, the second black city councilman in New York (succeeding Adam Clayton Powell on the latter's election to Congress).

Davis was recruited by the remarkable William L. Pat-

[18] *Labor Fact Book* (New York: International Publishers, 1931), pp. 136–37.
[19] Foster, pp. 458, 504.
[20] *Ibid.*, p. 457.

terson, son of a slave, who was more responsible for the successful defense of the Scottsboro boys, nine black youths accused in 1931 of raping two white women, than any other individual. Patterson's organization of mass-demonstration defenses in legal cases continued until 1951, when he led several hundred people to the South in an unsuccessful attempt to save the Martinsville seven, charged with rape, from execution. This was the last movement-size undertaking of the American Communist Party in its twenty years as the most influential radical force in the black community, but Patterson, now seventy-five years old and still a Communist, continues to be effective. His 1951 book-length petition to the United Nations, *We Charge Genocide,* is presently on the reading list of the Black Panther party. It was on his advice that the Panthers engaged a white attorney prepared to conduct a militant defense, Charles Garry, as lawyer for Huey P. Newton. It was also on his advice that the Panthers conducted the mass-demonstration "Free Huey" campaign in defense of Newton.

The creation in 1935 of the Congress of Industrial Organizations under militant Communist prodding had the consequence that black and white workers fought side by side for their mutual benefit in the rubber, auto, steel, and mining industries, as well as in the National Maritime Union and the West Coast International Longshoremen's and Warehousemen's Union. Black economic boycotts were organized. "Don't buy where you can't work!," the organizers shouted.

With the advent of World War II, black men once again came to the defense of the country. At first there was some hesitancy because of discrimination and segregation in the defense program. A. Philip Randolph threatened a massive black March on Washington in 1941 unless President Franklin D. Roosevelt brought a halt to discrimination in defense plants. Executive Order 8802, establishing the federal Fair Employment Practices Commission, did just that. It prohibited racial and religious discrimination in war industries, government training programs, and government industries. The planned march was called off.

Over a million black men served in the Armed Forces during the war. They served in all capacities. Black pilots were trained at an Army flying school in Tuskegee, Alabama, and in 1942, the *Booker T. Washington,* the first U.S. merchant ship to be commanded by a black captain, was launched. On the home front, black workers, taking advantage of the defense jobs which were now open to them, began to improve their economic status. The income gap between black and white families closed appreciably during the period of World War II and the Korean War. After this period the gap began to widen again, partly because pressure for hiring and upgrading of black workers fell off as the government successfully destroyed the Communist Party.

A. Philip Randolph, a master strategist, used the wartime period of international turmoil to advance the Negro cause. In 1948 he proclaimed to a Senate committee that he would advise black youths to refuse military induction unless segregation and discrimination were banned in the armed forces. Once more a President yielded to Randolph's threat, and Harry Truman directed that the armed forces provide "equal treatment and equal opportunity" to all personnel.

But executive orders were not sufficient to combat the virus of racism which afflicted white America. At the height of the war in 1943, a bloody race riot occurred in Detroit, Michigan, and thirty-four persons died. Earlier in that same year troops had to be called in when a riot broke out in Mobile, Alabama, following the upgrading of black workers at a shipyard. After the war there was a resurgence of Klan activity and southern terrorism. More ominously, automation was by then clearly the wave of the future, raising the specter of widespread technological unemployment.

Large numbers of blacks, by that time, were firmly lodged in northern cities and the activities of the Com-

munists and later of men like Randolph had made them
aware, if only vaguely, of the latent power which they
possessed. Important gains had been made during the war,
but these were now threatened by postwar developments.
For ordinary black people, particularly those in the northern cities, the question was how best to safeguard their
newly achieved economic and social status. Two forms of
black leadership projected programs designed to answer
this question. The first was represented by the NAACP and
the Congress of Racial Equality, which was organized in
1942. As early as 1945 NAACP lawyers had begun making
plans for a massive legal assault on the edifice of segregation. CORE activists favored the nonviolent, direct action
approach. In 1947, CORE in conjunction with the Fellowship of Reconciliation organized the first freedom ride,
then called a "Journey of Reconciliation." Its purpose was
to test the enforcement of a U. S. Supreme Court decision
outlawing segregation on interstate buses. Although the
NAACP and CORE differed in their tactics, they were in
agreement on the ultimate objective: to fight for racial
integration as the means for insuring black equality.

While these two organizations went about their work,
increasing numbers of blacks were turning to another
organization—the Nation of Islam, sometimes known as
the Black Muslims. The Muslims had been around since
the early 1930s, but their membership had never climbed
much above 10,000 in prewar years. In fact, by 1945, their
ranks had dwindled to about one thousand in four temples.
After the war, however, there was a steady growth both in
the number of members and in the number of Muslim
temples scattered in cities across the country. The NAACP
and integrationism were boosted to national prominence in
1954 when the U. S. Supreme Court handed down its
famous public school desegregation decision. Some people
thought the struggle was close to reaching a successful
conclusion. But this decision had little effect on the steady
growth of the Muslim organization. In 1955 there were
fifteen temples. This number rose to thirty temples in

twenty-eight cities by March of 1959. With the insight gained by the passage of time, it is now clear that the Muslim appeal was not diminished by the 1954 decision because their base was fundamentally different from that of the NAACP and CORE. Both CORE and the NAACP were middle-class organizations which directed their attention to attacking the legal forms of segregation which were prevalent in the South. The Muslims were strongest among working-class blacks who resided in the urban areas of the North. Court decisions and southern freedom rides had little or no effect on the concrete economic status of these blacks.

It was in the summer of 1930 that a mysterious "prophet," W. D. Fard, appeared in Detroit peddling raincoats and silks, and dispensing strange teachings about Africa, the white man, the Christian Church, and Islam. Soon he organized the first Temple of Islam, and by 1934, when Fard mysteriously disappeared, the movement had grown to eight thousand members. It was then that Elijah Muhammad came into power. Muhammad was Minister of Islam under Fard. Born Elijah Poole in Georgia, his family migrated to Detroit where he joined the new movement and was given his "original" Islamic name. His "slave name," Poole, was then dropped.

Under Muhammad's guidance Fard was deified and identified with Allah, and the Muslim movement grew into a dedicated, tightly disciplined bloc with a membership estimated in the early 1960s at between sixty-five thousand and one hundred thousand. Muhammad set himself up in a mansion in Chicago, where Temple No. 2, the Muslim headquarters, is located. The Muslims established a "university of Islam"; their temples are found in practically every major American city, and they are collectively engaged in far-flung business and real estate activities.

The Muslim ideology is compounded of a fantastic mythology coupled with elements of orthodox Islamic doctrine. The Muslims reject Christianity, which they regard as the "white man's religion," and instead have constructed their own version of Islam. Allah is seen as the "Supreme Black Man," and it is asserted that the first men were black men. C. Eric Lincoln, in his classic study of the Muslims, described their beliefs:

> The "originality" of the Black Nation and the creation of the white race by Yakub, "a black scientist in rebellion against Allah"—this is the central myth of the Black Muslim Movement. It is the fundamental premise upon which rests the whole theory of black supremacy and white degradation. . . .
> These devils [white men] were given six thousand years to rule. The allotted span of their rule was ended in 1914, and their "years of grace" will last no longer than is necessary for the chosen of Allah to be resurrected from the mental death imposed upon them by the white man. This resurrection is the task of Muhammad himself, Messenger of Allah and Spiritual Leader of the Lost-Found Nation in the West.[21]

With this resurrection the white slavemasters are to be destroyed in a catastrophic "Battle of Armageddon."

The Muslim program calls for racial separation and a complete economic withdrawal from white society; this is to culminate in the establishment of a separate black state. On the back page of each issue of *Muhammad Speaks,* the weekly Muslim newspaper, are detailed the Muslim demands.

> We want our people in America whose parents or grandparents were descendants from slaves, to be allowed to establish a separate state or territory of their own—either on this continent or elsewhere. We believe that our former slave masters are obligated to provide such land and that the area must be fertile and minerally rich. We believe that our former slave masters are obligated to maintain and supply our needs in this separate territory

[21] C. Eric Lincoln, *The Black Muslims in America* (Boston: Beacon, 1961), pp. 76–77.

for the next 20 to 25 years—until we are able to produce and supply our own needs.

Since we cannot get along with them in peace and equality, after giving them 400 years of our sweat and blood and receiving in return some of the worst treatment human beings have ever experienced, we believe our contributions to this land and the suffering forced upon us by white America, justifies our demand for complete separation in a state or territory of our own.

These obviously are long-term demands. In the interim the Muslims want equality of legal treatment, employment, and educational opportunities, although in the latter they want schools which are segregated by sex.

The Muslim organization grew in response to a perceived threat to the economic security of a certain class of black people. Black workers made significant occupational advances after 1940 in intermediate-level jobs such as operatives and kindred workers. But this category of workers was hard hit by technological unemployment due to automation. In 1960, for example, the unemployment rate in this category was 6.4 percent for males and 9.9 percent for females—a higher rate of unemployment than among any other category of workers except laborers.[22] At the same time that some black workers were moving into this new category, the demand for unskilled and semiskilled labor, categories in which blacks are traditionally overrepresented, was declining faster than black workers could be retrained for other lines of work.[23] Economic self-sufficiency of the race as a whole, the Muslims proposed, following a by now well-worn path, is the only solution to this problem. Racial integration is no answer, they contended, because it can't work.

The effectiveness of the Muslims was limited, however, by their religious mysticism, which alienated many

[22] Leonard Broom and Norval Glenn, *Transformation of the Negro American* (New York: Harper & Row, 1965), p. 118.
[23] *Ibid.*

blacks and obscured the question of how to change power relations in America, and by the fact that their organization served in large part as simply an alternative route to middle-class status for some blacks, rather than actively attacking the problem of general black oppression.

Nonetheless, the nationalist position was measurably strengthened in the middle 1960s when it became obvious to many observers that the integrationist civil rights movement had reached its peak and was in decline, having only minimally affected the lives of ordinary black people. This failure compounded the crisis which was precipitated at the close of the war years.

The next phase of nationalist expression followed the demise of the civil rights movement. The modern civil rights movement was launched by one of those little incidents which happen all the time, but which in a revolutionary epoch can assume awesome proportions. In December 1955, Mrs. Rosa Parks, a black woman weary from work, refused to give up her seat on a Montgomery, Alabama, city bus to a white man. The irate white bus driver had her arrested for this open affront to the unwritten, but, nonetheless, real southern behavioral code. The driver did not know, could not know, that southern blacks were like a coiled spring and that tension had reached the breaking point. Mrs. Parks was arrested little more than a year after the 1954 Supreme Court school decision, a decision which many southern blacks thought spelled the end of segregation. But the white South had responded in classic style and openly defied the Court ruling. The formation of the first White Citizens Council, in Indianola, Mississippi, just two months after the Court decision presaged the bitter struggle which was to come. Blacks, however, were in no mood for more procrastination. This was it. If talk of integration meant anything, now was time for the struggle to be joined and fought to its conclusion, whatever that might be.

Within two days the black people of Montgomery had begun organizing a massive boycott of the municipal buses. A young Baptist minister, Martin Luther King, Jr., who had arrived in town only months earlier, was named to head up the boycott. King was given the job probably because he was new and not identified with any of the factions which splintered the black community. It took more than a year for the bus boycott to succeed in finally forcing desegregation of public transportation facilities in Montgomery, but this struggle represented a clear victory for the nonviolent, direct action tactics advocated by the newcomer from Atlanta. The tactic of court struggle stressed by the NAACP was cast in a shadow, and King became a national leader.

King moved on to new battles. As he wrote in his account of the Montgomery drama, *Stride Toward Freedom*, the problem in that city was "merely symptomatic of the larger national problem," and he decided to go wherever necessary to attack this problem.[24] Nonviolent change for the better was possible, King believed, if only the federal government and liberal whites would back the Negro struggle.

It was this belief which, as the crisis of black America deepened, converted King into what some regard as a reluctant accomplice of the white power structure. As the years passed, the liberal establishment tried to use King to restrain the threatening rebelliousness of the black masses and the young militants. Thus one of the admitted purposes of his poor people's campaign, for example, was to channel that rebelliousness into a movement he thought could be as effective as Gandhi's had been. In the press his calls for nonviolence were frequently contrasted with the "rabble rousing" of black militants.

King could not repudiate this role because he was convinced that the establishment could be pushed and pressured to implement his program, provided that he did not move so far and so fast as to lose his white liberal support.

[24] *Stride Toward Freedom* (New York: Harper & Brothers, 1958), p. 189.

In 1957, King organized his Southern Christian Leadership Conference, composed then mostly of black ministers from ten states. With SCLC as a base, King led numerous economic boycotts and desegregation and voter registration campaigns in cities such as Albany, Georgia; Birmingham, Alabama; St. Augustine, Florida; and Selma, Alabama. Jailed and beaten frequently, he was nearly killed in 1958, when he was stabbed in the chest by a black woman, while he was autographing books in Harlem. In his wanderings, King seemed to be in search of a "new Montgomery"—the right confrontation or combination of demonstrations which would wake up white America and result in the granting of full equality to black people.

By 1963 and the March on Washington, King's dream was no closer to being realized. Already, even among some of those who demonstrated in support of it, there was the gnawing suspicion that the civil rights bill, if passed, would not be effectively enforced, that it was only another palliative. Critics sprang up where none had been before. King himself was accused of being opportunistic in his campaigns and of not seeing them through to the finish. A new breed of leaders, drawn from the northern ghettos or the fierce rural civil rights drives in the South, was growing into maturity. Black Muslim Minister Malcolm X challenged King's espousal of integration and nonviolence. Later, after he left the Muslims, Malcolm, a cogent and persuasive speaker, advocated the need for radical change —and many listened. Young, skeptical leaders were also being tempered in King's stepchild organization, the Student Nonviolent Coordinating Committee. These activists, mostly college students or ex-students, were beginning to examine political and economic exploitation, and the American government's perpetration of injustice not only at home but in foreign countries. In January 1966, SNCC left the fold of traditional civil rights activity by taking a stand in opposition to the Vietnam war and the military draft. The SNCC radicals felt they were involved in a movement of worldwide dimensions.

With the advent of the era of urban rebellions in 1964, it became painfully obvious that the civil rights movement had not altered significantly the plight of the black masses. The cry of "black power" articulated this awareness and presented a new departure for the freedom movement. Black control of black organizations and communities was demanded, and militants turned their backs on the goal of racial integration. The liberal reform strategy advocated by King and others came under suspicious scrutiny. Revolution replaced integration as the most used word of the day.

King had secured a leadership position in the top ranks of the civil rights movement by adapting the thrust of his actions and campaigns to the shifting sentiment and conditions within the movement. He trailed the militants, but often managed to bring along large numbers of ordinary black people, particularly in the South, to the new positions he adopted. His initial efforts were aimed at legal rights, such as the right to vote and desegregation of public facilities. As early as 1965, however, King urged President Lyndon B. Johnson to issue "unconditional and unambiguous" pleas for peace talks, but it was not until 1967 that he came out clearly against the Vietnam war, basing his opposition on his adherence to nonviolence and the fact that the war was draining funds from social welfare programs at home and thereby adding to urban unrest.

The Chicago open housing campaign in 1966 was King's first effort to deal with more basic internal issues. It ended without reaching its goal, but King regrouped his forces and late in 1967 began planning for a massive poor people's campaign in Washington. This new campaign was not to focus on civil rights but was to demand jobs and housing. Not only were blacks to be the beneficiaries, if it were successful, but also poor whites, Indians, and Spanish-speaking people. King sensed that he had to attack the economic problem because political rights were meaningless to a people held in economic bondage. When the Memphis garbage men went on strike and called on King to aid them, he readily accepted. The significance of that

strike by black workers was pointed out by Norman Pearlstine, writing in the *Wall Street Journal* of March 8, 1968:
"Negroes here [in Memphis] have found a weapon in the
sanitation strike that may be picked up elsewhere by civil
rights militants. In many communities, particularly in the
South, sanitation departments are predominantly Negro."
Pearlstine termed the alliance of black workers with civil
rights groups a powerful coalition. The hope that such a
coalition might give a new lease on life to a sinking civil
rights movement was shattered, however, by an assassin's
bullet.

Writing in *Look* magazine in the same month that he
was killed, King once again articulated his basic philosophy and his continuing hope: "We have, through
massive nonviolent action, an opportunity to avoid a national disaster and create a new spirit of class and racial
harmony. . . . All of us are on trial in this troubled
hour, but time still permits us to meet the future with a
clear conscience." Time, however, ran out, and the verdict
of guilty which history first passed on white America in
1619 was once again confirmed.

With the apparent failure of the integration movement
in the middle 1960s, black nationalism again became a visible force on the American scene. White journalists started
quoting the same nationalist spokesmen whom they dismissed as madmen before. Malcolm X was still called a
firebrand and an agitator, but the journalists realized now
that he spoke for many black people. This was confirmed
in 1966 when both SNCC and CORE openly embraced
nationalism. The subsequent Black Power Conference in
Newark and the revelation that the undeniably white Ford
Foundation was financing CORE completely stilled any
lingering doubts that black nationalism was nothing more
than a fringe phenomenon. One could be for it or against
it, but it was no longer possible to ignore nationalist sentiment.

If it is admitted that black nationalism is a serious component of black thinking, both in the past and present, the

question naturally arises why this ideology is vigorously advocated only during certain times of social stress. Does black nationalism exist only at certain historical junctures, or is it always there like the subterranean stresses which precede an earthquake?

It is usual to ascribe nationalist feeling to black "frustration" and to imply that this is a pathological response. But to understand outbursts of nationalism fully, it is necessary to delve into the social fabric of Afro-American life. The foregoing historical sketch strongly suggests that nationalism is an ever-present but usually latent (or unarticulated) tendency, particularly among blacks who find themselves on the lower rungs of the socioeconomic ladder. The members of this class traditionally exhibit a sense of group solidarity because of the open hostility of the surrounding white society. This hostility stems from the fact that whites historically have viewed this class of blacks as "irresponsible Negroes," the spiritual descendants of the "field niggers" of slavery. Whites not only held these beliefs but they acted upon them, treating ordinary blacks as a thoroughly worthless and despicable lot.

In addition to its historical origins, this white hostility also grows out of one of the hard facts of American economic life—that there is insufficient productive space in the American economy for twenty million black people. This is one reason why white workers today are among the worst bigots and racists. They know that their jobs, and consequently their economic security, are directly threatened by integration efforts. On the other hand, black workers cannot help but become increasingly conscious of the fact that the American economy is structured to preclude their full participation.

Black unemployment, especially among youth, normally assumes disaster proportions. For example, in the years since 1954, a period of unprecedented prosperity for the United States, the rate of over-all black unemployment, according to U. S. Labor Department statistics, has consistently stayed well above 6 percent, a situation that would be termed a major recession if it occurred among whites. Furthermore, the jobs which blacks do hold usually offer substandard wages and great instability. Even in recent years the overwhelming majority of employed black males have held low-paying jobs in the unskilled and semiskilled categories. At the same time, again relying on government findings, Negro life in general in the hard-core city slums is getting no better, and, in many instances, is growing noticeably worse.

Not only is the economic situation of the masses of blacks grim, but the prospects are that it will not improve, rather it will continue to deteriorate. This is due partly to the unregulated impact of automation. Leonard Broom and Norval Glenn, in a careful study of this problem, wrote the following conclusion in 1965:

> Mechanization and automation in industry and consequent decreased demand for unskilled and semiskilled workers are tending to push Negroes farther down in the economic hierarchy, and prospects do not seem good for an offsetting increase in Negro education and skills during the next few years. At best, a majority of adult Negroes will be rather poorly educated for another four or five decades, and in the absence of an extensive and unprecedented job retraining program, they are going to fall farther behind other Americans in economic standing.[25]

Since these words were written, various retraining schemes have been tried, not the "massive and unprecedented" program called for by these authors, but small-scale projects which have had commensurate results.

More recently a business writer corroborated the findings of Broom and Glenn:

> Negro gains in income, it is true, have been more rapid than whites' gains recently. However, the long-term trend has not been so favorable. In 1952, during the Korean-War boom, median family income for non-whites

[25] Broom and Glenn, p. 187.

climbed to 57 percent of the white figure. After a couple of dips and rises, it was only three percentage points higher in 1966. Even this gain largely reflects the movement of Negroes out of the South, where income levels are generally low. Relative gains *within* the South, and within the rest of the U.S., have been negligible.

The median figures, of course, lump together Negroes who are advancing economically with those who are not. The reality seems to be that *some* Negroes, especially those in the middle and upper income brackets, are gaining rapidly on whites, while others, especially slum dwellers, are losing ground in relative terms.[26]

Black workers and unemployed quite rightly conclude from these facts that there is no productive role for them in the structure of the American economy. In such a situation, as A. James Gregor argued in an insightful 1963 essay, a turn toward nationalism is a perfectly sane and rational response. "Negro nationalism is," Gregor concluded, "the spontaneous and half articulated answer of the lower-class and petty-bourgeois Negro to *real* problems little appreciated by white liberals and half-understood by the 'new' Negro middle class. Negro radicalism seeks solution to problems which afflict the Negro masses as distinct from problems characteristically those of the semiprofessional and white collar Negro bourgeoisie."[27]

If the general society which envelops a given ethnic group refuses to protect the economic security and human dignity of that group, then the only recourse is for the group in question to fall back upon its own resources. This is a logical conclusion. It is in the *application* of this conclusion that much confusion has arisen. What baffles many people, but is completely intelligible, as will be shown, is the tendency for this nationalism to withdraw into mystical, religious fantasies, escapist dreams of a massive emi-

[26] Edmund K. Faltermayer, "More Dollars and More Diplomas," *Fortune*, January 1968, pp. 222–24.
[27] A. James Gregor, "Black Nationalism," *Science & Society*, Fall 1963, p. 417.

gration to Africa or utopian hopes that American capitalism will somehow see fit to grant black people a chunk of its
territory.

Whites do not notice the substratum of nationalism
among ordinary blacks until it is verbalized. This nationalism has always existed in the cultural life of black people,
especially in their music, but most whites are unaware of it
until it finds a conscious advocate.

Intellectual advocacy, however, is largely a prerogative
of the articulate and educated—the black middle class.
Hence, whether nationalism finds verbal expression depends mainly on whether there are articulate, and
usually middle-class or middle-class-oriented, spokesmen
who are inclined to advocate this maligned ideology. This
inclination, in turn, is related to the ambivalent attitudes
which the black middle class displays toward the white
world and indeed toward its own blackness.

A number of writers have documented and described
this ambivalence.[28] Suffice it here to outline its major
features. The Negro middle class, not unlike middle classes
of other minority groups, is characterized by a desire to
separate itself from the masses. This is because it has
selected the white middle class as its reference group and,
therefore, tries to assume the values and attitudes (including prejudices) of this group. The black bourgeoisie identifies blackness with subjugation and shame. Furthermore,
because this class of Negroes has achieved middle-class
economic status, it seeks to dissociate itself from what it re-
gards as lower-class blacks and thereby establish itself as a

---

[28] E. Franklin Frazier (*Black Bourgeoisie*) and Nathan Hare
(*The Black Anglo-Saxons* [New York: Marzani & Munsell,
1965]) must be credited with drawing attention to the concept
of black middle-class ambivalence. They have been criticized,
however, for relying on impressionistic evidence and exhibiting
undue bias in their writings. Nevertheless, more "scholarly"
research has tended to confirm their conclusions about ambivalence. See, for example, "Color Gradation and Attitudes Among
Middle-Income Negroes," *American Sociological Review*, Vol.
31, No. 3 (June 1966), p. 365.

distinct group, worthy of inclusion in the great American mainstream. But unlike white minority groups, the black middle class can never win this general acceptance, precisely because of its blackness.

In white America, a change of name or religion means little if the skin is still dark. Middle-class Negroes know that they possess the income and/or education that would entitle them to full acceptance as middle-class Americans (something their poorer black brethren don't share), but white racism prevents this hope from being realized. This poses a continuing dilemma for the Negro middle class and results in the ambivalent attitudes it displays toward its own race and toward the white world.

Normally, the black bourgeoisie favors integration as the solution to the race problem. This is because integration operates in the individual self-interest of middle-class blacks. Racial integration promises to fulfill their dream of assimilation. Through integration they hope to be given the high-status, high-income jobs held by whites, to be allowed to move into predominantly white suburban neighborhoods and to be accepted as full participants in the social life of their white peers. In short, racial integration offers middle-class Negroes the pleasurable prospect of shedding their blackness.

But when white society, for whatever reasons, appears to shut the door on integration, the black bourgeoisie responds by adopting a nationalist stance. Like a child refused a stick of candy which it knew belonged to it by rights, the black bourgeoisie rejects the white world and flouts its blackness. It becomes loudly nationalist and threatens to rain destruction on the offending whites. Conferences are called, manifestos issued, and delegations are dispatched to confer with African leaders. Middle-class Negroes become nationalist advocates, and blacks who have been nationalists all along are accorded a new respect. All of this bravado works, of course, to soothe the injured egos of the black bourgeoisie. More importantly, it serves to legitimize the black bourgeoisie in the eyes of the black masses, who are led to believe that middle-class Negroes have at last "come home to their people." This temporarily shared nationalism also provides a convenient cover under which the black bourgeoisie can foist its business schemes, professional stratum, and general leadership upon the masses of blacks.

At such times the white media report that Negroes have suddenly gone nationalist, failing completely to point out which blacks are nationalist now and which have always been nationalists.

This then, in summary fashion, is the mechanism by which black nationalism comes to the attention of the white public. It is only when "respectable" Negroes take up the nationalist cry or give heed to "rabble rousing" nationalist spokesmen, that white America gives the matter any serious consideration. The fact that black nationalism normally lies hidden just beneath the surface veneer of black America is overlooked by mass media which are geared to crises, scandals, and otherwise spectacular developments.

Middle-class black students play a unique role in this process. To some extent they share the ambivalent feelings of their middle-class parents, but having been born and raised in the Negro middle class, it is easier for them to discern its weaknesses and illusions. At the same time, these black students, particularly the present high school and college generations, are less enchanted with the white world. They've heard the bitter stories told by their older brothers and sisters who went south or went north in a vain struggle to make the American Dream a reality for downtrodden blacks. These students identify, however hesitantly or confusedly, with the majority of their race, and their nationalism springs from conviction rather than from the rancor of wounded egos.

(2)

Human beings usually are able to make some suitable adaptation to the hard realities of life which are imposed by nature. They find it more difficult, in the long run impossible, to adapt when they know the burden is unfairly imposed by other men. But history and circumstance do not always offer the best conditions for open rebellion against tyranny. There are situations where one must look in unexpected places for the embryonic signs of revolt. This is especially true in cases where the oppressed group believes that the normal channels for change are closed, or when it is not even aware that such channels exist. Seeing no way out, the oppressed group looks for some other means of change, and if none exists, it is created out of the cultural fabric which is the only thing the oppressed can call their own. Thus traditional religious forms in some tribal and peasant cultures have been "modified and readapted, not only as vehicles for expressing grievances, but as powerful mechanisms of social integration and political cohesion during the earliest phases of armed resistance."[29] Examples of such revolutionary millenarian movements are found in the history of feudal Europe, particularly from the twelfth through the sixteenth centuries. These movements frequently culminated in peasant wars.

In more recent times millenarian movements have been widely distributed in the primitive and underdeveloped colonial areas of the world. The catalogue of these movements includes, for example, the ghost dance of the North American Plains Indians, the Cargo Cults of Melanesia, the Birsaite Movement of India, the Maji-Maji Rebellion in Tanzania, the Tai Ping Rebellion in China and others. These movements characteristically involved fantasies about the coming of the millennium, at which time the yoke of colonialism and white oppression was to be lifted.

[29] A. Norman Klein, "On Revolutionary Violence," *Studies on the Left,* Vol. 6, No. 3 (1966), p. 69.

Much energy is expended making "preparations" for the anticipated time of liberation. Some observers are inclined to dismiss millenarian movements as nothing more than escapist fantasies. But when an oppressed people becomes aware of its oppression, yet sees no secular or "normal" means of redress, then "revolutionary millenarianism poses a radical alternative—albeit utopian and concocted out of ritual eschatological fantasy—to the organization of colonial power."[30] Thus, the Cargo Cults which appeared in Melanesia shortly after World War I predicted the arrival of a steamship bearing the spirits of dead ancestors who were to bring with them the precious "cargo" of liberation. This cargo was to include flour, rice, tobacco, weapons, and other "trade" which the ancestors decreed belonged to the natives and not to the whites. The colonial whites were to be driven away in this process, and the cargo (symbolizing the land and its fruit) was to return to the hands of its rightful owners, the natives. The Cargo Cult thus gave expression to the then vaguely formulated nationalist ideas, and was in effect a "protonationalist" movement.

Peter Worsley, a British student of millenarian movements, has observed that such beliefs "have recurred again and again throughout history, despite failures, disappointments, and repression, precisely because they make such a strong appeal to the oppressed, the disinherited and the wretched. They therefore form an integral part of that stream of thought which refused to accept the rule of a superordinate class, or of a foreign power. . . ."[31] Worsley found that millenarian cults were likely to appear among the populations of colonial countries, discontented peasants, and among certain groups in the towns and cities of feudal civilizations where there was "dissatisfaction with the existing social relations and yearnings for a happier life."[32] Millenarian movements flower when

[30] Ibid.
[31] Peter Worsley, The Trumpet Shall Sound (London: MacGibbon and Kee, 1957), p. 225.
[32] Ibid., p. 243.

such groups seek to rid themselves of oppression but do not have at hand effective means of change. They therefore readapt traditional cultural forms and convert them into weapons, however "impractical," of revolution.

This is where so-called irrational elements creep into the picture. It must be understood, however, that it is not irrational for a people who are not familiar with Western technology nor in possession of a "rational" and completely worked out theory of social change to redefine and restructure familiar cultural forms in an effort to make them serve a liberating function. Within the context of available alternatives, and to a mind not enamored with formal Western logic, this is a perfectly rational and understandable choice. It is rational in the sense that it is an effort, based on available cultural materials, to connect cause with effect, or means with ends. It is not logical in a formal sense because it does not employ the scientific approach which has been distilled from Western culture. This is the difference.

A successful millenarian cult with a mass following performs an integratory function in the society which generates it. The cult overcomes the many divisions, schisms, and suspicions which characterized the colonized native society. This is because the cult bases its authority on an appeal to powerful religious symbols or universally agreed-upon cultural values in the native society which have been suppressed by the presence of an alien colonial culture. Thus religion and cultural values provide the leader of a cult with a means, and in the protonational period this is often the only effective means available, of uniting a divided people. That this unity is based on a program of illusions should not lead one to overlook the basic significance of millenarian cults. And that is that such cults can represent the first step in the developing of a revolutionary consciousness and program among a subjugated, colonial people.

Basically there seem to be two choices for the millenarian cult in the later stages of its development: It can be transformed into a revolutionary political movement, or it can drift off into passivity and irrelevance.

For Melanesia, we have seen a general trend in the development of the cults away from apocalyptic mysticism towards secular political organization, a trend from religious cult to political party and cooperative. This development is by no means unusual. But when secular organization has replaced millenarism, the cults which persist into the era of secular politics almost invariably lose their drive. The revolutionary energy is drained from them; they become passive. The day of the millennium is pushed farther back into the remote future; the Kingdom of the Lord is to come, not on this earth, but in the next world; and the faithful are to gain entrance to it not by fighting for it in the here and now with their strong right arms but by leading quiet, virtuous lives. This transition to passivism is particularly marked in two situations: where the cult has been defeated, and where political aspirations are no longer masked in religious forms, but are expressed through political parties."[33]

Worsley compares the escapist and passive trends in millenarian cults with revival movements among southern blacks. He argues that such revivalist religious movements derive from the fact that black people are largely restricted from participating in other institutional forms of American culture. What Worsley fails to note, however, is that an even closer connection exists between the activist phase of millenarian cults and traditional black nationalist movements as they have developed in this country. Like the millenarian cult, black nationalism arises in social conditions where oppression is perceived, but effective means for ending it do not appear available. The most widely promoted program for resolving the race problem is integration, but as noted earlier, this program has recurrently failed in its concrete application. It has been periodically and graphically demonstrated to black people that racial

[33] *Ibid.*, p. 231.

integration and assimilation are not today real prospects in America. Thus black people observe that the "normal" route to change is closed, and think that even social revolution, in the orthodox sense, is out of the question. The uninitiated conceive of black nationalism as terribly revolutionary. Actually, traditional black nationalism all too often represents a denial of the possibility of social revolution. At best, traditional black nationalism is a pre-revolutionary development. The traditional black nationalist views reform (i.e., integration) as an ineffective remedy which, in any case, cannot be administered. The whole history of black people's experience in America stands as a vivid testimony to the validity of this conclusion. It is a simple next step, therefore, to conclude that a revolution in the United States is impossible, too.

After all, is it not true that one of the best examples of an incipient revolutionary movement in recent U.S. history, the labor movement of the 1930s, has now become reformist and indeed a bulwark of racism? But if both reform and revolution are excluded as realistic possibilities, then the only alternatives left are religious and cultural fantasies about liberation. The traditional black nationalist cannot, of course, admit that these are nothing more than fantasies.

In this light the religious mysticism of the Black Muslims and the fantastic dreams of other traditional black nationalists now become understandable. The Muslims prophesied the coming of an Apocalypse in which the white man would be destroyed and the black man enthroned as ruler of the world. Other nationalists long for a return "home" to Africa, or hope fervently that America will see fit to grant black people a separate territory within the United States. The Western mind would label all of this as clearly irrational. But this obscures the contention that these nationalist sects are the prototypes which are laying the basis for a genuinely revolutionary movement.

Within the past few years, evidence has been mounting that traditional black nationalism is moving, at least in some instances, from the protonationalist phase into revolutionary nationalism. In other cases traditional black nationalism is developing into bourgeois nationalism which, not unlike the integrationist movement, is oriented toward reforms. In both instances black nationalism is becoming more "rational" and is trying to generate programs which address themselves to things as they are rather than to things as they exist in the minds of protonationalists.

The urban rebellions played a key role in retrieving black nationalism from the world of fantasy. Beginning in 1964 when there were fifteen outbreaks, these rebellions have shown a tendency to increase both in intensity and frequency. In 1965 there were nine rebellions; thirty-eight in 1966; 128 in 1967, including massive revolts in Newark and Detroit; and in the first six months of 1968 there were 131 urban rebellions, most of them triggered by the assassination of Martin Luther King. A significant proportion of the black population participates in these rebellions, not just a handful. A survey by the National Advisory Commission on Civil Disorders found that about 18 percent—instead of the commonly believed 1 percent or 2 percent—of black residents in major 1967 riot areas participated in the uprisings. The survey also found that the rioters, "far from being the riff-raff and outside agitators," were representative of the young adult black men in the ghetto. They were not newly arrived immigrants from the rural South; they were not unemployed; and they were not predominantly young teenagers. Finally, the study found that the overwhelming majority of black people do not unequivocally oppose riots. They may be ambivalent and deplore the violence in riots, but the majority feel that the rebellions will have beneficial consequences in improving black people's social and economic conditions.

The rebellions were a clear signal that black people would no longer tolerate the conditions under which they were forced to live. At the same time, the rebellions put nationalist leaders on notice that, while more black people might be inclining toward nationalism, they were not in the least interested in idle dreams or obscure mysticism. If the nationalist leaders had nothing more substantial to offer, the people would take to the streets and thereby declare their hatred for the bondage imposed on them. Thus the rebellions, spontaneous outbursts of repressed anger, forced the nationalist spokesmen to come to grips with the problem or to write themselves off as irrelevant cultural conjurers.

IV. BLACK POWER AND BOURGEOIS BLACK NATIONALISM

"The year 1967," wrote James Forman of SNCC, "marked a historic milestone in the struggle for the liberation of black people in the United States and the year that revolutionaries throughout the world began to understand more fully the impact of the black movement. Our liberation will only come when there is final destruction of this mad octopus—the capitalistic system of the United States with all its life-sucking tentacles of exploitation and racism that choke the people of Africa, Asia, and Latin America."[1]

There can be little doubt that Forman was right in pointing to 1967 as an important turning point in the history of black America. It was a year of unprecedentedly massive and widespread urban revolts. It was the year that so-called riots became an institutionalized form of black protest. Government agencies tallied some 164 "civil disorders" which resulted in eighty-nine deaths and insured property damage of sixty-seven million dollars. Uninsured property damage and indirect economic losses were estimated by some as exceeding five hundred million dollars. Clearly, 1967 was the Year of Rebellion.

Rebellion, however, connotes an undirected emotional outburst. It is what Albert Camus called an "incoherent pronouncement." The rebel may transform himself into a revolutionary—he may conclude that liberation really does require the "final destruction of this mad octopus"—but

[1] James Forman, *1967: High Tide of Black Resistance* (New York: SNCC International Affairs Commission, 1968), p. 1.

this is not an automatic consequence of the act of rebellion. In this sense, Forman overestimates the significance of the events of 1967. It would be a closer approximation to the truth to say that 1967 witnessed a dramatic upsurge in militancy and political consciousness among black people. It was this consciousness, however rudimentary, which imbued the rebellions with political meaning. While the rebellions did not constitute a conscious assault on American capitalism, they did involve attacks on some of its more easily accessible and obviously exploitative aspects. A brief examination of one of the more serious, but not atypical, ghetto rebellions will perhaps make this point clear.

(2)

Newark, New Jersey, is a drab city located on the Passaic River. Like many other municipalities hit by riots, Newark was a city in crisis. This was no secret, although public officials may have done their utmost to conceal and obscure the facts. Conditions were bad and were known to be bad. This is why *Life* magazine could call the Newark rebellion "the predictable insurrection." The city had a population of four hundred thousand, of whom more than 50 percent were black. Middle-class whites have been deserting Newark for the suburbs at an accelerating rate over the past twenty years. This altered the city's tax base, forcing steady increments in property taxes. But higher taxes prompted more whites (and those middle-class blacks who could afford it) to leave. Of those who remained in 1967, 74 percent of white and 87 percent of black families lived in rental housing.

Newark's black residents found themselves trapped in a deteriorating situation. Unemployment ran at between 12 percent and 15 percent. At the time of the July rebellion, there were some twenty-four thousand unemployed black men within the city limits. According to the city's application for planning funds under the Model Cities Act, Newark had the nation's highest percentage of bad housing, the greatest rate of crime per one hundred thousand residents, and the highest rates of venereal disease, maternal mortality, and new cases of tuberculosis. Newark was listed second in infant mortality, second in birth rate, and seventh in the absolute number of drug addicts. According to the 1960 census, more than half of the adult black population had less than an eighth-grade education.

Although Newark has a black majority, black people were largely excluded from positions of traditional political power, whether that be in city government or city agencies, such as the police force. The city government and police force were dominated by Italians, who ousted Irish politicians in the early 1960s.

Three developments—relating to police brutality, school policy, and ghetto housing—set the stage for the summer rebellion. Police brutality had long been an emotional issue in Newark, as in most other urban ghettos. The police force boasted fourteen hundred members—proportionately the largest police department of any major city—of whom 250 were black. In 1965 CORE organized a march to protest police brutality, and Mayor Hugh Addonizio conceded that there was "a small group of misguided individuals" on the force. The mayor, however, rejected a demand for a civilian review board.

A conflict over the board of education was provoked when it became known that the secretary of the board intended to retire. A black man—the city's budget director—with a master's degree in accounting was proposed to fill the post. In the black community it was felt that Wilbur Parker was the logical choice for the post since he was fully qualified, and at the time at least 70 percent of the children in the school system were black. But the mayor had nominated a white man who had only a high school education, and he refused to withdraw the nomination. In the weeks preceding the rebellion this became an emotion-laden issue in the black community. Large numbers of blacks disrupted board of education meetings. The situation ended in an unsatisfactory stalemate when the outgoing secretary decided to stay on the job for another year. This dispute over integrating the city's educational bureaucracy particularly incensed middle-class blacks, who viewed this bureaucracy as a potential vehicle of social mobility.

Coupled with the two foregoing developments, and leading up to the rebellion, was a heated controversy over the site selected for a proposed medical school. A 150-acre site in the predominantly black Central Ward had been chosen for the planned New Jersey State Medical School and Training Center. This site was three times larger than had been originally requested, and construction work would necessitate the removal of hundreds of black families from their homes. This created bitter resentment in the black community, and residents crowded the planning board hearing for weeks in a futile effort to have the medical school site decision reversed.

Thus the stage was set. Newark's black community was more and more alienated from the white-controlled city government. Tension was high. All that was required was a spark to set off the conflagration.

Early in the evening of July 12, John Smith, a black cab driver, was arrested by Newark police and charged with "tailgating" and driving the wrong way on a one-way street. Like countless other ghetto residents who run afoul of the cops, Smith was taken to the local precinct station and reportedly severely beaten. Because he was a cabbie, Smith's arrest was quickly reported by other black cab drivers over their radios. Within a short time word of the arrest had spread throughout black Newark, along with rumors of Smith's beating. A large and angry crowd gathered in front of the Fourth Precinct stationhouse. A delegation of civil rights leaders was allowed inside to have a look at Smith and his wounds. The delegation demanded that Smith be taken to a hospital for treatment; then two of the leaders returned to the sidewalk to pacify the crowd.

But the situation was already out of the hands of the leaders.

From the darkened grounds of the Hays Housing Project across the street, missiles and Molotov cocktails were hurled at the police station. The crowd grew more unruly. The leaders tried with little success to organize an orderly march on City Hall, but the attempted march fell into disarray as more rocks and bottles—probably thrown by youths from the housing project—crashed to the pavement or against the police building. At this point, policemen, wearing helmets, rushed out of the stationhouse and charged into the crowd. The crowd dispersed, and in a short while looting began nearby. The looting was sporadic and minor, however, and soon ended.

The next day the situation grew more serious. An evening rally called in front of the Fourth Precinct stationhouse to protest police brutality was broken up as police again charged into the crowd. The cops beat everyone and anyone with black skin, including a black policeman in civilian clothes and several black newsmen. Cursing and mouthing racial slurs, the club-swinging cops indiscriminately smashed into the throng.

The police repression was quickly followed by heavy looting which began on Springfield Avenue. Tom Hayden, a white community organizer who witnessed the rebellion, described what happened next:

> This was the largest demonstration of black people ever held in Newark. At any major intersection, and there are at least ten such points in the ghetto, there were more than a thousand people on the streets at the same time. A small number entered stores and moved out with what they could carry; they would be replaced by others from the large mass of people walking, running, or standing in the streets. Further back were more thousands who watched from windows and stoops and periodically participated. Those with mixed feelings were not about to intervene against their neighbors. A small number, largely the older people, shook their heads.

People voted with their feet to expropriate property to which they felt entitled. They were tearing up the stores with the trick contracts and installment plans, the second-hand television sets going for top-quality prices, the phony scales, the inferior meat and vegetables. A common claim was: this is owed me. But few needed to argue. People who under ordinary conditions respected law because they were forced to do so now felt free to act upon the law as they thought it should be. . . .

Economic gain was the basis of mass involvement. The stores presented the most immediate way for people to take what they felt was theirs. Liquor was the most convenient item to steal. The Governor's announcement on Friday morning that he would "dry the town out" came a little late. But liquor was hardly the sole object of the looters. Boys who had few clothes took home more than they had ever owned before. Mattresses were carried into apartments to replace a second-hand or over-used ones purchased on installment. New television sets, irons, tables and chairs, baseball bats, dishware and other household goods were carried out in armloads. People walked, ran, or drove off with their possessions. There were Negro gangsters and hi-jackers, with connections in the white mob network, on the scene too, but most of the people were taking only for themselves. One reason there was so little quarrelling over "who gets what" was that there was, for a change, enough for all.[2]

Although the looting was initiated by poor blacks, Hayden recounted that the black middle class soon became heavily involved in the action. They did so, Hayden explained, "because their racial consciousness cut through middle-class values to make property destruction seem reasonable. . . ."

There was no formal organization to the looting. It was a spontaneous outbreak. Black people were simply doing what they knew had to be done. Although there

[2] Tom Hayden, *Rebellion in Newark* (New York: Vintage, 1967), pp. 29–30, 32–33.

was no organization, the looting was not without logic. White-owned stores, the most visible mechanism of black exploitation, were the main targets of looters and arsonists. There were no attacks on "soul brother" businesses. However, many of these would later be demolished by police and National Guardsmen.

In the early morning hours of July 14, as the rioting began to diminish, Mayor Addonizio asked Governor Richard J. Hughes to send state police and National Guard troops. Within hours more than three thousand Guardsmen, called up from the surrounding white suburbs, and five hundred white state troopers started arriving in the troubled city. "The line between the jungle and the law might as well be drawn here as any place in America," Hughes announced. To his mind the black community was indeed a "jungle" which encroached upon and threatened to destroy so-called white civilization.

Using the pretext of gunning for snipers, the troops opened fire indiscriminately on Newark's black residents, according to Hayden. No snipers were killed and no one was arrested in the act of sniping. One fireman and one policeman were killed, but only *after* the troops were called in; and the circumstances surrounding their deaths were unclear. The reign of terror resulted in the deaths of more than twenty blacks, including six women and two children. Many blacks were killed while standing or sitting in front of their homes, or while otherwise engaged in innocuous activities. The body of one black youth was riddled by forty-five bullet holes.

After observing the rebellion and the brutal suppression of it, Hayden concluded that "the military forces killed people for the purposes of terror and intimidation."

Thus it seems to many that the military, especially the Newark police, not only triggered the riot by beating a cab-driver but then created a climate of opinion that supported the use of all necessary force to suppress the riot. The force used by the police was not in response to snipers, looting, and burning, but in retaliation against the successful uprising of Wednesday [July 12th] and Thursday [July 13th] nights.[3]

The Newark rebellion generated a new sense of militancy and unity in that city's black community. To many in the community the so-called riot was the celebration of a new beginning. But what this beginning represented, and where it would go from there, were uncertain. Hayden speculated that the rebellion signaled the rise of "an American form of guerrilla warfare based in the slums." While it is quite conceivable that this will be one of the long-term consequences of the urban rebellions, the immediate results in Newark were quite different.

The black community was aroused and unified. It was ready to move, although it did not know how or where to move. The black power demand for self-government appealed to many, but the question was how to transform this idea into a program of action. This situation represented a dramatic opportunity for militant black nationalists, who saw in Newark a chance for black people—under the leadership of the nationalists—to gain control of the city. Chief spokesman for the nationalists was poet-playwright LeRoi Jones. During the rebellion, Jones was beaten and arrested on charges of being in illegal possession of weapons. A few days later, on July 22, he told reporters: "Again and again . . . we have sought to plead through the reference of progressive humanism . . . again and again our plaints have been denied by an unfeeling, ignorant, graft-ridden, racist government." Now, he added, "We will govern ourselves or no one will govern Newark, New Jersey." Within a few months Jones' plans would become clear.

Early in 1968, a summit conference of black leaders resulted in the formation of the United Brothers of Newark. This group was to become the united black front of Newark

[3] *Ibid.*, p. 53.

similar in philosophy to Stokely Carmichael's Black United Front in Washington, D.C. Within its ranks was a cross-section of Newark's black leadership. Only the outright "Toms" were excluded. By utilizing their individual organizational bases along with their collective power, the members of the United Brothers have pushed the concept of black control and black unity.

In an interview with this writer in March 1968, Jones explained what he meant by black community control. "I think in the cities it means the mobilization of black people with black consciousness to take control over that space which they already inhabit and to achieve programs so that they can defend and govern that space and survive the onslaughts of white society."[4] In practical terms, this meant that the black nationalist had to be prepared to strike bargains. Black liberation, Jones once wrote, "will be achieved through deals as well as violence."[5]

Jones soon began to make the deals which he believed were necessary. In his capacity as spokesman for the United Brothers, Jones actively sought to quell the riots which developed after the murder of Martin Luther King. He believed that black control of Newark could be won through the ballot, not the bullet. On April 12, 1968, he participated in an interview with Newark Police Captain Charles Kinney, and Anthony Imperiale, leader of a local right-wing, white organization. During the interview, Jones suggested that white leftists were responsible for instigating the riots. The policeman then named Students for a Democratic Society (SDS) and the Newark Community Union Project as the troublemakers. While Jones did not make this specific charge, the inference was that he agreed. Later in the interview, it was suggested that Jones and Imperiale were working together with the cops to maintain the peace.

[4] *Guardian,* March 23, 1968, p. 3.
[5] LeRoi Jones, *Home: Social Essays* (New York: William Morrow & Co., 1966), p. 239.

A week later, Jones explained his position in an interview with the Washington *Post*. "Our aim is to bring about black self-government in Newark by 1970. We have a membership that embraces every social area in Newark. It is a wide cross-section of business, professional, and political life. I'm in favor of black people taking power by the quickest, easiest, most successful means they can employ. Malcolm X said the ballot or the bullet. Newark is a particular situation where the ballot seems to be advantageous. I believe we have to survive. I didn't invent the white man. What we are trying to do is deal with him in the best way we can. . . . Black men are not murderers. . . . What we don't want to be is die-ers." Jones added that he had "more respect for Imperiale, because he doesn't lie, like white liberals." Imperiale, he added, "had the mistaken understanding that we wanted to come up to his territory and do something. That was the basic clarification. We don't want to be bothered and I'm sure he doesn't want to be bothered."

An explanation for Jones' behavior can be at least partially surmised from the political context of Newark. In Newark militant black nationalists saw a chance to gain control of a major city, assuming that they could avoid being destroyed by the police or the right-wingers. From their point of view, then, it was of crucial importance to buy time and maintain the peace until a nonviolent transfer of power could be effected, hopefully in the 1970 municipal elections. A violent confrontation right now, the nationalists might argue, would be disastrous for their young and relatively weak organization. In the meantime, during this period of stalemate, and with the real power of the city government and the right-wing whites on the wane as their supporters emigrate from the city, every effort would be made to unify the black community around the aspiring new leaders and to eliminate potentially "disruptive" elements. Such elements may derive from two sources: independent political organizations with some black support, particularly such ones as the

Community Union Project, which also controlled one of the city's eight poverty boards; and, on the other hand, groups that advocate arming and violence against the establishment. Both of these existed in Newark, and the essential question was not whether they were white or black; right, left, or apolitical. The point was that they were working in the black community but were independent of the group seeking control and because they, too, might grow in strength, unlike the white establishment, they posed a serious threat to the nationalists. They had to be either incorporated into the nationalist organization or discredited.

Of course, as far as the police and Imperiale were concerned, Jones' statements were very useful since they publicly set one group of militants in the black community against another. The implication was that Jones was denouncing any blacks who associated themselves with the white leftist students, and also those blacks who were planning "terroristic" acts of violence. In short, Jones was used by the whites whom he opposes. The police and Imperiale were also playing a waiting game—waiting to exploit what they hoped were growing rifts among Newark's militant groups.

Jones might fall into the mire of opportunism and be used by the white establishment and right-wingers because, despite his denunciations of white liberals, his strategy of peaceful transfer of municipal power in Newark is based on an implicit faith that liberalism will triumph, and that those white businessmen and government leaders who control Newark will see fit to grant power to the new black leadership. This appears unlikely. Newark is an important transportation and industrial center. Even the most ardent white liberal leader would be reluctant to grant any semblance of real power to black militants in such a city. Much too much is at stake in Newark to allow "unstable" and inexperienced militant blacks to run the municipal government.

Yet, from the liberal point of view, some concessions must be made if future disruptions such as the 1967 riot are to be avoided. In Gary, Indiana, and Cleveland, Ohio, these concessions took the form of allowing black men of liberal or moderate political persuasion to become titular heads of local government. No real power relations were altered in these cities, but black people were supposed to get the impression that progress was being made, that they were finally being admitted through the front door.[6]

In Newark, where black people by the thousands have demonstrated their willingness to take to the streets, and where militants are actively building a citywide organization, such a strategy would have the additional advantage of occupying the militant leaders in electoral campaigns and traditional municipal politicking. And by making suitable overtures to the "reasonable" militants, convincing them that a nonviolent transfer of power is possible, white leaders could hope to use these militants to isolate the "extremists" and pacify the angry and unpredictable ghetto youths. In these machinations there is no intention of effecting a transfer of real power—although Newark, like Gary and Cleveland, may some day boast of a black mayor. The intent is to create the impression of real movement while actual movement is too limited to be significant.

In an interview Jones was asked if he thought the white power elite might be encouraging black militants to become embroiled in municipal politics as a way of diverting the

[6] Gary's mayor, Richard Hatcher, commented in a speech on the fact that visible black leadership by no means implies real black control: "There is much talk about black control of the ghetto," he said. "What does that mean? I am mayor of a city of roughly 90,000 black people, but we do not control the possibilities of jobs for them, of money for their schools, or state-funded social services. These things are in the hands of the United States Steel Corporation and the County Department of Welfare of the State of Indiana. Will the poor in Gary's worst slums be helped because the pawn-shop owner is black, not white?"

black movement from a possibly more revolutionary direction. He replied that while "a lot of slick young white men" might be thinking this, black people would never permit it to happen. "We intend to make this city represent the sentiment of black people, in whatever issue, and to take a stand according to the will of black people." He added that black "specialists" in "trade and taxes, municipal government and diplomatic relations with foreign countries" would in time address themselves to this question and, therefore, it was "premature" for him to respond to it.

This of course was no answer at all. It was, rather, an evasion and an implicit admission that Jones had not given the question serious consideration, and, therefore, was totally unprepared to sort out its implications. But this is exactly the kind of question that those who would call themselves militants must always have in the forefront of their thoughts. Any strategy for black liberation must be based not only on the needs and demands of black people, but, if it is to succeed, it must also be designed to counter the anticipated response of the opposition. Any strategy that does not meet this condition—no matter how militant, nationalist, or revolutionary it may be—is almost certainly doomed to failure: The white establishment that rules this country has had great experience in distorting and co-opting the simplistic militancy which for too long has been the hallmark of the black movement.

Jones' implicit reliance on liberalism also does not take into consideration the fact of the gradual breakup of the liberal establishment, not only in Newark but throughout the country, over the past several years. There has been a steady polarization in American politics since the death of John Kennedy, and there is no reason to think that this trend will be reversed in the near future. While fascism is not an immediate issue, the growing strength of reaction in this country bodes ill for any hopes of peaceful change. Accordingly, a strategy for achieving black self-government at the ballot box will be reduced to mere tokenism, and it can be expected that any efforts to win anything more than token representation and control will be forcibly resisted. Under such circumstances, it is folly for black militant leaders to talk about a choice between the ballot and the bullet. The choice is not theirs to make. As the forces of reaction gain strength, especially at the local government level, opposition becomes entrenched and adamant, and any means necessary will be freely employed to halt the advance of black liberation. "When the Black Panther comes," says Anthony Imperiale, "the White Hunter will be waiting." If black people are not consciously prepared and organized to meet this eventuality, then the genocide which it has become fashionable to denounce will be an all too tangible reality.

In the summer of 1968 the United Brothers campaign to establish black control of Newark went into high gear. Specifically, the object was to elect a black mayor in 1970 and to put two black men on the city council in the November 1968 elections. To this end a Black Political Convention, sponsored by the United Brothers, was held in Newark June 21-23, 1968. The three-day convention, which attracted as many as one thousand people, chose two candidates to run for the city council. The convention also endorsed resolutions calling for a commuter payroll tax on nonresidents, opposing the construction of an interstate route and other highways that would cut through the black community, demanding that the Model Cities Program be under the direction and control of the black community, demanding black community control of the schools, and calling for the development of a police-community relations program, hiring of more black police, and a complete review and revision of the judicial system.

The sole dissident voice raised at the convention was that of Phil Hutchings, the new program secretary of SNCC. In an unpublished essay, Hutchings summarized his criticisms of the black militants' strategy in Newark.

If there is a weakness in the United Brothers approach it is the question of whether or not black control of Newark by 1970 can actually fundamentally change the lives of blacks in the city. It is no secret that economic power is moving to the suburbs and that Federal government insistence on regional planning and a metropolitan approach will guarantee that black power in any city will not mean for black people what it once meant for the Anglo-Saxon WASPs, Irish, Jews, and Italians. In the long run Newark (though now a pace-setter) cannot be separated from what happens around the nation, and no amount of black businesses or cooperatives (not to mention black capitalists) will ever overcome the entrenched and neo-colonialistic white corporate power in this urbanized technological society. Black control of some cities where blacks are the majority (or have a plurality) is not the answer to racism in 20th Century America. It may be that black people will have to have blacks in power over them within the confines of this system before they can truly recognize the necessity to organize against capitalism as well as the racist aspects of America.

What happened in Newark was not unique. Similar attempts to build black united fronts were taking place around the country. There was the Black United Front of Washington, D.C., the North City Congress in Philadelphia, the United Front in Boston, the Black United Conference in Denver, and the Black Congress in Los Angeles, to mention a few. All of these were coalitions which sought to alter power relations in the cities where they existed. They sought to establish some measure of black control or influence in those cities. They faced the same dangers of manipulation and co-optation which confronted the United Brothers. Again like the Brothers, they had to come to grips with the threat of gradual takeover by more conservative blacks who have little desire to serve the community.

The simple but unfortunate fact is that the militants are usually less well organized than the Urban League, NAACP, SCLC, preachers, teachers, and social workers who are invited to participate in the united fronts also. Consequently, it is relatively easy for these representatives of the privileged black bourgeoisie to take control of organizations ostensibly dedicated to militant reform, to enabling black people to assume control over their own lives. If this process of takeover goes unchecked, the united front is transformed into an instrumentality serving the interests of the black middle class alone. The needs of the popular black masses go by the board, and a new oppressive elite assumes power. It is only to the extent that the united fronts serve the needs and aspirations of the great bulk of black people that they can be regarded as progressive organizations. To the extent that they fall into the hands of a privileged and opportunistic elite, they become simply an added burden strapped to the back of black America.

LeRoi Jones, as remarked, was not operating in a political vacuum. Others were following a similar course. The ouster of Harlem Congressman Adam Clayton Powell from the House of Representatives prompted CORE to concretize its interest in electoral politics. On January 16, 1967, Floyd McKissick issued a call for a conference to create a national black political structure. "No political machinery now in existence," he said, "is available to us through which our just hopes and aspirations can be achieved." He told reporters that the proposed structure would be "an apparatus, not a [political] party." This apparatus would decide whether to support the Democratic or Republican parties or "develop an independent platform which it will attempt to sell to the Democrats or Republicans." McKissick added that black people were moving toward bloc voting throughout the United States. He said that both national political parties had failed blacks, and he sought to "elevate the black man to a state of equality in the decision-making processes of government." He expressed the hope that the proposed political structure would become a "formidable bloc" by the time of the 1968 national elections.

Thus CORE was in the contradictory position of espousing greater black involvement in electoral politics even though it was precisely in this sphere—with the humiliating ouster of Powell—that black people had just suffered a significant political defeat. But the temptations of electoral politics were too great to be denied. The proposed conference never took place, but CORE and its tacit ally, the Black Power Conference, moved progressively closer to becoming little more than political lobbies advocating reforms, taking whatever political crumbs they could garner for themselves.

CORE was to take other curious turns, and eventually ally itself with an arm of the very power structure which it claimed to be fighting. Early in 1967 the Ford Foundation made grants of several hundred thousand dollars to the NAACP and the Urban League. A few months later the Foundation gave one million dollars to the NAACP Legal Defense Fund's new National Office for the Rights of Indigents. But for the purpose of urban pacification these groups were less than satisfactory, since there was serious doubt as to how much control they exercised over the young militants and frustrated, ghetto blacks who were likely to be heaving Molotov cocktails during the summer. If its efforts to keep the lids on the cities were to succeed, the Foundation had to find some way to penetrate militant organizations which were believed to wield some influence over the angry, young blacks who are trapped in the urban chaos.

The first move in this direction occurred in May 1967, when the Foundation granted five hundred thousand dollars to the Metropolitan Applied Research Center (MARC), a newly created organization in New York with a militant-sounding program headed by Dr. Kenneth B. Clark, a psychology professor who at one time was associated with Harlem's anti-poverty program. When it was organized the previous March, MARC announced that its purpose was "to pioneer in research and action in behalf of the powerless urban poor in northern metropolitan areas." Clark's strategy was to get the large corporations involved in the ghetto. "Business and industry are our last hope," he once remarked. "They are the most realistic elements of our society." Interestingly, in a brochure MARC compared itself with the semi-governmental RAND Corporation, which does research for the Air Force. The difference between the two, according to the brochure, is that MARC is not associated with the government, nor is it limited to research. It is also an action organization.

One of MARC's first actions was to name Roy Innis, then chairman of the militant Harlem chapter of the Congress of Racial Equality, as its first civil rights "fellow-in-residence." The May 11 announcement also stated that the Reverend Martin Luther King, Jr., president of the Southern Christian Leadership Conference, and the Reverend Andrew Young, one of King's chief aides, had "agreed to take part in the fellowship program."

Innis received a six-month fellowship. "The civil rights fellowships," wrote the New York *Times* on May 12, "are designed to give the leaders an opportunity to evaluate their programs and tactics and undertake long-range planning." MARC's staff was to aid the leaders in their studies, and the fellows were to draw salaries equal to those they received from their organizations or from private employment.

Clark said he had also discussed fellowships with Floyd McKissick, national director of CORE; Stokely Carmichael, then chairman of SNCC; Whitney Young of the Urban League and Roy Wilkins of the NAACP.

MARC's next move was to call a secret meeting of civil rights leaders for May 27. The meeting was held at the home of Dr. Clark. Subsequently, another such meeting was held June 13 at a Suffern, New York, motel among Clark and leaders of nine major civil rights groups. At the conclusion of that meeting, Clark announced a joint effort to calm Cleveland's racial tension. He said the "underlying causes of unrest and despair among urban ghetto Negroes, as well as clear indications of their grim, sobering and costly consequences, are found in classic form in Cleveland."

Clark did not mention that the Ford Foundation had been trying to "calm" Cleveland since 1961 by financing various local research and action projects. But Cleveland blew up in 1966, and further serious rumblings were heard in the early spring of 1967.

Clearly, a new approach was needed in Cleveland, and the stage was set for the Foundation's first direct grant to a militant group—the Cleveland chapter of CORE. The Foundation announced on July 14 that it was giving $175,000 to the Special Purposes Fund of CORE to be used for "training of Cleveland youth and adult community workers, voter registration efforts, exploration of economic-development programs, and attempts to improve program planning among civil rights groups." In explaining the grant, McGeorge Bundy said that Foundation staff and consultants had been investigating Cleveland "for some months." In fact, he said, "it was predictions of new violence in the city that led to our first staff visits in March."

Apparently realizing that the grant might give the impression of a close relationship developing between the Foundation and CORE, Bundy added: "The national officers of CORE have dealt with us on this matter in a businesslike way, and neither Mr. Floyd McKissick nor I supposes that this grant requires the two of us—or our organizations—to agree on all public questions. It does require us both to work together in support of the peaceful and constructive efforts of CORE's Cleveland leadership, and that is what we plan to do."

It must be said that CORE was vulnerable to such corporate penetration. In the first place, they needed money. Floyd McKissick in 1966 had become national director of an organization which was several hundred thousand dollars in debt, and his espousal of black power scared away potential financial supporters.

Secondly, CORE's militant rhetoric but ambiguous and reformist definition of black power as simply black control of black communities appealed to Foundation officials who were seeking just those qualities in a black organization which hopefully could tame the ghettos. From the Foundation's point of view, old-style moderate leaders no longer exercised any real control, while genuine black radicals were too dangerous. CORE fit the bill because its talk about black revolution was believed to appeal to discontented blacks, while its program of achieving black power through massive injections of governmental, business, and Foundation aid seemingly opened the way for continued corporate domination of black communities by means of a new black elite.

Surprisingly, to some, Core's program, as elaborated by Floyd McKissick in July 1967, was quite similar to the approach of MARC. Both organizations see themselves as intermediaries whose role is to negotiate with the power structure on behalf of blacks and the poor generally. Both suggest that more government and private aid is necessary, and both seek to gain admission for poor blacks and whites into the present economic and political structure of U.S. society. McKissick, who became the second CORE official to accept a MARC fellowship, criticized capitalism, but only because black people were not allowed to participate fully in it.

Within a few months the Ford Foundation could apparently view its grant to Cleveland CORE as a qualified success. There was no rebellion in Cleveland in the summer of 1967, and in November, Carl Stokes became the first Negro mayor of a major American city—a fact which temporarily eased tensions in the ghetto. "We are not satisfied with the speed with which the program has moved," said James Cunningham, a consultant retained by the Foundation to monitor the project, "but it has shown real potential. I see it as a flowering of what black power could be."

The first phase of the project was an intensive voter registration drive in three slum wards in August. This was followed by a voter education program to instruct black people on voting procedures and to get them to the polls. This program included mailings and meetings with candidates. The net result of this phase of the program was to aid in the election of Carl Stokes, a fact of which Cleveland CORE boasted in its report on the project.

Another part of the program, designated as a "youth leadership training program," began in November. In all, some sixty-two youths, ranging in age from seventeen to twenty-one, were involved in this project. The project was designed, according to the CORE report, "to identify and train urban ghetto youth in those learnings and skills which can serve as an alternative to frustration and violence. . . ." To this end the youngsters attended classes on black history, African history, and social science. They were taught skills in canvassing, interviewing, and recording community opinions. There was apparently little discussion of who would ever read (not to mention act upon) their interviews and reports of community sentiment. Some of the staff of this project were taken on visits to black-owned businesses in Chicago. In short, youths who had no faith in the "system" were taught that if only they could resocialize themselves, they might fit in after all.

The director of the youth training program, Philip Carter, said his project hoped to show that "the legitimate hostilities and aggressions of black youth" could be "programmed" into socially acceptable channels. He expressed the hope that the youths being trained will become "young black urban renewal specialists, young black sociologists, and young black political scientists." He did not say—and did not need to say—in whose interest these young black experts would be put to work. The mere fact that there aren't any genuinely black-controlled educational institutions guarantees that if they are to work, they must work in the interest of continued white domination of every facet of black life.

Militant rhetoric was used to cover up the co-optative nature of this project. "Our job as an organization," said

Arthur Evans, a member of Cleveland CORE and national first vice chairman of the organization, "is to prepare people to make a decision on revolution or not. The choice is whether to take land and resources and redistribute them." The evidence of the Cleveland CORE project suggests that CORE decided against revolution.

This militant rhetoric deceived no one, least of all those who financed the project. In his annual report for 1967, McGeorge Bundy dismissed "the preachers of hate" as so much "spume on the wave of the past," but he concluded that "no one who has dealt honestly with legitimately militant black leaders will confuse their properly angry words with any conspiracy to commit general violence. . . ." So much for Mr. Evans' cagey talk about revolution.

Unfortunately for Bundy, "legitimately militant black leaders" do not necessarily speak for or represent anyone but themselves. The violence which hit Cleveland the next year should have amply demonstrated this fact.

Developments at CORE's convention in Oakland, California, early in the month of July 1967, provide further insight into that organization's strategy. One of the more important events at that meeting was the presentation of an impressive twelve-page report by Roy Innis's Harlem chapter. The report gave a summary of Harlem CORE's "program for the gaining of control or the creation of institutions in our community. . . ." "We call this," the report stated, "a program of separate but not segregated institutions." In the area of economics, the report announced that Innis, as chapter chairman, had joined with a group of young black men in Harlem in organizing a "small business investment corporation that will have a broad-based stockholding membership." The organization was to be known as the Harlem Commonwealth Council, Inc., and Innis became a member of its board of directors. Referring to HCC, the report continued: "Money will be raised in the black community that will be matched 2 to 1 by small business loans, and this money will be used to invest in or

to create businesses in Harlem, or possibly light industry."
Thus Harlem CORE was pioneering in formulating a
strategy for the rise of black capitalism.

In the field of education, Harlem CORE reported that
in March it had launched its demand for black control
of the schools in Harlem by proposing the creation of an
independent board of education for Harlem selected and
completely controlled by and responsible to the black people of Harlem. According to the proposal, integration had
failed, and the only way to achieve quality education for
Harlem's youngsters was through community control of its
schools. Harlem CORE set up a Committee for Autonomous Harlem School District and began organizing support for the proposal.

Interestingly, the following November, McGeorge Bundy
recommended that New York City's school system be
decentralized into thirty to sixty semiautonomous local
districts. Bundy had been named head of a special committee on decentralization at the end of April after the
state legislature directed Mayor Lindsay to submit a decentralization plan by December 1 if the city were to qualify
for more state aid. Lindsay, an astute political liberal, insisted that decentralization was "not merely an administrative or budgetary device, but a means to advance the
quality of education for all our children and a method of
insuring community participation and achieving that goal."
Bundy's proposal would allow for not one but possibly
several school boards for Harlem. Harlem CORE's school
board committee therefore found itself in the position of
being on the same side as the New York *Times* in giving
critical support to the Bundy plan, while both the New
York City Board of Education and the United Federation
of Teachers (UFT) opposed it. Bundy and the *Times* saw
that decentralization could be modified and applied in a
manner that would not seriously change the over-all functioning of the educational system, while the UFT was so
blindly engrossed in immediate problems that it failed to
realize that its long-term interests lay neither with the
school board nor in the course proposed by Bundy.

Tension between teachers and black parents had risen as a result of a three-week teachers' strike that fall. The teachers thought parents were attempting to usurp their professional rights and privileges. The parents, on the other hand, attacked the teachers as racists and the destroyers of their children. Bundy was well aware of this escalating tension when his report, *Reconnection for Learning,* was being written. But he also knew that the teachers had in their union an established mechanism for channeling their discontent. The parents had no such channel, and there was always the danger that their anger, having no institutionalized outlet, might escalate into violence. Hence it was an urgent necessity for the parents in some way to be "reconnected" to the schools if disruptive conflict were to be avoided. The mechanism for accomplishing this end appeared to be limited school decentralization, which would allow some parent participation—thereby mitigating dangerous clashes—while at the same time precluding genuine community control of the schools by masking central control under a new façade.[7]

[7] A year later, in October 1968, when the New York City school system was in the throes of yet another crisis, Bundy would go so far as to play the role of self-appointed spokesman for the militant parents. He charged that the teachers and staff professionals were more to blame for the crisis than the reform-minded parents and community forces. "It is deeply puzzling to me," he lamented, "how those professionals who are concerned with the future welfare of the teaching staff can be successful if they remain in a state of warfare with those [blacks and Puerto Ricans] whose children make up more than half of the enrollment of the schools." The effect of Bundy's statement was to further reduce the possibility of any alliance between teachers and parents against the school board and city government by driving in further the wedge between the two former groups. The militant reformers in the black community were led to believe that their real friends were found among the corporate elite rather than among white professionals and teachers. Regardless of the respective merits of the parents' and teachers' mutual suspicions, Bundy's move could only increase these hostilities, and it amounted to a splitting tactic.

CORE's Oakland meeting was shaken briefly by a rebellion of dissident nationalists who thought that the strategy of separate community institutions was too limited in scope. The nationalists wanted CORE to endorse complete separation of blacks from white America. They sought to have the organization approve the idea of a separate black state. They also wanted CORE to exclude white members. On this latter point a compromise was reached and the convention agreed to strike the word "multiracial" from the section of the organization's constitution that describes its membership. White liberals loudly decried this compromise. The New York *Times,* for example, lamented editorially that "white co-strugglers have been given a clear message that they will be relegated to second-class citizenship within the organization. To put it bluntly, CORE membership now stands for racial *inequality.*" CORE, however, was no longer attuned to this traditional white liberal view of the meaning of racial equality. In the second half of the sixties, having a quota of white members was no longer required to legitimatize a black freedom organization. (And neither was white membership necessary to insure that a black organization conformed to the desires of white society. Indirect control and manipulation of the black liberation movement was the hallmark of the new liberalism, which even went so far as to endorse black power and black separatism—not to mention black capitalism—as a means of sidetracking black revolution.)

The programmatic thrust of the CORE convention was outlined a few weeks later by McKissick. As the occasion of his remarks, McKissick denounced the statement condemning riots issued by Martin Luther King, A. Philip Randolph, Roy Wilkins, and Whitney Young. Their statement approved violent repression of the riots and said in part: "Killing, arson, looting are criminal acts and should be dealt with as such. Equally guilty are those who incite, provoke and call specifically for such actions. There is no injustice which justifies the present destruction [by "rioters" or retaliating troopers?] of the Negro community." Mc-

Kissick replied that history would record the ghetto explosions that summer as the beginning of the "black revolution" and as "rebellions against repression and exploitation." In a tactfully worded statement, McKissick accused the four civil rights leaders of opportunism: "We believe that it is unfortunate that our brothers felt it necessary to condemn Black Men for rebelling against that which oppresses—that they found it opportune to decry the violence of the victim. It is fruitless to condemn without offering solutions and it can only force Black People to question those who condemn."

"We wouldn't have the violence if someone hadn't made some mistakes," said the CORE leader. He then went on to outline CORE's program for correcting these "mistakes." Some of his specific proposals sounded remarkably like what Harlem CORE had recommended:

> Black people seek to control the educational system, the political-economic system and the administration of their own communities. . . .
> Ownership of the land area in places such as Harlem must be transferred to the residents of Harlem—individually or collectively. Existing governmental programs such as the Demonstration Cities Program, the Federal Housing Authority, the Commerce Department Programs, along with contributions from private industry, must be coordinated to accomplish this end.
> Ownership of businesses in the ghetto must be transferred to Black People—either individually or collectively. . . .

These paragraphs suggest certain economic changes, but they leave unanswered the critical question of in whose interest is economic power to be exercised? Simple transference of business ownership into black hands, either individually or collectively, is in itself no guarantee that this will benefit the total community. Blacks are capable of exploiting one another just as easily as whites.

It was this ambiguity, however, that opened the way for CORE to move toward black capitalism. What had begun as a Harlem CORE project was now shaping up as the over-all strategy of national CORE. Black power was slowly but relentlessly coming to be equated with the power of black business. This despite the fact that black business had never been a powerful social entity.

Most ghetto businesses tend to be marginal operations such as beauty salons, barbershops, small grocery stores, and other retail and service businesses. In 1967, one-quarter of all businesses in Harlem, for example, were black-owned, but in all of New York City only a dozen or so black-owned or -managed enterprises employed more than ten people. Commenting on the plight of black business, *The Negro Handbook* noted that

> The number of Negro-owned restaurants and other eating places according to Department of Commerce statistics, declined by one-third between 1950 and 1960; other retail outlets declined by a slightly larger percentage. In addition, the number of funeral directors dropped by six percent between 1950 and 1960, the number of barbers decreased by over 16 percent, and while there has been an increase in the number of Negro-owned motels and hotels, they have obviously lost a sizable portion of their most desirable clientele. In the field of cosmetic manufacture, Negro firms have lost ground, as the field has become increasingly attractive to large firms producing cosmetics for the general market.
>
> Thus, over the past decade there has been a gradual and steady erosion of the position of the Negro business community.[8]

The history of black business fails to disclose any significant ventures in steel, automobiles, telephone, railroads, and most other major industrial fields. The white corporate oligopoly has excluded blacks from the mainstream of American corporate endeavor, except in certain areas of banking, insurance, and publishing. But in at least two of these areas the black businessman is largely fighting a rearguard action.

[8] *The Negro Handbook* (Chicago: Johnson, 1966), p. 215.

It is in the field of insurance that great inroads have been made into the Negro market by the large white corporations which formerly shunned the Negro policy-holder. Where formerly the large national companies were only willing to sell a Negro a policy at higher rates, or an industrial policy, the Negro consumer is [now] sought for ordinary insurance coverage.[9]

In 1948, the National Negro Insurance Association could claim to have sixty-two member companies with assets of over 108 million dollars. As of 1963, *The Negro Handbook* listed eighty-nine black insurance firms, with total assets of only twenty-six million dollars. The top ten white firms alone claimed assets of over 100 *billion* dollars in 1967.

As for banks, in February 1969, Dempsey J. Travis, president of an association of Negro mortgage bankers, told a conference that the number of black-owned commercial banks, for instance, had declined to twenty in nineteen cities from forty-nine in thirty-eight cities in 1929. At present there is very little that would suggest any reversal of these over-all trends.[10]

Moreover, in cities where a significant black business class exists, it usually is a conservative force rather than a militant advocate of reforms.

[9] *Ibid.*

[10] A survey of businesses in San Francisco, for example, published in November 1968, found that "black businessmen are typically engaged in small, marginal, neighborhood kinds of operations. . . . The great majority of proprietors are limited by a lack of education suited to business management. They are undercapitalized and located in predominantly depressed areas where they are limited to a black clientele. The major weakness is that they are not engaged in the more profitable and complex kinds of businesses, nor are they located in the prime commercial districts." It also noted that "A crucial deficiency [still] is the lack of businesses which produce goods." The report did not attempt to explain why this condition exists, however. (See *Black Business in San Francisco.* This is a special report prepared by the Plan of Action for Challenging Times, Inc. PACT was founded in 1963 by two black professional men who sought to promote black capitalism.)

The proposed CORE program tried to reverse the general downward trend and create new and expanded black businesses by demanding that existing white-controlled economic enterprises be transferred to black ownership. However, such a transfer could alter economic realities in the ghetto only if ownership and control of business activities became collective and community-wide. Individual ownership or limited-stock corporations restrict effective control (and resulting benefits) to a narrowly circumscribed class of persons within the black community. If the community as a whole is to benefit, then *the community as a whole must be organized to manage collectively* its internal economy and its business relations with white America. Black business firms must be treated and operated as *social property,* belonging to the general black community, not as the private property of individuals or limited groups of individuals. This necessitates the dismantling of capitalist property relations in the black community and their replacement with a planned communal economy. But CORE had no intention of tampering with the "free enterprise" system.[11]

McKissick chose to ignore the ramifications of these considerations in his anxiety to project CORE as *the* most prominent and serious organization in the militant black movement. CORE, he concluded his statement, stands ready "to serve as a coordinating agent to assist all Black People, of any philosophy." Subtly addressing himself to those with money to spend and who want to put out the flames in the cities, he contended that if CORE's programs were "adequately funded and fully implemented" then it just might be possible to "alter the future of America from its present self-destructive course."

[11] Several months before the July program was announced, McKissick had made clear his position on capitalism in testimony before a Senate committee. "You tell us to live under the capitalistic system," he said. "Well, brother, give me a chance to make it in the system."

(3)

CORE was not the only militant black group to be snared by corporate liberalism and reformism.[12] The Newark Black Power Conference fell into the same trap. It was at this conference, held in July 1967, that the split in the black power movement between rebels and revolutionaries became manifest.

Initial plans for the conference were made at the behest of Adam Clayton Powell somewhat less than a year prior to its actual convening. In the fall of 1966 Powell called a Black Power Planning Conference at the Rayburn House Office Building in Washington. He appointed a five-man committee which was charged with organizing the conference. Heading up the planning committee was an Episcopalian minister, Dr. Nathan Wright, who was executive director of the Department of Urban Work of the Episcopal Diocese of Newark.

The conference took place only a few days after the Newark rebellion. Yet it was held at a white-owned hotel in downtown Newark, and a registration fee of twenty-five dollars per participant was charged. Both of these facts provoked angry grumbling among some of the delegates who felt that the location selected and the fee mitigated against grass-roots participation. In this they were right. The delegates were largely middle-class blacks and professional militants.

[12] The general attack on reformism in this study is not meant to imply that there is no role for reforms in a revolutionary struggle. In a struggle to transform an oppressive society, it is indeed necessary to fight for certain reforms, but this requires that those who are oppressed are conscious (or made conscious) of how the reforms fit into an over-all strategy for social change. All too often black leaders hail piecemeal reforms—and mindlessly advocate reformism—while overlooking the fact that frequently reforms serve mainly to salvage and buttress a society which in its totality remains as exploitative as ever.

The black power meeting was attended by some thirteen hundred persons from 190 organizations, forty-two cities, and thirty-nine states. The basic conclusion reached at the conference was that black people should organize to get their "fair share" of the American pie. If this effort fails then, according to one resolution, "massive efforts will be launched to disrupt the economy. . . ."

Resolutions passed dealing with economic matters included statements supporting "buy black" campaigns, neighborhood credit unions, upgrading of black workers, establishment of a guaranteed annual income, and establishment of a black economic power fund to provide money to cooperative business ventures in black communities.

In the political sphere the conferees voted to establish a black power lobby in Washington, demand the reseating of Powell, elect twelve more black congressmen in 1968, and demand that police captains assigned to black neighborhoods be black.

In the educational field the conference followed the by then familiar path of calling for black control of school boards in black communities.

Although the conference was described by the New York *Times* as evidencing the "radicalization of the moderates," many disgruntled militant delegates felt that the meeting was all too moderate in its basic assumptions.

A manual distributed by conference organizers to workshop leaders opened with the statement: "Ethnic groups in America have developed their own solidarity as a basic approach toward entry into the American mainstream." While not disputing the need for solidarity, one youthful delegate declared that "we don't want to enter America's polluted, dirty mainstream but to carve out an altogether new river." An older delegate said: "I don't want to be exploited by a black man any more than I want to be exploited by a white man. You've got to change the whole system."

This dispute over basic premises of the black power movement permeated many workshop meetings. Some delegates spoke of "filling the gaps in the present system" and "pumping the system for all it's worth." Others denounced capitalism and urged black people to "burn it all down and create something new." "Something new" was left undefined.

Typical delegate attitudes were voiced in the youth workshop:

"Black youth today," said a man in African garb, "can't see how they're going to get their share of the system and so their mood is to burn it down."

"I want to burn the system down," responded a young woman, "but not in such a way as to hurt black people. I happen to think that co-ops are the best way to put a big torch to Chuck's [the white man's] system."

"I think capitalism is the most successful system although it's the youngest," retorted a well-dressed man. "Co-ops just replace one form of bureaucracy with another. The black community should get behind those black people who have made it in the system."

"The capitalist system hasn't worked for us in the four hundred years we've been under it," answered a young delegate wearing a cap and dark glasses. "Capitalism is the most successful system of enforced exploitation in the world, I agree. It's the latest model of slavery."

The youth workshop debate was resolved in favor of a boycott of white-owned businesses and a "buy black" campaign.

The question of economic co-operatives in black communities also came up in other workshops. A pro co-op resolution was passed in the plenary session, though several delegates expressed doubts privately as to whether black-controlled co-operatives could seriously alleviate the economic depression of black people in a white-dominated capitalist economy.

A workshop on "cooperation and alliances" rejected

alliances with the white power structure but agreed on little else. "At this historic moment any struggles to take back some of this bread [money] to the African-American community, I'm for," declared one workshop member. Another favored socialism, and a third argued that a fight for reforms would educate black people to the defects in the system. A "brief summary" of the workshop's conclusions prepared by a militant delegate and read at the plenary session called for alliances with "those forces in various stages of conflict" with the status quo; it was not voted upon because moderate members of the workshop rejected the summary statement as "inaccurate."

Some delegations voiced suspicion about the purpose of the conference. Several termed it an "operation" to round up support for Powell. Others feared that an alliance of moderate leaders in the conference was trying to win control of the black power movement. One delegate jokingly commented that more alliances were being forged in the corridors of the conference than were being discussed in the workshop on alliances.

The meeting was described by Wright in the opening session as a "study conference where we can think about issues in terms of empowerment." But even this description was not accepted by all. "Was this to be another conference just to allow the brothers to blow off steam?" asked a veteran of many conventions. "Was this to be just another cynical attempt to obscure fundamental issues in clouds of diffuse rhetoric?"

A surprise resolution was introduced at the opening session which called for the conference to "strongly endorse the black revolution in all its glorious manifestations," including ghetto revolts. After a lengthy parliamentary hassle, the resolution was tabled. The conference eventually adopted a resolution supporting armed self-defense.

Perhaps a better understanding of what the conference was all about can be gathered from an examination of Nathan Wright's conception of black power. Wright, a pacifist, deplores the "painful excesses" in the "current call to the banners of black power." In his book, *Black Power and Urban Unrest*, published a few days before the conference, he stated, "Black Power in terms of self-development means we want to fish as all Americans should do together in the main stream of American life."[13] More specifically, Wright virtually equated black power with black capitalism: "Undoubtedly the most strategic opportunity which our American capitalistic system has to preserve or strengthen itself lies in the possibility of providing the Negro community with both a substantial and an immediate stake in its operation at every level."[14]

Where most black leaders are fond of talking of ways of alleviating unemployment, Wright blandly accepts the necessity of chronic unemployment under capitalism.

Some economists believe that the economic system which is traditional in our culture calls for a fluid reservoir of untapped resource at its base. If such a reservoir is needed, as may be assumed from its sustained existence, the rudimentary economic problem becomes a potentially explosive social problem when the group at the bottom is not heterogeneous—being almost entirely of one ethnic group comprising both the well-trained and some who should be there—all through social injustice.[15]

Put in plain English, what Wright is suggesting here is that rather than working to reduce or eliminate unemployment, what is really required is integration of the ranks of the unemployed. Such integration would ease the "potentially explosive social problem" posed by having so many blacks without jobs.

As for those who already enjoy economic security and power, Wright's version of black power can also be helpful. "The co-operative efforts of black and white executives,

13 New York: Hawthorn, 1967, p. 62.
14 *Ibid.*, p. 92.
15 *Ibid.*, pp. 18–19.

. . . for the sake of sharing power to increase power and benefits, can be one of the most creative thrusts in this sphere, again for the good of the nation—and individual self-interest."[16]

Wright's approval of this "black-and-white-together" scramble for corporate power and individual advancement represents a betrayal of the black liberation struggle. Not only is he an apologist for corporate capitalism and its depredation of the working population and the poor, but he advances also, as an implicitly positive value, one of its prominent ideological features—one that is particularly destructive of concern for social welfare—selfish individualism.[17] In this respect Wright is like the native intellectual in a colonial country who cannot relinquish Western values, including individualism, which he has been taught by his colonial masters.

As Fanon argued, in a serious liberation struggle aimed at creating a new society, individualism should be among the first of the old habits to disappear:

> The native intellectual had learnt from his masters that the individual ought to express himself fully. The colonialist bourgeoisie had hammered into the native's mind the idea of a society of individuals where each person shuts himself up in his own subjectivity, and whose only wealth is individual thought. Now the native who has the opportunity to return to the people during the struggle for freedom will discover the falseness of

[16] *Ibid.*, p. 43.

[17] In America the ideology of individualism serves as a safety valve. Social unrest is curbed by the hope fostered among the discontented that at least some of them, as individuals, can climb out of the misery that cloaks their lives. Thus individualism counters the growth of group or class consciousness and hinders the development of an awareness of the social nature of exploitation. Black leaders who espouse individualism, therefore, are acting against the general interests of the popular masses, of black people as a group. They are simply fueling the illusions which have been the steady diet of black people since the Civil War.

this theory. The very forms of organization of the struggle will suggest to him a different vocabulary. Brother, sister, friend—these are words outlawed by the colonialist bourgeoisie, because for them my brother is my purse, my friend is part of my scheme for getting on. The native intellectual takes part, in a sort of *auto-da-fé,* in the destruction of all his idols: egoism, recrimination that springs from pride, and the childish stupidity of those who always want to have the last word. Such a colonized intellectual, dusted over by colonial culture, will in the same way discover the substance of the village assemblies, the cohesion of people's committees, and the extraordinary fruitfulness of local meetings and groupments. Henceforward, the interests of one will be the interests of all, for in concrete fact *everyone* will be discovered by the troops, *everyone* will be massacred—or *everyone* will be saved. The motto "look out for yourself," the atheist's method of salvation, is in this context forbidden.[18]

Actually, the connection between the Black Power Conference and corporate capitalism was more than merely ideological. After the conference ended, Wright revealed that it was partially financed by some fifty American corporations which, Wright said, "were not pressured" into contributing. In explaining why these white-controlled companies would pay for a black power meeting, Wright simply referred to his definition of black power as meaning "self-development" by powerless blacks.

By the time of the Philadelphia Black Power Conference the following year, there was no longer even the slightest effort to conceal that this meeting was partly a front for channeling black militancy into the arms of the corporate capitalists. For example, the invitation to the meeting was sent out on Clairol Co. letterhead stationery and was signed by Benjamin Wright, Market Development Manager for Clairol. Benjamin Wright also happens to be

[18] Frantz Fanon, *The Wretched of the Earth* (New York: Grove Press, 1963), p. 38.

the brother of Nathan Wright. Enclosed with the invitation was a copy of a speech given by the president of Clairol in June 1968. The Clairol chief told his audience that at first the term black power "very frankly filled me with dread." But this was no longer the case now that he understood black power to mean "equity" and "empowerment," that is, "ownership of apartments, ownership of homes, ownership of businesses, as well as equitable treatment for all people." The corporation president announced that business now recognizes that by actively attacking the human and economic waste represented by ghettos "we can increase our Gross National Product by a solid 10% within three years."

This is obviously good news for business. Ghetto reconstruction offers the prospect of becoming a new vehicle for corporate growth and expansion. Ghetto residents should welcome this corporate invasion, according to the Clairol man, because "Only business can create the economic viability for equity. And only the businessman can make equity an acceptable social pattern in this country." The message to the audience was clear: Forget black militancy and all this foolish talk of revolution! Rely on the American businessman, for it is only he who has the power—and now the will—to promote black "self-development." Of course, a fair rate of return must be guaranteed for the businessman's investment of time and resources in the ghetto, but then a national government which has seen its anti-poverty programs flop and watched cities go up in flames will be only too happy to underwrite this new and promising venture in ghetto pacification.

(4)

Although Nathan Wright's thinking provided the major ideological underpinning of the Black Power Conferences, another important intellectual current was evident at the gatherings. This was cultural nationalism, and its chief exponent at the Newark meeting was Ron Karenga, who also was a member of the Continuations (Plans) Committee. Karenga spoke at a plenary session and was honorary chairman of one of the workshops. Subsequent to the Newark conference, Karenga, together with LeRoi Jones, have become major national spokesmen for black cultural nationalism.

Karenga is leader of a cultural nationalist group in Los Angeles called US (as opposed to "them"). The son of a Baptist minister, he was well on his way to a comfortable slot in the black middle class before he became a militant after the Watts rebellion of 1965. He had earned a master's degree in political science from the University of California, and earlier he had been the first black elected student body president at a junior college in Los Angeles. Karenga founded US following the Watts uprising. "The revolt was the catalyst," he explained. "It put a new light on things."

A brilliant orator and past master in the use of militant rhetoric, Karenga was described by the *Wall Street Journal* as "typical of many militants who talk looting and burning but actually are eager to gather influence for quiet bargaining with the predominantly white power structure." Following the assassination of Martin Luther King, Karenga met secretly with Los Angeles Police Chief Thomas Reddin, and he played an important part in preventing the outbreak of riots in that city.

Cultural nationalists place primary emphasis on the development of black cultural and art forms as a mechanism of black liberation. Karenga, with whom Jones is in virtually complete agreement, has a theory of the cultural revolution and how this must necessarily precede the political revolution. "The revolution being fought now," Karenga maintains, "is a revolution to win the minds of our people. If we fail to win this one, we cannot expect to win the vio-

lent one."[19] Karenga contends that the main problem of
the black person in America is "that he suffers from a lack
of culture. We must free ourselves culturally before we free
ourselves politically." This leads Karenga quite naturally
to conclude that "nationalism is a belief that black people
in this country make up a cultural Nation." He defines
this cultural nation in terms of intangible commonalities:
common past, common present, and a common future.
"Black values" are also included as part of the black cultural nation.

For Karenga, culture takes precedence over everything
else. He maintains that for black people, blackness is their
ultimate reality, as the ultimate reality for whites is their
whiteness. To his way of thinking the black freedom struggle
is a fight for the right of self-determination, race pride,
and the pursuit of blackness, with heavy emphasis on the
latter two elements.

Proceeding from his basic premise, Karenga concludes
that

> Racist minds created racist institutions. Therefore you
> must move against racism, not institutions. For even if
> you tear down the institution that same mind will build
> them again.

> Economics, specifically, is not the issue.

> The international issue is racism, not economics. White
> people are racists not just capitalists. Race rules out
> economics and even if it doesn't wipe it out completely
> it minimizes it. Therefore we conceive of the problem to-
> day not as a class struggle but a global struggle against
> racism.

Karenga does not, however, rule out economics altogether; he believes that black people "can only reach a

[19] This and subsequent quotes are from Karenga's pamphlet,
The Quotable Karenga, copyright © 1967 by US Organization, Los Angeles.

stage of economic force through a cooperative economic system," and that "you cannot have political freedom without an economic base." What all of this means concretely is best indicated by the fact that Karenga firmly allied himself with the Black Power Conferences and Wright's opportunistic conception of black nationalism.

The cultural nationalism being advocated by Jones and Karenga had several weaknesses when viewed in the light of black liberation which it claims to seek. In the first place, in their political and economic program, both Jones and Karenga have allied themselves with the reformist nationalists and placed almost exclusive emphasis on electoral politics, black-owned small businesses, and "buy black" campaigns. Some of the problems of this program have already been discussed.

Revolutionary nationalists are strongly critical of the cultural nationalists' fascination with traditional African culture. The revolutionary nationalists feel that this emphasis on blackness can be reactionary and might possibly lead to a kind of black fascism in the United States. Huey Newton, imprisoned Minister of Defense of the Black Panther Party, expressed this when he said:

> Cultural nationalism, or pork chop nationalism, as I sometimes call it, is basically the problem of having the wrong political perspective. It seems to be a reaction instead of responding to political oppression. The cultural nationalists are concerned with returning to the old African culture and thereby regaining their identity and freedom. In other words, they feel that the African culture will automatically bring political freedom. Many times cultural nationalists fall into line as reactionary nationalists.
>
> Papa Doc in Haiti is an excellent example of reactionary nationalism. He oppresses the people but he does promote the African culture. He is against anything other than black, which on the surface seems very good, but to him it is only to mislead the people. He merely kicked

out the racists and replaced them with himself as the oppressor. Many of the nationalists in this country seem to desire the same ends.[20]

In their fascination with Africa, the cultural nationalists seem to believe that black culture and art alone will somehow bring about a revolution. "Black art initiates and supports change," says Ron Karenga. This belief has had two consequences. First of all, it has allowed a passive retreat into "blackness" on the part of some of those who call themselves revolutionaries. These so-called black revolutionaries measure their militancy by how much "black awareness" they have or how "bad" they can talk. Verbal militance thus replaces action, and the net result is passive nonresistance to oppression. Secondly, the fascination with African culture and art has led to a distortion and a vulgarization of the whole idea of black culture. Black culture has become a badge to be worn rather than an experience to be shared. African robes, dashikis, dresses, and sandals have become standard equipment not only for the well-dressed black militant, but even for middle-class hipsters who have gone Afro. Business firms advertise hair sprays especially suited for natural styles, and some of the shrewder cultural nationalists have turned a profit peddling African trinkets and clothes to naïve young blacks. How this activity relates to black liberation is difficult to understand; except it certainly aids the economic liberation of those who are cashing in on the fad.

The cultural nationalists are also notorious for their chauvinistic attitude toward black women. Karenga's conception of the function of black women is best expressed in his own words:

> What makes a woman appealing is femininity but she can't be feminine without being submissive.
> The role of the woman is to inspire her man, educate their children and participate in social development.

20 *The Movement*, August 1968.

Equality is false; it's the devil's concept. Our concept
is complementary. Complementary means you complete
or make perfect that which is imperfect.
The man has any right that does not destroy the collective needs of his family.
The woman has the two rights of consultation and
then separation if she isn't getting what she should be
getting.

Chauvinism is also quite evident in the matter of birth
control. Black militants (usually males) have taken a very
hard line on this question, vehemently contending that it
amounts to genocide. Birth control, they say, is simply the
white man's way of controlling nonwhite populations, or
decimating some of them, such as blacks in the United
States. Typical of this position was a statement issued last
year by a group calling itself the Black Unity Party of
Peekskill, New York. The statement called on black women
to spurn birth control pills and contended that "in not taking the pill we must have a new sense of value. When we
are producing children we are aiding the revolution in
the form [of] nation building."

For some time black women uncomplainingly accepted
chauvinist attitudes and remarks by male black nationalists.
They reasoned that black men had been castrated by four
hundred years of white domination and now that the men
were regaining and asserting their manhood, a few excesses were to be tolerated. But the birth control issue provoked an angry response from a group of poor black
women—most of them housewives, domestics, or welfare
recipients—in nearby Mount Vernon, New York. The
women were certainly opposed to genocidally enforced
sterilization, but they argued that self-administered birth
control devices gave them greater leeway to be good
mothers and good freedom fighters. "Poor black women
in the U.S. have to fight back out of our own experience
of oppression," they said in a letter to the men. "Having
too many babies stop [sic] us from supporting our chil-

dren, teaching them the truth or stopping the brain-washing, as you say, and fighting black men who still want to use and exploit us."

They then charged the male militants with exhibiting class bias:

> But we don't think you're going to understand us be-cause you are a bunch of little middle-class people and we are poor black women. The middle-class never un-derstands the poor because they always need to use them as you want to use poor black women's children to gain power for yourself. You'll run the black community with your kind of black power—You on top! The poor understand class struggle!

Black women rightly reject blatantly reactionary attitudes on the part of male nationalists. The women do so be-cause they know it makes no sense to talk about national liberation if women still are to be cast in the roles of serv-ants and baby factories. They understand in a way the men do not, that the liberation of the group, to be meaningful and progressive, necessitates the liberation of its most op-pressed members. From their perspective, it is black women, and especially poor black women, who are at the rock bottom of the American social heap. They bear the double burden of being oppressed by society in general because they are black and of suffering at the hands of their men because they are women.

It is obvious from such statements as those made by Karenga that many black nationalists are completely un-aware of the lessons learned by revolutionary nationalist movements in other countries, particularly Cuba and Vietnam.[21] National liberation does not come bearing a stamp, "For Males Only." And if it does, as has become

---

[21] For a thoughtful survey of the status of Vietnamese women, see Mai Thi Tu, "The Vietnamese Woman, Yesterday and Today," in *Vietnamese Women* (Vietnamese Studies No. 10, Hanoi: 1966). It is available in the United States at China Books and Periodicals, 2929 24th St., San Francisco, Cali-fornia.

apparent in Algeria, then that stands as one indication of an incomplete revolution, a revolution which has not fulfilled its promise.

Cultural nationalism, then, when considered as a separate ideological current, has serious drawbacks. This by no means implies, however, that there is no need for a deepening awareness of black culture and history. Revolutionary nationalists would probably agree with Huey Newton's position, expressed in an interview in March 1968:

> We believe that it's important for us to recognize our origins and to identify with the revolutionary black people of Africa and people of color throughout the world. But as far as returning, per se, to the ancient customs, we don't see any necessity in this. And also, we say that the only culture that is worth holding on to is revolutionary culture, for change, for the better.

It was this revolutionary cultural and psychological awareness that laid the foundation for the recent nationwide black student revolt. Certainly this development was no retreat into reaction, but cultural nationalism can become just that if it is not firmly incorporated into a revolutionary political movement.[22]

(5)

In his massive study, *The Crisis of the Negro Intellectual,* Harold Cruse tried to avoid the pitfalls into which Jones and Karenga stumbled. Cruse was not a public figure at the Black Power Conference, but his writings have done much to shape nationalist thinking. Cruse himself is a black radical and nationalist of many years' experience. In addition, he brought to his work intimate knowledge of the inner machinery of the older white Communist move-

[22] Former SNCC leader Rap Brown, realizing this, was fond of quipping that there are too many blacks sporting natural hair-dos but still burdened by processed minds.

ment and its serious failings. He is clearly committed to black people and to their liberation, and he raises serious questions as to why so many black intellectuals have not exhibited in their actions a similar concern. The outcome is a passionately compelling intellectual treatise. At times his passion grates against reason, and he displays occasional discursive drifts, but there can be little doubt that Cruse is among the critical figures helping to shape an indigenous Afro-American radicalism. Hence, an examination of his work is a pressing necessity.

Although he is a nationalist, it is not meaningful to say that Cruse is a cultural nationalist in the same sense in which this term is applied to Jones and Karenga. Cruse is unique. He stands outside the pale of accepted categories. To begin with, he does not arrive at his nationalism out of any mystical fascination with black art and culture. Art and culture are the substance of his concern, but not because of any peculiar power which they exercise over the minds of men. Rather, art and culture are important because of the special role they play in the political and economic matrix of America. Unlike some cultural nationalists, Cruse claims that he does not assign culture a higher priority than politics and economics.[23] Instead he insists that the three must be carefully fused together in any viable black radical program. His main criticism of black intellectuals and the white left is that they have given precedence to politics and economics while playing down or totally discounting the cultural aspect.

Cruse postulates his own idea of the cultural revolution, and he arrives at this concept using three separate but related arguments.

For him the social reality of America is grounded not solely in class divisions, as the Marxists would have it, but primarily in ethnic group divisions. The United States is

[23] His primary concern, however, *is* culture, and it is this that opens the way to defeat for his program of revolution.

a mosaic of such groups, each vying for power and control over the others as well as control over natural resources. The schoolbook version of America as a melting pot is patently untrue. It is rather in competitive, largely unassimilated ethnic groups that the American reality is found. Cruse does not, however, rule out the idea of class struggle. He maintains simply that in America class struggle is subordinate to ethnic group struggle.

Two ethnic groups are of particular concern to black people, in Cruse's estimate, because taken together they dominate all aspects of Afro-American life. White Anglo-Saxon Protestants, as *the* dominant ethnic group in America, control all aspects of black economic and political life. They also have usurped and commercialized black culture to their own pecuniary advantage. On the other hand, Negro protest against this rank exploitation (except for nationalist groups like the Garveyites and the Muslims) has been carefully molded by Jews. It was the Jews of the Communist Party and the old white left generally, and more recently the young Jewish civil righters, who formulated and shaped the thrust of Negro protest activities. This Jewish leadership has worked to the detriment of black people, Cruse argues, because it was based more on the inner dynamics of the Jewish ethnic group than on the objective requirements of black liberation. Jews were able to assume this role because of their influence in the Communist Party, an organization which from 1929 to 1951 was the major vehicle for the expression of black unrest.

Blacks are on the losing end of American ethnic group conflict, according to Cruse, because they fail to recognize it for what it is, and they do not grasp that the crucial arena for this conflict is the cultural front. The cultural front is crucial because it is here that the conflict is openly expressed. While it may be pretended that economically and politically America is homogeneous, on the cultural plane, this pretense becomes an obvious façade, and the underlying ethnic reality is exposed. "America," Cruse says, "is

a nation that lies to itself about who and what it is. It is a
nation of minorities ruled by a minority of one—it thinks
and acts as if it were a nation of white Anglo-Saxon
Protestants."[24]

America "thinks and acts as if it were a nation of white
Anglo-Saxon Protestants" because it is precisely this group
which controls the cultural apparatus (mass media, performing arts, etc.) of the country and, therefore, is in a
position to control ideas and values. Hence, "For American society, the most crucial requirement at this point is
a complete democratization of the national cultural ethos.
This requires a thorough, democratic overhauling of the
social functions of the entire American cultural apparatus. First of all: For whom, and in whose interest,
does the cultural apparatus exist in America? Does it exist
for the social needs, the social edification, the spiritual
uplift, the cultural development, solvency and morale of
all the diverse minority groups in America? Or does it
exist solely, and disproportionately, for the social suprem-
acy, the group narcissism, and the idealization of the white
Anglo-Saxon Protestant minority?"[25] This struggle for cultural democracy, the cultural revolution, thus becomes
absolutely essential in order to expose, and finally effectively deal with, the group reality of American life.

The cultural revolution, also, flows from another premise
held by Cruse. Following C. Wright Mills, Cruse believes
that it is the intellectuals who are the real agents of historical change, particularly in underdeveloped societies, because the intellectuals, like certain parts of the proletariat,
are acutely aware of national oppression. But the intellectuals are conscious of the dynamic of social change also,
and, in some instances, are able to apply this knowledge to
their concrete situation. Hence, it is left to the revolutionary intellectuals to motivate and guide the masses.

This guidance must take place in the cultural field, at

24 Cruse, p. 456 (New York: William Morrow, 1967).
25 *Ibid.,* p. 457.

least initially, because it is here that the intellectual, like the artist, operates.

The special function of the Negro intellectual is a cultural one. He should take to the rostrum and assail the stultifying blight of the commercially depraved white middle-class who has poisoned the structural roots of the American ethos and transformed the American people into a nation of intellectual dolts. He should explain the economic and institutional causes of this American cultural depravity. He should tell black America how and why Negroes are trapped in this cultural degeneracy, and how it has dehumanized their essential identity, squeezed the lifeblood of their inherited cultural ingredients out of them, and then relegated them to the cultural slums. They should tell this brain-washed white America, this "nation of sheep," this overfed, overdeveloped, overprivileged (but culturally pauperized) federation of unassimilated European remnants that their days of grace are numbered.[26]

This impassioned exhortation is apparently supposed to prod black intellectuals out of their lethargy and force them to assume their responsibilities as agents of social change, makers of the cultural revolution. "The Negro movement is at an impasse precisely because it lacks a real functional corps of intellectuals able to confront and deal perceptively with American realities on a level that social conditions demand."[27]

Finally, Cruse asserts the need for a cultural revolution in his analysis of American capitalism and its weaknesses. Writing in *Liberator* magazine in November 1963, Cruse says:

We American Negroes exist in essentially the same relationship to American capitalism as other colonials and semi-colonials have to western capitalism as a whole. Yet, when other [S]emi-colonials of the colored world rebel against the political and economic subjugation of

26 *Ibid.*, pp. 455–56.
27 *Ibid.*, p. 472.

western capitalism, it is for the aim of having the freedom
to build up their own native industrial bases for themselves. But our American Negro rebellion derives from
the fact that we exist side by side with the greatest industrial complex the world has ever seen, but which
we are not allowed to use democratically for ourselves.
Hence, while the Negro rebellion emerges out of the
same semi-colonial social conditions of others it must
have different objectives in order to be considered revolutionary. In other words, we must locate the weakest
sector of the American capitalist "free enterprise" front
and strike there. But where is that weak front in the free
enterprise armor? That sector is the cultural front. Or
better, it is that section of the American economic system that has to do with the ownership and administration
of the cultural communication in America, i.e., films,
theaters, radio and television, music performing and
publishing, popular entertainment booking, performing,
management, etc. In short, it is that sector devoted to
the economics and aesthetic ideology involved in the
cultural arts of America. If the Negro rebellion is limited
by a lack of original ideas to "fit the world into a theo-
retic frame" then it is only in the cultural areas of American life that such new ideas can have any social meaning. What is meant here is that the only observable way
in which the Negro rebellion can become revolutionary
in terms of American conditions is for the Negro movement to project the concept of Cultural Revolution in
America.

Cruse does not explain in this article why he thinks the
cultural sector is the weak link in American capitalism, nor
does he say how the cultural revolution is to come about.
In *The Crisis of the Negro Intellectual* Cruse simply re-
states in altered form his assertion of the economic importance of the cultural apparatus: "Mass cultural communications is a basic industry, as basic as oil, steel, and
transportation, in its own way. Developing along with it,
supporting it, and subservient to it, is an organized network of functions that are creative, administrative, propa-
gandistic, educational, recreational, political, artistic, eco-

nomic and cultural. . . . Only the blind cannot see that whoever controls the cultural apparatus—whatever class, power group, faction or political combine—also controls the destiny of the United States and everything in it."[28]

The most serious flaw in Cruse's work is this failure to establish, by argument or evidence, his central thesis concerning the salience of the cultural apparatus and the projected cultural revolution. He evidences an unfortunate tendency to substitute rhetorical assertion for reasoned argument.

In the achievement of American "democratic cultural pluralism" is found the essence of Cruse's program for launching the black revolution. This means decentralizing the ownership and administration of the cultural apparatus as a crucial step toward creating genuine democracy among America's diverse ethnic groups. This task is to be performed by the black "creative intellectuals" because, Cruse contends, in America "there is now *only one* group of American creative intellectuals who have the motivation (or at least the potential) for democratizing American culture and forcing the return of the public arts to the people. These are the new young generation of Negro intellectuals. . . ."[29] These creative intellectuals form a special class which includes writers, poets, playwrights, musicians, composers, conductors, directors, actors, critics, artists, etc. It is this class, usually socially and economically privileged, to which Cruse assigns the function of leadership.

If Cruse's program were carried through, it would consequently exacerbate already existing class divisions and tensions in the black community. This is something of a paradox, since Cruse is also an advocate of democratization and equality. Upon closer examination, however, it becomes clear that Cruse only espouses more democratic relations among various ethnic *groups*. As for the internal

28 *Ibid.*, p. 474.
29 *Ibid.*, pp. 98–99.

structure of the Afro-American ethnic group, his only
criticism is that old-line leaders and the black bourgeoisie
have failed in the task of securing group equality for black
America. He sees in the intellectual class, especially young
intellectuals, blacks' only hope of getting beyond the impasse created by the failure of the civil rights movement.

Cruse's elitism goes so far as to call for the creation of a
new black middle class, apparently to be composed largely
of the black intelligentsia, "organized on the principle of
cooperative economic ownership and technical administration."[30] He believes that such an administrative class
"would be more responsible to the community in social,
political and cultural affairs than middle classes based on
free enterprise and laissez-faire economics."[31]

This may or may not be true, but it is precisely the
creation of a new, invigorated black bourgeoisie which is
high on corporate America's agenda for the black colony.
From the corporate standpoint, such a class would help to
stabilize the ghettos and provide a subtle means of social
control. It definitely would not be a revolutionary force.

This is illustrative of one of Cruse's dilemmas. He devotes a thick book to tracing and explaining the failures of
the black intellectuals; yet he falls back upon this same
class for black salvation. A new nationalist synthesis cannot be achieved, he contends, "until the Negro intellectuals as a class are prepared to lead the way. . . ." But
how is this possible when Cruse, following sociologist Milton M. Gordon, also maintains that the black intellectual
is, "in the main, socially detached from his own Negro
ethnic world . . ."? Cruse answers that the hope lies in the
young intellectuals who somehow are expected to "first
clear the way to cultural revolution by [undertaking] a
critical assault on the methods and ideology of the old-
guard Negro intellectual elite."[32] But this does not answer
the class question.

30 *Ibid.*, p. 89.
31 *Ibid.*
32 *Ibid.*, p. 99.

As in the case of all black professionals, their middle-class orientation creates an ambivalence which is extremely difficult to overcome. Are black intellectuals somehow different? Cruse admits that the answer is no. Thus: "Middle-class Negroes have rejected the basic art expressions of the Negro folk in music, dance, literature and theater." And: "Negro creative intellectuals, if not already of middle-class origins, adopt middle-class values." Hence: "Negro creative intellectuals as a stratum tend toward total acceptance of racial integrationist premises."[33] Thus, while some individual black intellectuals may free themselves of their background, black intellectuals *as a social stratum* are identified with the black middle class and its ambivalent attitudes. Plead with them though he may, Cruse cannot change this class reality.

Cruse speaks of structural changes in societal forms and cultural "revolution," but the essence of his program can be reduced to a call for "democratization" of America's cultural apparatus. He wants genuine "pluralism" instituted in the cultural life of the country. Herein lies another weakness in his program for revolution. For American capitalism is quite willing to allow "cultural democracy" so long as that does not interfere with established power relations. Cruse is not unaware of this possibility. "One of the keys to understanding the effectiveness of any tactic, idea, strategy or trend in the Negro movement, is to determine how well the American system can absorb it and, thus, negate its force. To repeat, the American social system quite easily absorbs all foreign, and even native, radical doctrines and neutralizes them. The same applies to the doctrines of the Negro movement. In fact, it applies all the more, simply because this movement is more native than others and therefore more intimately connected to the inner American social dynamic."[34] Apparently, Cruse thinks this dynamic does not apply to his program.

[33] *Ibid.,* pp. 83–84.
[34] *Ibid.,* p. 36.

But at a superficial level, the mass media have been "democraticized" in the last two years, and black people have made their debut on the American cultural stage. Blacks have become very visible on television and in mass circulation magazines. Of course, the roles that they play (e.g., in "Julia," "I Spy," "The Mod Squad," and "Mission: Impossible") have nothing to do with cultural nationalism but are rather the white cultural establishment's effort to "absorb" Negro cultural protest.

To say the least, this absorption is being carried out in a crude and implausible fashion.[35] The Negro characters in these productions have not the faintest relation to the reality of black life. One may ask if black youngsters in this age are *actually* expected to identify with black men who are cops or spies working for whites and black women who are so incredibly bourgeois as to be hardly identifiable as blacks? The answer is yes. The media are not trying to project a picture of black life as it is, but rather they are telling black TV viewers how they are *expected* to act if they want to make it in white America. Television thus plays the role of a socializing mechanism, probably second only to public schools, devoted to inculcating blacks with white middle-class values.

News media have increasingly dropped the term "Negro" in favor of the cultural nationalist "black." (Even the U. S. Treasury Department, after a quick survey to see which way the wind was blowing, announced it would start using the term "Afro-American" in its press releases.) Concomitantly, blacks are appearing more frequently in "nonracial" roles in television commercials and in magazine advertising.

One of the most successful efforts to absorb black cultural nationalism into otherwise totally white-oriented television programming was last summer's seven-part CBS News Special on Black America. The series ranged over

[35] More sophisticated are the productions of New York's Negro Ensemble, which is underwritten by the Ford Foundation.

black history, music, Africa, black soldiers, and a few minutes were even given over to a discussion of separatism (only to come up with statistics purporting to show that most blacks don't like the idea). The series was particularly interesting because, despite its official tone of sympathy for blacks, it revealed, once again, the deep gulf which exists between the attitudes of average blacks and those of average whites. Where blacks want to talk about "race relations" in terms of discrimination or racism, to whites the same phrase conjures up images of riots and destruction.

The "Black America" series largely steered clear of any serious discussion of the views of "extremists" like Stokely Carmichael and Rap Brown. It sought instead to legitimize the ideas of more moderate advocates of "black pride" such as CORE's Floyd McKissick and Congressman John Conyers of Detroit. More sophisticated media people, however, are dissatisfied with this failure to grapple with the black militants. Jack Gould, television critic of the New York *Times*, criticized television's new "constructive therapy" efforts on the grounds that there is a "veritable censorship ban" on black militants.[36] Gould was concerned with reaching and pacifying militant black youngsters, "the very persons who do not hesitate to go into the streets and spearhead the disturbances that concern the nation as a whole." He argued that it was insufficient to "merely afford added comfort and reassurance" to the parents of the young blacks by airing the shopworn opinions of supposedly respected Negro leaders. What was really needed, Gould stressed, was for black youths to see Stokely Carmichael, for example, intellectually demolished on a television screen. Carmichael's "pat phrases," he said, "could be taken care of in relatively short order." This should be followed by "a mature exposé of his [Carmichael's] political thinking, his aims for what he says should be a better America, how he proposes to go about winning

[36] Gould, New York *Times*, June 2, 1968.

them and the influence of his recent global jaunt on his philosophy." Gould was clever enough to know that no white man could successfully destroy Carmichael in the minds of young black rebels. He, therefore, suggested that this dirty little task be assigned to Mrs. Martin Luther King with entertainer Harry Belafonte acting as referee. This "absorbing confrontation between the outstanding advocates of non-violence and violence" would then be beamed coast-to-coast for all potential rioters to see whose political blood was spilled.

So progresses the "cultural revolution." Of course, asinine television programs and insidious proposals by white television critics are unacceptable to Cruse. Cruse sought a basic change in ownership and administration of the cultural apparatus, not simply a facial uplift. But it cannot be denied that by adding a few black faces on television, the medium which probably has the greatest impact on the black population, the white cultural rulers have taken a major step toward co-opting, distorting, and eventually nullifying Cruse's program—and this because Cruse's program could be reduced to a demand for an extension of democracy into the cultural field.

American capitalism has demonstrated that it is quite capable of extending "democracy" into almost any field, cultural or political, without altering its fundamental structure or existing power relationships. But unless the latter are changed, "ethnic group democratization" becomes merely another meaningless shibboleth like "racial integration"—and it does little to help the black community as a whole.

(6)

The political and economic programs proposed by cultural nationalists usually are quite similar to, if not identical with, the program of reformist nationalists, most notably the Congress of Racial Equality. CORE's embracement of black capitalism was completed at its 1968 convention in Columbus, Ohio. The theme of that meeting was "Black Nationalism: CORE's Philosophy for Survival," but these seemingly militant words served as a cover for CORE's retreat into the arms of corporate capitalism. It was a curious convention in that all workshop resolutions, the product of three days of work by the several hundred delegates, were tabled. To add to the confusion an open schism, which some said threatened to become violent, erupted between the national office and CORE's Brooklyn chapter.[87] Despite these gyrations, the conven-

[87] Actually, the break did not become known to many delegates until after the convention was over. It was the tension of this impending public schism, however, which led to the tabling of workshop resolutions. The split with Brooklyn CORE revolved around questions relating to the national structure of CORE, self-defense of black communities, cooperation with white businesses and foundations, and conflicting programs of nationalism. Brooklyn CORE chief Robert Carson demanded a restructuring of CORE to give power to regional chairmen instead of the national office. He also advocated a massive campaign against genocide, including the creation of a black police or protection agency and the arming of black communities. Carson charged that CORE, in working with white corporate interests, was betraying the liberation struggle. "We feel," he said, "there cannot be any negotiations with industry and capitalism since capitalism is what put us [black people] in the situation we're in. We feel capitalism should be destroyed." In a press conference after the convention, Floyd McKissick responded to Carson's charges by lashing out at "disrupters and political losers" who "made certain false statements regarding CORE."

At the root of the split were conflicting approaches to the question of nationalism. Carson, unlike Roy Innis, is an advocate of relocation and total separation of the black population in the United States. For example, a resolution, which Carson said reflected the thinking of his group, was passed by one of the convention workshops stating that "black self-determination is impossible in close proximity to whites." It called for the "establishment of a national homeland for black people either in the southeastern section of the U.S. or in the combined area of South West Africa and the Union of South Africa." Roy Innis termed this document "fantastic," and immediately all workshop resolutions were tabled.

tion struggled along and finally reached agreement on a unique nationalist program—a program which grew out of several years' thinking by black nationalists within CORE. The leading spokesman for nationalism within CORE, Roy Innis,[38] explained his program in a lengthy presentation to the delegates. Innis first explained that black power "is the methodology for the implementation of the goals of black nationalism." Black nationalism, he said, "is the philosophy of self-determination of an oppressed people." He said that blacks must seek "liberation by any means necessary and pragmatic." He went on to differentiate between segregation, integration, and nationalist separation. A necessary condition of segregation is racial separation. But this is not sufficient to define and understand segregation. Equating the two simply confuses and obscures the underlying economic realities. For segregation also means that, even in all-black communities, control over public institutions (schools, welfare, police, etc.), private business, and the flow of goods and services is exercised overwhelmingly by whites, not blacks. Thus while whites and blacks are physically separated under segregation, whites are able to control and manipulate blacks to the advantage of the former.

In terms of control, racial integration is no better, Innis contended. Even in a racially integrated or heterogeneous society, whites would continue to hold economic power and exercise control over the integrated blacks. The blacks, not being owners, managers, or administrators of any major institutions, would have no choice but to continue to yield to this white control. Hence, for Innis, the determining factor in the race issue hinges on the question: Who exercises effective institutional control over black people? On this score segregation and integration must both be counted failures because neither alters basic power relations within the society.

[38] Following this convention, Innis was named national director of CORE.

The only acceptable solution, Innis argued, is the nationalist solution. By this he meant institutional and geographic separation of "natural sociological units" and redefinition of these as political units. Mere institutional decentralization is not sufficient because real power would still rest in white hands. Innis instead called for parallel institutional systems, "completely separate and different." Parallel structures are necessary to effectively counteract the institutional racism which facilitates the exploitation and oppression of black people. It is not the individual racist who is most dangerous to black people, Innis stated; rather it is racism which, over hundreds of years, has become enshrined in American institutions and now poses the gravest threat to the existence of black people. Innis believes that predatory and unreformed capitalism is incapable of rooting out and destroying this institutional racism. Therefore, he concluded, only through complete institutional separation can black people defend themselves against the debilitating effects of racism.

Innis rightly attacks institutional racism as a prime enemy of black liberation, but in the reasoning that leads him to this point there is confusion about the relationship between capitalism and racism. Indeed, one could get the impression from Innis that there is no intrinsic connection between the two, and it is simply accidental that they happen to co-exist in the United States. The historic growth of American racism out of capitalist-inspired slavery and the subsequent institutionalization of this racism are simply ignored. Innis treats capitalism and racism as givens, which require no further probing in themselves.

With this much said by way of introduction, Innis then elaborated his program. Termed the "Economic Theory of Nationhood" in CORE's new constitution, it calls for the complete takeover by blacks of all economic, political, and social institutions in black communities for the purpose of fostering the economic development of these communities. Innis cautioned the delegates that discussing black economic development is tricky business, since much

186   BLACK AWAKENING IN CAPITALIST AMERICA

depends on who is talking. For example, by "economic
development" the government means opening up more
jobs. This is an unacceptable palliative, Innis said. To men
such as Senator Jacob Javits and the late Senator Robert
Kennedy, he continued, black economic development
means bringing white corporations into the ghettos to
create jobs.[39] This also is unacceptable. "A modern nation," Innis asserted, "becomes viable through the creation of capital instruments. We can't make money through
jobs. You make money through owning capital instruments: land and other properties."

How are these "capital instruments" to be secured?
Innis answered by suggesting that the way to economic
development lay in foraying into the political arena in an
effort to gain control of key public institutions, such as
schools. He attacked school decentralization plans, such
as the one developed recently in New York City, on the
grounds that they do not provide for any real transfer of
power to the local level. He charged that the New York
plan merely arranged for a redistribution of power between
the Board of Education and the mayor, with the teachers'
union trying to pick up some of the crumbs. It is necessary for blacks to take full control of the schools in their
communities, he maintained. Then, one of the first economic development programs could be "supplying goods
and services to schools in our areas by setting up black
companies." He explained that such companies could later
diversify, and, thereby, expand and strengthen an independent economic base in black communities. Thus political action (e.g., taking control of the schools) becomes a
means for building black capitalism.

Innis's strategy was unwittingly based on the assump-

[39] Kennedy, for example, had two community development
corporations in Brooklyn's Bedford-Stuyvesant, the nation's second largest black community. The two organizations encouraged huge white-owned corporations such as International
Business Machines to relocate in the area in order to increase
employment.

tion that American political democracy actually works the way it is described in school textbooks. That is, that political power is based upon the will of a majority of the people in a given geographic area. If this were the case, then there might be hope for instituting black capitalism along the lines suggested by Innis. But political power in America is dependent upon those who control valued resources and critical institutions, not vice versa. And those who have this power cannot be voted out of their positions by the public at large, because the base of their power lies outside the formal political sphere. Their base of power lies in the corporations and the large public institutions which are interdependent, but largely removed from the sway of public pressure.

Innis was not altogether unaware of the problems posed by the gap between the myth and the reality of political democracy and political power in this country. He told the delegates that his program would necessarily require a "new contract between blacks and whites." Arguing that the U. S. Constitution is outdated, he called for a new political arrangement which would define black communities as political units and "secure the ability to re-allocate the wealth within [our] system." He contended that blacks must be recognized as a special interest group for which appropriate provisions must be made in a new social contract. This, of course, was very close to Cruse's demand for "ethnic democracy" in the United States. But where Cruse saw "ethnic democracy" in cultural terms, Innis is a political animal who approaches the matter as a political problem. Since black people are becoming the largest minority, if not outright majorities, in increasing numbers of American cities, any new social contract, to be acceptable to blacks, must redefine the structure of cities so as to grant political autonomy to the black communities. Such an arrangement, Innis said, would create a nation of dispersed city-states, "a series of islands with land separating us." The United States would thereby become a multinational federation.

Why will white America agree to this plan? Innis answered flatly: "We have the ability to withdraw a sacred commodity from America: peace and tranquility." Actually, white America is not monolithic, and it is possible to isolate the "petty urban barons" who control the ghettos from other white interest groups, including the national ruling structure, by graphically demonstrating that these "urban managers" are no longer controlling and operating their cities efficiently. By appealing to the self-interest and desire for peace of various elements of the white population, he concluded, it is possible to get a change of management and have the central cities turned over to black control. In this respect, it will be seen, Innis's thinking closely parallels that of more sophisticated members of the white power structure.

Needless to say, it is highly unlikely that such a rearrangement will come about, and, when everything is examined, the prospects for the urban black masses successfully to employ some kind of ethnic group model of advancement are, at best, dim. Social critics Frances Fox Piven and Richard A. Cloward, writing in the March 30, 1968 issue of *New Republic,* concluded that "local government has been greatly weakened since the heyday of the ethnic urban machine. Localities now collect a mere seven percent of tax revenues, while the federal government collects two-thirds. This fiscal weakness underlies the great vulnerability of local government to national centralized power. . . . The national government is using its multitude of existing programs for localities to form a new system of metropolitan-wide bureaucracies. This new level of government will impose federal policies on localities in the course of channeling grants-in-aid to them." This "metropolitanism" will also serve to cushion the impact of urban black voting majorities on American politics and political priorities.

The new informal national governing structure which is emerging in this process may be considered broadly "friendly" to black people, even some militants, but this favorable attitude has little effect on the hard realities of economic life. As in so many other areas of social life, conscious personal intention is a relatively minor factor in determining social function or consequence. Where the spoils of city office once went to the ethnic poor, friends and families of the successful politician, in the form of jobs, rakeoffs, and favors, this process is now being reversed in favor of the new nationwide business and political elites. "In pace-setting cities such as New York, Philadelphia, and Boston . . . the spoils never really reach the urban community at all. As in Rockefeller's massive Urban Development Corporation (or Philadelphia's West Philadelphia Corp. and Boston's Redevelopment Authority), the benefits go directly to the interests represented by the trustees: the state commissioners of commerce, banks, insurance and planning coordination, plus five corporate leaders (who represent national firms). Special real estate tax exemptions and other lures have been instituted to make sure that outside private developers join in the operation. In the face of these interests, municipal regulatory powers—always fragile—disintegrate altogether. Each of the development corporations mentioned above possesses power to override local regulations, such as zoning codes, whenever and wherever an attractive investment site should appear." (Carol Brightman, *Viet-Report* magazine special issue on "Colonialism and Liberation in America," Summer 1968, p. 5.) With this kind of competition from mushrooming urban development corporations, the "insiders," the urban black bourgeoisie and black poor, can hope only to scavenge a few of the crumbs.

Genocide is the alternative to the CORE program, Innis contended. He told the CORE delegates that for the white power structure the choice of options will be based on anticipated costs. He thinks genocide is much more expensive, both in terms of money and in terms of white lives.

Perhaps the best illustrations of what could be expected from Innis's program are to be found in Harlem and Cleveland. In the former, the Harlem Commonwealth Council

(HCC), of which Innis is a director and whose executive director, Donald Simmons, was moderator of the CORE convention workshop on economics, has undertaken what it terms "the economic regeneration of a community through the control of its capital goods and services." HCC advises black businessmen and aids them in planning and in securing loans. In its progress report for the spring of 1968, HCC said: "We believed from the very beginning that one root problem of Harlem is that almost no one who lives there *owns* anything. History has taught us that progress depends on the regenerative processes of capital goods. It is not enough to attract white-owned industry to Harlem. Finding jobs for blacks is not enough either, critical as it is to HCC's daily function. Both of these become enough only if we can develop Harlem's capital."

Harlem CORE itself announced plans to purchase a department store on 125th Street and use the income to finance the organization. In a brochure appropriately entitled "Black Power Is Black Business," the group pointed to the resentment which is created by money being drained out of black areas by white merchants. "We believe this is bad for black people, bad for white people, bad for the economy, bad for America. Harlem CORE sees an opportunity to begin erasing the hostility, defeatism and powerlessness of Harlem today by putting Black Power into business. . . ." Thus for Harlem CORE, at least, black power very definitely came to mean the power of black business. Unfortunately for CORE, as was noted earlier, the power of black business is mostly an illusion, since black businessmen have been unable to enter into successful competition with the gigantic corporations which dominate the economy.

Cleveland is where CORE operated its voter registration and education program which was financed by the Ford Foundation. The effect of this program was to aid in the election of Negro mayor Carl Stokes. "The Target City Project voter drive contributed significantly to this political decision," Cleveland CORE boasted in its report to

the Columbus convention. However, the riot which occurred in Cleveland later that summer was a strong indication that not all blacks thought the election of a Negro
mayor would seriously change their lives or alter power
relations in Cleveland. It was apparently only the CORE
leadership which clung to this belief.

Other work supposedly done on behalf of the black
community under the Ford grant included a research
project which became the basis of five of the eight major
workshops at the CORE convention. These five workshops were concerned with ways of establishing black-
owned corporations which would engage in trade in the
black communities, with white America, and with Africa,
Asia, and Latin America.

(7)

In summary, CORE and the cultural nationalists draped
themselves in the mantle of nationalism, but upon examination it is seen that their programs, far from aiding in the
achievement of black liberation and freedom from exploitation, would instead weld the black communities more
firmly into the structure of American corporate capitalism.
This reformist or bourgeois nationalism—through its chosen
vehicle of black capitalism—may line the pockets and boost
the social status of the black middle class and black intelligentsia, but it will not ease the oppression of the ordinary ghetto dweller. What CORE and the cultural nationalists seek is not an end to oppression, but the transfer
of the oppressive apparatus into their own hands. They
call themselves nationalists and exploit the legitimate nationalist feelings of black people in order to advance
their own interests as a class. And chief among those interests is their desire to become brokers between the white
rulers and the black ruled.

Speaking of the role played by the national middle class
in a colonized nation, Frantz Fanon wrote: "Seen through
its eyes, its mission has nothing to do with transforming the

192 BLACK AWAKENING IN CAPITALIST AMERICA

nation; it consists, prosaically, of being the transmission line between the nation and . . . neocolonialism."[40] This role of intermediary—which offers many rewards—is being increasingly assumed by the militant, nationalist black middle class in this country.

[40] Fanon, *The Wretched of the Earth*, p. 124.

V. CORPORATE IMPERIALISM
VS. BLACK LIBERATION

In recent times black militants have developed a habit of pointing to the city as the most important battleground of the black revolt. After all, they remark, it is urban America which already has felt the most fierce blows of black rebellion. And they cite statistics showing that two-thirds of all blacks living outside the South reside in the nation's twelve largest central cities and cite projections that within a generation most, if not all, of these cities will have solid black majorities. At the same time in just about every other major American city, blacks are, or soon will become, the largest ethnic minority. Since the cities provide the hubs of the country's communications and transportation facilities, as well as house much of its industrial plant, financial enterprises, and government agencies, it is obvious that what the militants say cannot be lightly dismissed.

White America is well aware of the facts cited by militant spokesmen, although liberal whites prefer to use the broader (and more delicate) phrase, "urban crisis," when referring to the troubled cities. To them the cities present not a battleground but a crisis to be managed. It is normally only those whites immediately affected by this crisis—local government and police officials, National Guard commanders, scared homeowners—who speak frankly about the possibility and likelihood of open warfare in the nation's urban areas. But whether one calls it an urban crisis or a state of civil war, the fact remains that the cities are in trouble and something has to be done to bail them out.

Several interlocked responses to this problem were forth-coming from white America.[1] On the one hand there was the orthodox liberal who prescribed more New Deal welfarism as an antidote to riots. More antidiscrimination legislation and expanded antipoverty programs would suffice nicely, he contended. But the orthodox liberal was in for a rude awakening if he only listened to the shrill voices emanating from the embattled metropolises—voices demanding more policemen, more troops, more weapons, heavier armor, and tougher laws. To those in the front lines, in what some have termed the second Civil War, there could be no talk of concessions to the other side. The only thing that mattered to them was getting the material and legal support they needed to put down the savage insurgents who stalked city streets by night. But, between these two camps, there has arisen a third force: the corporate capitalist, the American businessman. He is interested in maintaining law and order, but he knows that there is little or nothing to gain and a great deal to lose in committing genocide against the blacks. His deeper interest is in reorganizing the ghetto "infrastructure," in creating a ghetto buffer class clearly committed to the dominant American institutions and values on the one hand, and on the other, in rejuvenating the black working class and integrating it into the American economy. Both are necessary if the city is to be salvaged and capitalism preserved.

(2)

Typical of the welfare liberal's reaction to the black revolt was the June 1966 White House Conference on Civil Rights. The conference brought together the usual variety of "interested" parties: public officials, businessmen, labor leaders, educators, and civil rights leaders. It

[1] Here we are primarily concerned with "racial" aspects of the problem, not with fiscal or regulatory policies, although all are related.

recommended the usual package of welfare state reforms: expanded job opportunities (even though the conferees admitted that even in an economy approaching full employment, joblessness among blacks would remain a persistent problem), job training and counseling programs, more stringent enforcement of civil rights laws, passage of open housing legislation, and integration of the public schools. No new ideas were forthcoming from this conference.

But New Deal-type reformism was undergoing a serious crisis of its own. The welfare liberals were attacked by black militants for their paternalistic racism. From the right, they were assaulted by conservatives who identified the cause of the riots in the liberals' "coddling" of blacks. Finally, America's corporate leaders were becoming impatient with a welfare state, which seemed to be toppling into chaos because of incompetent management.

The *coup de grâce* was administered to the welfare liberals by a recalcitrant Ninetieth Congress. The legislators were responding both to the outcry against "crime in the streets" and to economic pressures imposed by the Vietnam war. Antipoverty, education, Model Cities, and rent supplement programs were drastically cut back as economy measures, and the legislators sat on bills such as one which would have expanded unemployment benefits for the jobless. They even rejected a rat control bill.

Instead, Congress passed "law and order" measures, aimed at curbing crime by providing federal funds to upgrade local police forces, making possible wire-tapping under court order, and Congress, in effect, overturned U. S. Supreme Court rulings which police officials claimed were hampering the conviction of suspected criminals. The Ninetieth Congress did, however, approve a bill which bans racial discrimination in the sale or rental of most housing, but the price for this concession to the civil rights lobby was an antiriot provision which makes it a felony for anyone to cross state lines with the "intent" of inciting or organizing a riot. This provision was admittedly

aimed at curbing the movement of black militants such as
Stokely Carmichael and Rap Brown.

(3)

Side by side with the welfare mentality, there exists the
police state mind. The term genocide expresses the gut-
level response of many blacks to what they perceive as a
growing threat of violent repression. This is no idle fear.
The hundreds of blacks who have been killed or wounded
as "rioters" are only the most obvious testimony supporting
this conclusion. While some whites have pooh-poohed talk
of massive repression, many blacks believe that the attitude
of Chicago's mayor, Richard Daley, is a more accurate
indication of the real mood in the country. In the aftermath of last year's April riots, which followed the killing of
Dr. King, Daley announced that he was "disappointed"
that policemen had not been given shoot-to-kill orders.
Daley said he had instructed his superintendent of police
that law enforcement officers were expected to "shoot to
kill an arsonist or anyone with a Molotov cocktail. . . ."
He also said that cops should "shoot looters to detain
them."

Daley's statements provoked an indignant reaction from
white liberals and civil rights leaders. "We are not going
to shoot children in New York City," retorted Mayor John
Lindsay. But this was far from enough to remove the
nagging suspicion in the minds of black people that Daley
spoke for a larger section of white America than did
Lindsay. Moreover, New York police have shot black and
Puerto Rican children, the mayor's words notwithstanding.

Black newspaper readers knew that Wilmington, Delaware, a city of eighty-five thousand people, nearly half of
them black, had been occupied by heavily armed National
Guard troops following the King riots, and was *still* under
occupation seven months later at the time of the national
elections.

The elections themselves were no cause for comfort. The "law and order" campaign probably reminded older blacks of similar sloganeering by another aspirant to public office who declared:

The streets of our country are in turmoil. The universities are filled with students rebelling and rioting. Communists are seeking to destroy our country. Russia is threatening us with her might, and the republic is in danger. Yes, danger from within and without. We need law and order! . . . Elect us and we shall restore law and order. We shall by law and order be respected among the nations of the world. Without law and order our republic shall fall.

These words were not spoken by Hubert Humphrey, or Richard Nixon, or even George Wallace. They are an excerpt from a campaign speech made in Hamburg, in 1932, by Adolf Hitler. The frightening thing was that in modern America these words had an uncomfortably familiar ring. With no great stretch of the imagination one could literally hear them being uttered by "responsible" public figures, past and present.

Black suspicions were reinforced by press reports of a mushrooming domestic arms race, which could be interpreted only as a direct threat to black survival. At the end of 1968, a major manufacturer of antiriot equipment boasted that 1968 had been a good year for his industry, and he expected 1969 to be even bigger. Cities across the country were stockpiling arms, buying tanklike armored vehicles, building up huge caches of ammunition and tear gas, and arming their policemen with helmets and high-powered rifles and shotguns. Newark spent three hundred thousand dollars for bulletproof helmets, armored cars, antisniper rifles, and large quantities of tear gas. Chicago spent a little more than half that amount on three helicopters designed to serve as airborne command posts during riots. State police in Virginia got themselves six armored cars at a hefty thirty thousand dollars each. The

Los Angeles sheriff's department showed a little Yankee ingenuity and built its own armored vehicle for an economical seven thousand dollars. Equipment like this obviously was not intended for routine police work. These were preparations for warfare.

And this is exactly the way many law enforcement and military officials viewed the riots. A National Guard officer in Maryland pulled no punches. To him the riots were guerrilla warfare. "These people [black rioters] have been learning the lesson of Vietnam," complained Maryland's Adjutant General Gelston. In an article entitled "The Second Civil War" (*Esquire*, March 1968), author Garry Wills quoted Detroit's police commissioner as saying: "This is revolution, and people have not become aware of that. . . . This is not just mob or gang fights. It is a question of the survival of our cities." As though to emphasize that he wasn't kidding, the commissioner asked Detroit's Common Council for nine million dollars' worth of antiriot equipment, including battle cars and machine guns.

After the 1967 rebellions, the development and production of antiriot and exotic weaponry became a booming business. B&H Enterprises promoted its "R-2 multipurpose armored personnel carrier" to local police. The machine can accommodate fifteen men in a carpeted interior and it can either, depending on what the "riot fighters" inside think is appropriate, spray crowds with tear gas or address them through a built-in PA system. But the B&H product had to compete with Cadillac Gage's "commando police vehicle," which is amphibious, seats twelve, and is equipped with a body which can be electrified to shock anyone who is so foolish as to attack it with his bare hands.

General Ordnance's Chemical Mace, a disabling spray that causes dizziness, nausea, and a feeling of suffocation, came into general use in 1967. Other exotic "nonlethal" weaponry for the complete policeman's arsenal included "Instant Banana Peel," a powder which can be sprinkled on sidewalks and when wetted down produces a slippery surface guaranteed to down any who venture upon it.

Then there is the "Curdler," a noisemaking device which delivers such a brain-numbing screech that it disrupts normal thought processes in the hearer. For the real anti-riot connoisseur, only the imagination limited what he could buy. Author Wills got hold of a brochure published by the Institute for Defense Analyses. The Institute, by the way, because of its research activities in counterinsurgency (whether of the foreign or domestic variety), has been the target of student demonstrations around the nation. The brochure described the latest devices that enable the diligent riot stopper to "Foam . . . rioters, pepper them, festoon them in long swaths of chewing gum, mark them with invisible dyes, with odors undetectable except by dogs or instruments, snow them up inside drifts of plastic confetti, prick them with tranquilizers, rinse them down with electric sluices, stay them with hoses."

Lethal hand-held weapons, now available to local law enforcement agencies, include a lightweight semiautomatic shotgun which can be fired with one hand, and which is equipped with a small spotlight for picking out targets on dark nights. For antisniper work, there is the Stoner gun, a weapon which is powerful enough to propel a shell through the brick walls of apartment buildings.

Hardware is only one part of the antiriot mania. Additionally, city governments hurriedly passed ordinances giving mayors increased powers to set curfews, close businesses, and seal off areas of their cities. In New York, for example, the city council approved in April 1968 a bill —requested by Lindsay—which empowered the mayor to declare a state of emergency for up to fifteen days in the city, to impose curfews, prohibit pedestrian and motor traffic, halt the sale of alcoholic beverages, and close places of public assembly. The measure also prohibited the sale of gasoline unless it was delivered directly into the tank of a vehicle. (Apparently the city fathers thought that once the gasoline was in the tank it couldn't be gotten out again.)

Such ordinances, however, take effect only after a riot

has started. To prevent riots, the police mentality thinks in terms of police-state techniques such as sending large numbers of spies, police agents, and informers into the ghettos. Young people are especially prized recruits for these growing police espionage networks.

To make police occupation and infiltration of the ghetto more palatable, black men are being vigorously recruited as policemen. Special efforts are made to recruit black Vietnam veterans, whose military training and discipline are thought to make them ideal candidates for police academies.

Attempts to camouflage the overtly repressive nature of the police were also tried with the setting up of experimental storefront precincts, satellite stations, and neighborhood task forces in cities such as San Francisco, Oakland, Los Angeles, Baltimore, Atlanta, and New York. Under the guise of "improving community relations," these scattered police outposts in the ghetto provide a base for surveillance of the surrounding hostile terrain.

Another twist in the riot preparations of some police departments included arming white civilians and training them in the use of weapons. The Kansas City, Missouri, police department set up a six-week course for teaching civilians how to use firearms. Police Chief Clarence Kelly reasoned that since private citizens were buying guns "for protection," they might as well be taught—by the police—how to use the weapons most effectively. In Dearborn, Michigan, an all-white community near Detroit, the city sponsored a six-hour course in the use of pistols for local housewives. Police in Highland Park, another Detroit suburb, provided gun training to local merchants. And in Detroit itself, an all-white group called "Breakthrough" set up a gun club to train its members.

Late in 1967 the Iowa Sheriffs Association voted to establish a three-hundred-man vigilante force to handle "emergency situations." The move followed a December antiwar demonstration by students at the University of Iowa. The plan, to organize and arm civilians as an ad-

junct to the sheriff's office, was dumped after meeting
strong opposition from state officials. But the plan was
revived in January, in Chicago, by Cook County Sheriff
Joseph I. Woods, who proposed establishing a private
paramilitary force under his direct control. The volunteer
"riot control squad" was needed, Woods contended, to put
down anticipated disorders in Chicago over the summer,
particularly at the time of the Democratic Convention.
Woods got one thousand volunteers almost overnight.
Vigilantes have also been active in Newark. A white
group called the North Ward Citizens Committee, headed
by Anthony Imperiale, the man with whom LeRoi Jones
has had some dealings, not only gave its 1550 members
gun training, but it also claimed to own an armored truck
and a helicopter. Even rural villages are getting into the
act. The *Bucks County Gazette,* published in New Hope,
Pennsylvania, a small town fronting on the Delaware River,
ran an article in February 1968 urging the creation of a
thirty-six-man vigilante force in case a rebellion in nearby
Trenton or Philadelphia should "spill over" into the surrounding countryside.

Beyond these purely hometown activities, there were
interconnected efforts to beef up state and federal repressive apparatuses. Following the 1967 rebellions, state
National Guards, under presidential orders, launched a
thirty-two-hour crash program in riot-control training for
Guardsmen. Additionally, the states were authorized to set
up some 125 new Guard units. Most of the new units were
to be military police units "specifically oriented to state riot
control requirements." Meanwhile, Guard units started
holding special exercises with local and state police, designed to work out problems of communications and
chain of command.

On April 23, 1968, the U. S. Army announced that it
was adding five more brigades, or ten thousand troops, to
the fifteen thousand men on regular antiriot duty. The
troops are intensively trained in putting down civil disturbances. The new units were added because more than

twenty-two thousand Army troops had to be sent into Chicago, Baltimore, and Washington to handle rebellions following the assassination of King. To coordinate the movement of these troops with local and state law enforcement agencies, riot control centers have been set up by the Pentagon for every area of the country. These are equipped with advanced communications gear and special wall maps of cities and towns.

To reduce reaction time in a potentially explosive situation, computers are being used to predict likely rebellion areas and suggest troop deployment patterns.

Most major cities also have detailed "emergency mobilization plans" which provide for virtually instantaneous sealing off of ghettos, arrest of militant leaders, and movement of armed troops to preselected areas. These plans alone run to several volumes. They allow for close cooperation and coordination among local, state, and federal agencies in quelling a civil disturbance.

To many blacks, the logical next step in these preparations for repression was the setting up of concentration camps. And a rash of rumors claiming that exactly this was being done flashed through black America in 1967 and 1968. Stokely Carmichael, Rap Brown, and other militants frequently argued that blacks were a surplus population in the United States which was pensioned off on welfare rolls. But the rebellions, said the militants, had prompted white America to make plans for a "final solution" to the race problem by permanently ridding itself of the troublesome blacks. Martin Luther King was moved, just six days before he was killed, to say: "I see a ghetto perhaps cordoned off into a concentration camp. I haven't said there was a move afoot, just that it is a possibility. The more there are riots, the more repression will take place, and the more we face the danger of a right-wing take-over, and eventually a Fascist society."[2]

The white press at first ignored this growing fear and then sought to exorcise it by claiming that it was based on

[2] *Look*, May 28, 1968.

myth. The Washington *Post,* for instance, ran a long article in March 1968 which contended that "there is no evidence that a concentration camp system exists or is planned. . . ." A *Look* magazine article in May of that year stated flatly: "A probing into every available official record and a running down of every current rumor yield no evidence either of physical preparations or of plans by the Federal Government for mass-level incarceration of Americans. . . ."

But blacks recalled the forced evacuation of more than one hundred thousand Japanese Americans to "relocation camps" in 1943 and the confiscation of their property. If it happened once, why couldn't it happen again?

To date, the most authoritative study of detention camps in the United States is a sixty-page booklet written by free-lance journalist Charles R. Allen. The booklet was published in 1966 by the Citizens Committee for Constitutional Liberties. Under Title II of the 1950 Internal Security (McCarran) Act six detention camps were set up. Construction began in 1952 and was completed in 1954. Title II gives the President power to proclaim an "internal security emergency" in the event of "any one of the following: (1) Invasion of the territory of the United States or its possessions, (2) Declaration of war by Congress, or (3) Insurrection within the United States in aid of a foreign enemy." In the event of such a proclamation by the President, the Attorney General is authorized to apprehend and detain "in such places of detention as may be provided by him . . . all persons as to whom there is reasonable ground to believe that such person probably will engage in or probably will conspire with others to engage in acts of espionage and sabotage."

The McCarran Act was passed over President Truman's veto. In his veto message, Truman warned: "It is not enough to say that this probably would not be done. The mere fact that it could be done shows clearly how the bill would open a Pandora's box of opportunities for official condemnation of organizations and individuals for perfectly honest opinions. . . . The basic error of these sections is that they move in the direction of suppressing

opinion and belief . . . a long step toward totalitarianism."
Construction of the detention camps began at the height
of the McCarthy hysteria which followed the Korean War.

J. Edgar Hoover and the Federal Bureau of Investigation have primary responsibility for determining who would
be placed in detention camps. Since Hoover considers most
rebellions to be "Communist-inspired" (i.e., in the language of the McCarran Act, inspired by "foreign enemies"), it requires no great stretch of the imagination to
see how the law could be applied.

Allen toured five of the six McCarran Act camp sites
and found them either fallen into disuse, no longer in
existence, or put to other use by the U. S. Bureau of Prisons. *Look* senior editor William Hedgepeth visited the
camps more recently and found the following:

—The Allenwood, Pennsylvania camp, covering forty-
two hundred acres, is operated by the Bureau of Prisons as
a minimum-security prison, mostly for draft resisters.
Camp administrator P. A. Schuer claimed he had heard
nothing about plans to shift the camp to McCarran Act
uses.

—The Avon Park, Florida camp was leased in the late
fifties from the Air Force by the state of Florida for use
as a facility in its own prison system.

—The Florence, Arizona camp—used for prisoners of
war in the 1940s—now serves as a minimum-security
federal jail for about eighty persons awaiting trial.

—The Wickenburg, Arizona camp's buildings still stand
unused, but the property itself supposedly has been returned to a private lessor.

—The El Reno, Oklahoma camp's detention barracks
have been dismantled by the Bureau of Prisons, which
now maintains the property for "beefherd pastures."

—The Tule Lake (Newell), California camp has the
most disturbing past, because it held 22,500 Japanese
Americans during World War II. It has been divided up
among numerous new owners, including the township of
Newell.

According to Allen, the federal government maintains the right of re-entry to the camps at Wickenburg and Tule Lake. Based on buildings in existence in 1966, he estimated the total combined capacity of the six camps at 26,500.

Hedgepeth viewed Allen's pamphlet with a slightly jaundiced eye. He quoted officials as saying there was no need for the camps and that Congress hadn't appropriated any money for detention camp purposes in many years. Hedgepeth took his inquiry as far as then Attorney General Ramsey Clark, who declared that there "have been and will be no concentration camps" in the United States. Yet Hedgepeth could not himself categorically deny that concentration camps would ever be used in this country. In fact, he admitted that "Military planners in Washington *do* acknowledge that detention of dissenters, on at least a limited basis, could conceivably take place should prolonged, simultaneous and seemingly coordinated urban riots reach such grand-scale, nationally disruptive proportions as to require the declaration of martial law."

A couple of weeks before Hedgepeth's article was published (but probably after it was written), the House Un-American Activities Committee released a sixty-five-page report which suggested that "guerrilla warfare" in the cities could be countered by widespread use of detention centers. Since urban guerrillas would be declaring a "state of war," the report contended, they could expect to "forfeit their rights as in wartime." It continued ominously: "The McCarran Act provides for various detention centers to be operated throughout the country and these might well be utilized for the temporary imprisonment of warring guerrillas." For ghettos in which guerrilla activity is recurrent, the HUAC report suggested the use of identification cards for the residents which would be issued by an office for "the control and organization of the inhabitants."

So there it was. And all according to the well-tested Nazi formula. Population expert Philip M. Hauser put the matter bluntly when he said that America has two choices. Either the country can make a heavy investment aimed at eliminating ghettos or it can suppress rebellious blacks. "If we are not prepared," he continued, "to make the investment in human resources that is required, we will be forced to increase our investment in the police, the National Guard, and the Army. And possibly—it can happen here— we may be forced to resort to concentration camps and even genocide."³ Hauser favored the first alternative, but there are probably many white Americans who would just as soon see the latter implemented. There was a third alternative, however, which Hauser did not consider— namely the corporatist program which will be examined shortly.

The question was, is it likely that repression approaching genocidal proportions will be employed against insurgent black communities in the near future? To begin to answer this question, it must first be recalled that hard-core advocates of massive repression tend to be either local officials (mayors, police chiefs, etc.) or representatives of the right wing, such as HUAC.

With the growing tendency toward centralization of effective power at the national level, there is a corresponding diminution in the ability of local officials to take independent action in implementing what they feel should be done in any given situation. Moreover, local police forces are being brought under pressure to "professionalize" themselves, that is, to bring their operations in line with national standards and practices. In August 1968, for example, the Justice Department offered the states 4.35 million dollars under the 1968 crime control law. This was the first federal money ever designated to prepare for and help avert rioting in the cities. The funds were to be used by local law enforcement agencies for a variety of purposes, including extra training, planning and cooperative arrangements with other law enforcement agencies, special units, preparation of guidelines for personnel, acquisition

³ San Francisco *Examiner*, September 1, 1968.

of equipment, and public education aimed at reducing community tensions and grievances. The net effect of such programs is to transform police departments from purely local institutions into agencies charged with implementing national policy. This is deemed necessary in order to streamline local operations and to allow maximum planning and coordination in dealing with those areas of crime which the national government chooses to combat.

As for the right wing, groups such as HUAC are useful to the national power structure because they can harass and intimidate dissident elements of the population. However, these groups do not set national policy. HUAC, for instance, has not produced a single piece of new legislation in many years. Yet HUAC exists, and probably will continue to exist, because of the services it renders in making trouble for vociferous dissenters.[4]

What, then, is national policy as it applies to urban revolts? Since the revolts are themselves recent phenomena, it should first be observed that before 1967 there was apparently no unified policy for dealing with them. After the massive rebellions of that year, however, a policy was formulated and was experimented with during the riots which broke out following the murder of Dr. King. That is the policy of containment. Nearly seventy thousand National Guard and federal troops were called to duty to deal with the riots which hit some 125 cities at that time. The troops did their job with a minimal use of violent force.[5] They were instructed to tolerate a certain level of arson and looting, and to use their weapons only when

[4] In 1969 it was modernized by the addition of "liberal" members, and its discredited name was changed to the House Committee on Internal Security.

[5] There was no repeat of the indiscriminate shooting which, for example, characterized the actions of National Guard troops in the 1967 Newark rebellion. In Washington, D.C., which experienced a major revolt, only twenty shells were expended by troops. To put the matter in grim but graphic terms, only forty-six persons were killed in all of the April riots, whereas nearly that number were killed in the 1967 Detroit rebellion alone.

absolutely necessary. The watchword was to exercise restraint and hold down fire.

This policy evolved out of a series of studies and meetings held in 1967 at top governmental levels. Participants in the meetings included Ramsey Clark, Cyrus Vance, government lawyers, police chiefs, military personnel, and some civil rights people. After the broad outlines of the policy were worked out, a broad range of government, police, and military personnel were invited to meetings in early 1968 designed to convince them of the efficacy of the proposed policy.

The essential ingredients of this policy can be summarized as follows: (1) Have available large numbers of troops especially trained in riot control techniques and stationed at points around the country from which they can easily motor or be airlifted to trouble areas; (2) instruct the troops to hold their fire, but give them substantial leeway in the use of tear gas and in making arrests; (3) have local authorities impose curfews and then arrest anyone who violates the curfew. The basic idea is to make a massive show of force while minimizing the actual use of force.

Detailed plans for implementing this policy on a nationwide basis were drawn up beginning in March 1968, under the code name "Garden Plot," and, as noted previously, it was given a relatively successful trial run during the April riots.

Although the new riot policy calls for restraint in the use of violent force, this is not done for humanitarian reasons. Some officials have tried to argue that it was the government's desire to minimize deaths that led to the adoption of the new policy. But this was hardly a plausible account of the motives of a government which had wreaked so much destruction in Vietnam. Ramsey Clark probably spoke part of the truth when he said that shooting rioters would "alienate the minorities and induce those who are not disposed to violence now to adopt terrorist and guerrilla tactics." In this he was eminently right, since history shows that in many instances revolutions are as much organized by the overly repressive measures taken by a panicky government as they are by the agitation of conscious revolutionaries. There is considerable disagreement over just how much actual sniping there has been in the recent riots, but indiscriminate retaliatory gunfire by policemen and troops is probably the best way to guarantee that in the future there really will be snipers on those rooftops.

A second and closely related reason for the policy of restraint was the belief of the policy-makers that alienated blacks could be won back to the American system, and that this course would be less disruptive to the society at large than a policy of severe repression.[6] Hence it was necessary to contain the riots, but not bear down with an iron fist, because this would further alienate an already greatly dissatisfied and volatile group. Furthermore, containment of the riots would buy time for the second prong of the new policy to take effect: an intensive program to convince black people that they as a group have a stake in the American system.

[6] This should not be interpreted to mean that repression will diminish. On the contrary, as American society is further polarized by domestic dislocations and the repercussions of foreign military adventures, it can be anticipated that there will be a steady, although gradual increase in the level of repression. What is being argued against here is the notion that genocidal repression is likely in the immediate future. In terms of the national power structure, there seems to be no real ground for this belief.

However, as the general level of repression gradually escalates, it can be expected that one of the favorite tactics of police forces will be more frequently employed—namely, decapitation of militant groups and movements. This is especially so since the U. S. Supreme Court has upheld the constitutionality of state conspiracy laws. More and more militant leaders (white as well as black) are likely to be arrested on charges of conspiring to bomb, assassinate, and otherwise engage in illegal activity, even where there is very little evidence to substantiate these charges. As a consequence there is an urgent need for a national organization devoted to mass, political defense.

This program will be examined in the following pages, but it is now necessary to consider another point. One of the prime objections raised by conservatives to the new riot policy is that it tolerates property destruction. This is true, and the small ghetto businessman and landlord are heavily hit by riots. This loss is acceptable, however, because the American economy is increasingly organized around large-scale economic units. These units may be located in cities, but they are not usually found in the slum areas that are likely to spawn rebellions. It is only if the rebellions spread outside the slums that the nation's industrial facilities, for example, are seriously jeopardized. Hence, another argument for the containment policy.

The only major industry that is threatened by the riots is the insurance industry. Insured losses in the Watts rebellion alone totaled an estimated forty million dollars. While this does not begin to compare with the insured losses which may result from natural disasters such as hurricanes (Hurricane Betsy in 1965 racked up insured losses of three-quarters of a billion dollars—an amount probably several times as great as the insured loss in all the racial riots in recent history), still, since riots have become recurrent, the figures do begin to add up and the insurance industry feels the pinch.

But a remedy is in sight. Legislation proposed by an Advisory Panel on Insurance in Riot-affected Areas, headed by New Jersey Governor Richard Hughes calls for the federal government to establish a National Insurance Development Corporation to which insurance companies would contribute a portion of their premiums in order to pool the risk. NIDC would provide reinsurance to these companies for riot and civil commotion peril in all lines of property coverage. Federal funds would back up large losses. In short, under this plan, insurance companies could continue to operate at a profit, even in riot-torn areas, since the federal government would underwrite any large losses they might incur. Moreover, according to the Chicago *Daily News* (April 8, 1968), the Hughes panel also recommended voluntary plans to assure all property owners fair access to insurance and federal tax deferral "to increase the capacity of the insurance industry to absorb costs." Thus any small ghetto businessman who can afford the premiums (naturally there would have to be increases in riot-prone areas because of the increased risks) would be assured of coverage against losses. And the insurance industry, backed by the federal treasury, would be quite happy to continue with business as usual.

(4)

The bulk of this study to this point has been devoted to an examination of how some black militant groups[7] have

[7] Moderate black groups also have a role to play in the program of black capitalism. The National Urban League, for example, has adopted a flexible posture. The Urban League is a service organization which tries to prod government, industry, business, unions, and foundations to provide black people with jobs and training. For instance, in 1967, it found forty thousand jobs for blacks, got better jobs for another eight thousand, and undertook on-the-job training in thirty-seven cities. For some time the organization has sought, in response to the anger in the ghettos, to give itself a more militant image. In the spring of 1967, the New York branch launched a magazine called *Probe*. The magazine made free use of militant rhetoric and endorsed cultural nationalism. The head of the Washington Urban League flirted with Stokely Carmichael's Black United Front early in 1968 and even became a member of that group's seventeen-member steering committee. Urban League chief Whitney Young got a warm reception at the 1968 CORE convention when he announced that the League "believes strongly in that interpretation of black power that emphasizes self-determination, pride, self-respect and participation and control of one's destiny and community affairs." He called for the creation of more black capitalists, although he opposed the idea of an independent black economy.

Whether the League's "new image" will legitimitize it in the eyes of ghetto militants remains to be seen. But it certainly has done so in the eyes of the corporate elite. In 1968 the League announced plans to spend five million dollars over the succeeding two years in aiding black businessmen in some eighty-seven cities. The funds for this project were to come from the Ford, Field, Carnegie, and Rockefeller Foundations.

used the nationalist sentiment of the black masses to advance the class interests of the black bourgeoisie. It is now necessary to look at the other side of the picture and investigate the manner in which the white corporate elite also has used the rhetoric of black nationalism in helping itself establish neocolonial control of the black communities.

The urban uprisings of 1967 made it painfully obvious to America's corporate leaders that the "race problem" was out of control and posed a potential threat to the continued existence of the present society. McGeorge Bundy spoke for a significant section of American business opinion when he insisted time and time again that resolution of the race question "is now the most urgent domestic concern of this country." The endemic racism which had functioned to the advantage of an adolescent capitalism was, in this view, in dire need of serious alteration as it spawned disruption in the mature capitalist society. Blacks must be brought into the mainstream of the economy if they no longer would remain docile while confined outside of it. This did not mean that every black person should be transformed into a capitalist. Rather it implied the creation of a class of capitalists and corporate managers within the black community. The theory was that such a class would ease ghetto tensions by providing living proof to black dissidents that they can assimilate into the system if only they discipline themselves and work at it tirelessly. A black capitalist class would serve thereby as a means of social control by disseminating the ideology and values of the dominant white society throughout the alienated ghetto masses.

Speaking of the related phenomenon of tokenism, Baran and Sweezy pointedly observed:

> The theory behind tokenism, not often expressed but clearly deducible from the practice, is that the black bourgeoisie is the decisive element in the Negro community. It contains the intellectual and political elite, the people with education and leadership ability and experi-

ence. It already has a material stake in the existing social order, but its loyalty is doubtful because of the special disabilities imposed upon it solely because of its color. If this loyalty can be made secure, the potential revolutionizing of the Negro protest movement can be forestalled and the world can be given palpable evidence—through the placing of loyal Negroes in prominent positions—that the United States does not pursue a South African-type policy of *apartheid* but on the contrary fights against it and strives for equal opportunity for its Negro citizens. The problem is thus how to secure the loyalty of the black bourgeoisie.[8]

Coupled with the thrust toward black capitalism and black management is a much-touted effort to integrate black workers into the economy, particularly those whom industry designates as the "hard-core unemployed." These are persons who, when measured against normal hiring standards, simply are unemployable. They have no marketable skills. And the young among them swell the ranks of rioters. Reclamation of this group, which in 1967 numbered in the hundreds of thousands, would have the further advantage of adding about one billion dollars annually to national output, while at the same time subtracting millions from welfare costs. But, as remarked before, most of the training and retraining programs tried to date have had at best only limited success due in part to their limited scope.

Beyond opening up jobs in industry and training potential workers, some provision also must be made for those who are too old to be retrained, or are tied down by child-raising, or suffer from physical or psychosocial impairments which make it impossible for them to work. In the past this task was assigned to the welfare system. But the welfare system itself is in crisis and, as the Riot Commission's report stated, ". . . our present system of public assistance contributes materially to the tensions and social

[8] Paul A. Baran and Paul M. Sweezy, *Monopoly Capital* (New York: Monthly Review Press, 1966), pp. 272–73.

disorganization that have led to civil disorders," because
the welfare system is built upon a labyrinth of federal,
state, and local legislation which sometimes conflicts with
itself and which requires a cumbersome inefficient bureaucracy to administer it. The Commission recommended
the establishment of a simplified "national system of income supplementation," which not only would make payments to traditional welfare recipients, such as elderly
people and women with children, but which also would
encompass employed persons working at substandard hours
or wages and those among the unemployed for whom there
are no jobs (i.e., the technologically unemployed). Backing
for some type of guaranteed income scheme has been
growing, and such a program quite possibly will be implemented in the foreseeable future.[9]

The emergence of corporations and corporate liberals
as leaders in the effort to resolve the urban crises became
apparent in August 1967 with the formation of the
National Urban Coalition. Organized in Washington, the
Coalition was an alliance of some twelve hundred business,
labor, religious, civil rights, and government leaders. In
its ranks were such corporate leaders as Roy Ash, president
of Litton Industries, a major aerospace company; Henry
Ford II, chairman of the Ford Motor Company; David
Rockefeller, president of the Chase Manhattan Bank;
Frederick J. Close, chairman of the Aluminum Company
of America; and Andrew Heiskell, chairman of Time, Inc.
Heiskell and New York's Mayor John Lindsay acted as
co-chairmen of the group's steering committee. John Gardner, former Secretary of Health, Education, and Welfare,
became chairman.

Announcing that it had committed itself "to programs
instead of promises," the Coalition proceeded to set up

[9] It should be observed that President Nixon has expressed opposition to such proposals. However, support for a guaranteed
annual income is evident among a wide range of business and
political opinion. See also Robert Theobald (ed.) *The Guaranteed Income* (New York: Doubleday, 1966).

subsidiary groups in cities around the country. Gardner called for greater black involvement in meeting the urban crisis, arguing that stability in the cities could not be achieved "until we bring into the same conversation all significant leadership elements that hold power or veto power in the life of the community." He also announced that it would take twenty-five years and perhaps two hundred billion dollars to finally solve the urban crisis.

Another major organization in the government-business partnership was the National Alliance of Businessmen. The Johnson Administration set up NAB early in 1968, and Henry Ford II was appointed chairman. Part of its function was to act as a "one-stop service for businessmen in dealing with the federal government." Many businessmen had complained bitterly about the frustrations involved in dealing with several government agencies at once. "We had to get approval from one state and three Washington agencies for money, and this was time-consuming," said one executive. "In my opinion, no businessman has that kind of time."

NAB set high goals for itself: five hundred thousand jobs for hard-core unemployed by 1971—one hundred thousand of them by June 1969—and some two hundred thousand jobs in the summer of 1968 for youth out of school. With much fanfare, Ford began visiting other businessmen, urging them to sign pledges that they would hold a certain number of job openings for hard-core cases. The hard-core cases were to be drawn from fifty key cities which NAB listed as most in need. But despite a well-publicized beginning, NAB had to concede that its campaign to find temporary jobs for the summer of 1968 was a good bit less than successful.

In return for the businessmen's efforts, Johnson promised that 350 million dollars would be made available to cover "extraordinary" costs involved in training and supportive services.[10] He also sent to Congress a housing bill

[10] Nixon, also, promised to provide incentives to business for training and hiring the hard-core unemployed.

designed to subsidize the construction industry by enabling the federal government to charter construction consortiums and grant them tax concessions to bring their returns up to the level of other forms of investment.

Writing in a special issue of *Fortune* magazine devoted to "Business and the Urban Crisis" (January 1968), Max Ways discussed business' newfound interest in the racial crisis. First noting the "sluggishness and ineptitude" with which the government and most social institutions have responded to the crisis, Ways went on to write:

> . . . Since mid-year of 1967, and largely as a response to the race crisis, [the] business attitude toward the problems of the city is shifting. The ardent efforts of the nation's business institutions will be especially needed, because they have qualities demanded by the double crisis of the Negro and the city. Modern corporations are flexible and innovative. They are accustomed to sensing and meeting and evoking the changing desires of the public. Above all, they practice the difficult art of mobilizing specialized knowledge for action—i.e., the art of managing change.

Moreover, Ways wrote, business can hope to succeed where the government had failed because "Business is the one important segment of society Negroes today do not regard with bitter suspicion."

To still any remaining doubts in the minds of his businessmen readers, Ways said rehabilitation of the cities promises to open up the era of the "public market" when whole communities "will need to buy [for their residents] cleaner air and rivers, better scientific research, better techniques of learning, better traffic control." If these demands are to be met, Ways asserts, clearly the great corporations will play a large part in supplying them. "One can imagine, say, a private contractor selling an antipollution service to fifty neighboring towns and cities." This is not a far-fetched dream. There is no logical reason why the corporations cannot profitably enter the field of public works and public service on a massive and independent basis. There is a great opportunity for business here, and it appears that ghetto reorganization will be the pilot project.

One of the more vigorous units set up by the National Urban Coalition was its New York City branch. The New York Coalition was headed by Christian A. Herter, Jr., a Mobil Oil Corporation vice president. Roy Innis of CORE sat on the Coalition's board of directors. In May 1968, the organization announced plans to raise some four million dollars from private sources. Within a month the group had accumulated more than half of the amount it sought. A third of the money was to be turned over to Mayor Lindsay's Summer Program to keep the peace in the city's streets.

Part of the money was also to go to two new corporations created by the New York Urban Coalition. The corporations were to begin operations in July. One was the Coalition Development Corporation, the purpose of which was to provide managerial and technical advice to ghetto businessmen. The second was the Coalition Venture Corporation, and its purpose was to make available risk capital to ghetto businessmen. The idea for these corporations stemmed from an eighteen-page report drafted in March by the Coalition's Economic Development Task Force. "One major goal of the New York Coalition," the report began, "is to foster self-sustaining social and economic growth in the ghettos." The task force was assigned the job of determining how best to achieve this goal. "Historically," the report continued, "minority groups have been chafed and been constricted in their economic and social growth by having to live in a society where the means of generating capital frequently have been held by individuals who lived outside the minority community."

The task force concluded that ghetto businessmen are handicapped by a critical shortage of business know-how and a chronic lack of venture and operating capital. It recommended (1) that a management assistance corporation be set up "to provide managerial and other assistance to help the entrepreneurs maximize their effective use of current and future resources"; (2) that a small business investment corporation be created and licensed by the Small Business Administration "to provide equity capital and make long-term loans to ghetto entrepreneurs," and (3) the establishment of a venture capital corporation to provide funds for new investments. Within a few months the first and third proposals were implemented.

On the surface these recommendations would appear to be free of any taint of white manipulation and control. The Coalition was simply creating a mechanism for providing black entrepreneurs with the business information they required and the capital that has been denied them by the big, white banks downtown. Charges such as those leveled by Innis against Robert Kennedy's corporate endeavors in the Brooklyn ghetto would seem out of place here. Yet, when the Coalition's proposal is examined more closely, the thin but tough strings which would tie black capitalists to the corporate power structure are revealed.

In the first place, the boards of directors of each of the proposed Coalition corporations were to be the same "in order to ensure close coordination." This board would set general policy guidelines, and beneath it there would be a review committee charged with relating the guidelines to actual practice. Specifically, the review group would be concerned with establishing specific requirements for assistance, reviewing and approving (or rejecting) specific proposals, and suggesting what financial arrangements should be made. Furthermore, the review committee would have the authority to mandate the involvement of the development corporation in any projects in which it thinks this is desirable. Thus, the review group determines which ghetto businesses are funded, and it has the power to appoint what is in effect a monitor in those enterprises about which it has reservations.

The review committee itself was to consist of individuals drawn from the membership of the Coalition, representatives of financial institutions, and community representatives. Review of specific proposals would be conducted by "proposal teams" composed of five persons. The make-up of these teams is important. Two members would be drawn from the staff of Coalition corporations, two from financial institutions, and one from the community. Hence, the "proposal teams" would be securely controlled by exactly the same corporate interests which control the Urban Coalition itself, although there would be a semblance of community participation.

Investment proposals would be judged on the basis of several criteria, including location in a ghetto, providing employment opportunities to ghetto residents and "social utility." This latter phrase was nowhere defined in the report, but some insight into its meaning is shed by the following paragraph:

> Ghetto residents complain that most of the businesses in their areas are controlled by "outsiders." . . . Real and imagined abuses and deception by the outside shop-owners are major causes of discontent. This discontent implicitly or explicitly has linked "business-white-abuse" in ghetto minds so that distrust is not only of whites in business, *but of business itself. Therefore, to the extent possible, the concepts of business as a beneficial force . . . must be promoted to gain active support of the community as a whole.* [Emphasis added.]

Consequently, those proposals which, among other things, promise to help spread in black communities the corporatist mentality of business as a "beneficial force," would likely be judged by the review group as having "social utility."

Also, criteria for assessing individual applicants were listed in the task force report. In addition to criteria relating to the soundness of the applicant's business plans, the reviewers must also seek evidence of "a strong desire to succeed as an independent businessman"; evidence of a "sustained effort toward an objective, such as holding a job, accumulating savings, getting an education, or supporting a family"; evidence of the applicant's "energy and willingness to work much more than forty hours a week"; and evidence of "his understanding of his need for counseling and advice and a willingness to accept it."

In sum, it must be concluded from the foregoing that far from being a "no-strings-attached" program, the endeavors of the New York Coalition amount to a sophisticated mechanism for selecting and aiding persons in the black community who are to be programmed into the new class of black capitalists. The review group selects only those applicants who meet predetermined personal, socio-ideological, and financial standards. These standards would tend to favor those applicants who already exhibit traditional middle-class virtues of thriftiness, hard work, and devotion to family. The development corporation then acts as a subtle means for socializing the selected individuals into the corporate world, i.e., inculcating in them those values, attitudes, and practices which are deemed desirable by the corporate groups which back the Coalition. Thus, in concrete example, can be seen how the New York corporatists' plan would generate a black capitalist buffer class firmly wedded (in both financial and ideological terms) to the white corporate structure.[11]

One of the first endeavors of the New York Coalition in this direction was the granting in late 1968 of a substantial loan to the New Acme Foundry in Harlem. The Foundry was to produce bronze, aluminum, and nonferrous metal castings for valves and fittings for the petroleum

[11] The members of the existing black business class are not opposed to these plans so long as they are assured of "equal" status in the corporate world. Thus Berkeley G. Burrell, head of the National Business League, told a group of white business leaders in Newark in April 1968 that it was necessary to end the "system of plantationship" which white-dominated corporations have supported in the past. "What is needed," he went on, "is a positive and truly meaningful partnership of the haves and the have-nots that will place capable black men side by side with capable white men in an entrepreneur effort that can succeed."

industry, bases and parts for street lamps, elevator gear blanks, parts for door locks, and medical instruments, among other products. The Foundry was expected eventually to sell shares to the Harlem community, but until that time the Harlem Commonwealth Council would be the principal shareholder. Rozendo Beasley and Donald Simmons, both HCC officers, were named, respectively, president and chairman of the board of the Foundry.

The New York Coalition makes a good example because its activities are more subtle than many other corporate efforts to penetrate and control the ghettos. The use of semiautonomous development corporations avoids the stigma of white interference and allows for maximum financial maneuverability. The more distasteful aspects of corporate manipulation and control—the kind of thing Innis complained about—are removed by one step and further glossed over by the attractive promise of community participation. However, the essential purpose for putting black power into business—the creation of a stabilizing black buffer class which will make possible indirect white control (or neocolonial administration) of the ghettos—is still guaranteed by the structure of the program.

The concept of community development corporations was given a significant boost in July 1968 with the introduction in Congress of a so-called Community Self-Determination Act. The Act enjoyed the bipartisan sponsorship of thirty-five senators and was endorsed by CORE. It calls for the inclusion of the poor into the economic system as "earners, producers, owners and entrepreneurs," and aims at "developing order, stability and participation" in the system. The Act would set up development corporations in black communities. These corporations would sell shares to local residents, and in many ways would operate as ordinary stock companies, but they would also exercise broad powers usually reserved to government agencies or indigenous community organizations. They could for example, plan urban renewal programs and speak for the community in many areas of public policy. A National

Community Corporation Certification Board would loosely supervise the development corporations, but effective control would likely rest in the hands of a professional bureaucratic elite, as was true under the antipoverty program.

At this juncture it is important to observe that the neocolonial thrust of corporate efforts in the ghetto is not necessarily correlated with the personal intentions of businessmen. Indeed, many of them are sincere reformers. Rather, this neocolonialism is an inevitable product of the structure of corporate capitalism. And one of the most significant structural aspects of modern American capitalism is the growing importance of planning by individual firms.

Some believe that black capitalism offers the best hope for achieving black self-determination. A recent report on black business in San Francisco cited a "growing consensus" that a viable, self-determined black community could be "created by the participation of black citizens in the mainstream of American economic activity and a sharing of the disposable capital which results."[12]

This belief, however, is not justified. Perhaps at the turn of the century it might have been, but, today, the American corporate economy, especially the industrial sector, is characterized by widespread planning. The free market is being replaced by a market controlled by and subservient to the large corporations. This was made necessary by the rise of modern large-scale production with its concomitant requirements of heavy capital outlays, sophisticated technology, and elaborate organization. To operate efficiently, such a complex and expensive system cannot rely on the vicissitudes of a free market. It requires careful planning, from procurement of raw materials to sale of the finished product to the consumer.

But corporate planning is antithetical to black self-determination. Corporate planning involves the subtle but nonetheless real manipulation of consumers in order to

[12] *Black Business in San Francisco.*

maintain and regulate demand for products. It involves corporate control of sources of supply and of labor. Genuine black self-determination would necessarily upset this process of manipulation and control, at least in the black communities (and there is a thirty-billion-dollar market in these communities alone). Consequently, if planning is to prevail (and the tendency is toward tighter and more pervasive corporate planning), then black self-determination can never be more than a chimera.

Concretely, this means that any black capitalist or managerial class must act, in effect, as the tacit representative of the white corporations which are sponsoring that class. The task of this class is to ease corporate penetration of the black communities and facilitate corporate planning and programming of the markets and human resources in those communities. This process occurs regardless of the personal motivations of the individuals involved, because it stems from the nature of the corporate economy itself and the dependent status of the fledgling, black capitalist-managerial class.

When this same process occurs between a major power and an underdeveloped country it is called neocolonialism. This latter term has been used in this study to describe corporate activities in the ghetto, because these efforts, as should by now be quite evident, are analogous to corporate penetration of an underdeveloped country. The methods and social objectives in both cases are identical.

Industry and the foundations quickly joined in implementing the program of creating a black capitalist and managerial class. Among the many projects undertaken were:

—Aerojet-General, a subsidiary of General Tire & Rubber Company, set up Watts Manufacturing, an independent, black-managed company. The company, organized in 1966, already has several hundred employees and makes tents for the government, and wooden crates and metal components for conveyors. The aerospace industry, in general heavily dependent on the government for lucrative defense contracts and troubled by the prospect that peace might break out, is particularly interested in the business of urban reform and redevelopment, a field which has been described as "a potentially vast new nonaerospace market for the aerospace industry's engineering skills."

—Xerox Corporation helped blacks (including militants) in Rochester, New York, set up a one-million-dollar-a-year business. Xerox was also sponsor of the TV series "Of Black America."

—A group of business and civic leaders in Philadelphia pledged one million dollars to underwrite business and self-help projects in that city's black community. The funds are to be administered by a united front group called the Black Coalition.

—A new plant was set up in Hunter's Point, a black area in San Francisco which produces corrugated and chipboard shipping containers. The new container corporation is black-owned, -operated, and -managed. Formation of the company was arranged through Crown Zellerbach, a major producer of corrugated containers. Part of the capital was put up by the Bank of America's Venture Capital subsidiary. The Bank of America in California, incidentally, has also made several million dollars available in loans designed to "promote home ownership and home improvements" in the ghetto. The bank had to lower some of its standards in order to approve the loans, but bank president Rudolph Peterson, believes that "keeping cities from becoming slums is profitable, too."

—In Atlanta the Chrysler Corporation announced that it planned to deposit 1.2 million dollars annually in the black-owned Citizens Trust Bank. Chrysler also said that similar arrangements were being made with the black-owned Bank of Finance in Los Angeles and a new bank being organized in Detroit.

—Business schools around the country have introduced courses on "the social responsibilities of business." Black power advocates have been brought onto campuses to "tell it like it is" to the business students. In return, students at some schools have taken on the task of giving managerial advice to black businessmen.

—Prudential, the world's largest insurance company, was shaken by the Newark uprising. The company has some forty million dollars invested in buildings, plant, and equipment in Newark, and is that city's biggest taxpayer. The company became concerned when it realized that it was surrounded by a hostile black community. It now is using its vast financial expertise to aid ghetto businesses. It revamped its hiring policies to bring in more blacks, and committed more than eighty-five million dollars in ghetto loans. Following the 1967 riots, the insurance industry as a whole agreed to earmark a total of one billion dollars for ghetto projects, chiefly in housing.

—In Oakland, home of the Black Panthers, the Ford Foundation granted three hundred thousand dollars to a minority contractors' group called the General and Special Contractors' Association of Oakland. The money has enabled association members in the Bay Area to bid on big construction jobs that in the past were out of their reach because of discrimination and lack of capital. Ford also announced plans to make available ten million dollars, a large part of which will be invested in black and other minority-group businesses. At about the same time the Taconic Foundation, which has supported civil rights and voter education projects, proposed a massive "multifoundation fund, or consortium, that would permit a pooling of risks" and enable the foundations to invest in business enterprises for "socially oriented" reasons.

In June 1968, the *Wall Street Journal* made a preliminary assessment of the success of corporate efforts dealing with the racial and urban crises. The *Journal* surveyed fifty major corporations, among them the top twenty-five industrial giants, and each of the five biggest banks, insurance companies, merchandisers, utilities, and transportation companies. The survey found these companies "playing a significantly larger role in the civil rights arena than they did five, or even two, years ago," but the results were hardly anything to brag about. The *Journal* pondered the social responsibilities of corporations, but many of the executives interviewed were quite candid about this subject. "If the cities continue to deteriorate, our investments will inevitably deteriorate with them," explained Paul A. Gorman, president of the Bell System's Western Electric Company. U. S. Steel's chairman, Roger M. Blough, sternly warned that if business doesn't do something "it is a very reasonable expectation that business will experience a serious degradation of the climate which allows it to operate profitably." A chain store spokesman expressed what was probably in the backs of the minds of many corporate executives when he said simply: "We're vulnerable."

The *Journal* survey reported on a number of instances in which corporations were aiding black businesses, hiring more black workers, and upgrading those already on the payroll. But the survey also unintentionally revealed two major problems which the corporations are incapable of handling and which threaten to subvert these efforts. Part of the reason that black unemployment is so high is that black workers have traditionally held the jobs which are now being eliminated by mechanization and computerization. At least one company in the survey reported that the percentage of blacks on its payroll had actually declined for this reason. But the pace of mechanization and automation, uneven though it is, cannot be halted because of the competitive need of individual corporations to increase efficiency and reduce costs in order to maintain profits and growth, and improve their relative standing *vis-à-vis* other companies.[13] On the contrary, it can be expected that the pace of automation will accelerate, putting more minority group and other workers without special skills out of work.

The second problem is this: In the event of a recession, most of the corporate programs would be seriously undermined. "In a serious recession, we will have a very

[13] It is this factor which also precludes *socially oriented* planning in a capitalist society.

serious problem," said James Roche, chairman of General Motors. What Roche meant was that a recession would force curtailment or complete stoppage of ghetto aid programs and cutbacks in hiring. Layoffs would probably result and, of course, blacks, who have least seniority, would be the first to go. Roche's observations reveal the precarious nature of the corporate programs, predicated as they are upon continued prosperity. But continued prosperity in the United States is heavily dependent upon the status of the international capitalist system, and this is something over which American corporations and banks do not yet have complete hegemony. Any serious dislocations in this system (e.g., monetary crises) which depleted corporate surpluses now available would sweep away black capitalism and reveal its insubstantial nature.

Even less dramatic changes in the economic climate, such as inflation-curbing spending cutbacks by the Nixon Administration, could well have serious adverse effects on embryonic black capitalism. In the past, clampdowns on inflation have been followed by recessions of greater or lesser magnitude: Unemployment rose, the stock market fell, and business went into a slump. There is no reason to believe this pattern will not be repeated, and some experts have predicted that over-all unemployment may well climb above 4 percent in 1969. Black capitalism and ghetto redevelopment, plumes on the wave of a booming economy, would be blown away by the harsh wind of recession if the wave breaks.

It is interesting to note that Richard M. Nixon was the first major public figure to thrust the concept of black capitalism into the public spotlight. Nixon opened the subject in a radio broadcast in Milwaukee on March 28, 1968, in which he declared that the country must give black people a better share of economic and political power or risk permanent social turbulence. "By this," Nixon said, "I speak not of black power as some of the extremists would interpret it—not the power of hate and division, not the power of cynical racism, but the power

the people should have over their own destinies, the power
to affect their own communities, the power that comes
from participation in the political and economic processes
of society."

Nixon followed up this intriguing overture in subsequent broadcasts. In a broadcast on April 25, Nixon declared: "For too long white America has sought to buy
off the Negro—and to buy off its own sense of guilt—with
ever more programs of welfare, of public housing, of payments *to* the poor, but not *for* anything except for keeping
out of sight: payments that perpetuated poverty, and that
kept the endless, dismal cycle of dependency spinning
from generation to generation. Our task—our challenge—
is to *break* this cycle of dependency, and the time to begin
is now." Warming up to his subject, Nixon continued,
"What we do *not* need now is another round of unachievable promises of unavailable federal funds. What we *do*
need is imaginative enlistment of private funds, private
energies, and private talents, in order to develop the opportunities that lie untapped in our own underdeveloped
urban heartland." He urged that incentives be provided
to industry "to make acceptable the added risks of ghetto
development and of training the unemployed for jobs." He
said that black success stories would show that "the way to
the American Dream is not barred by a sign that reads,
'Whites Only.'"

Another bridge between what he called the developed
and underdeveloped segments of American society is black
capitalism.

Using the language of black militants, Nixon criticized
present welfare payments because "They create a permanent caste of the dependent, a colony within a nation."
He praised the "forward-looking" efforts of the Urban
Coalition.

In this broadcast Nixon confronted the issue of property
rights vs. human rights. "It's long been common practice
among many to draw a distinction between 'human rights'
and 'property rights,' suggesting that the two are separate

and unequal—with 'property rights' second to 'human rights.' But in order to *have* human rights, people need property rights—and never has this been more true than in the case of the Negro today."[14] This bland assertion was probably intended as Nixon's answer to those who argue that in the ghetto the property rights of the owning classes have all too frequently been the sole justification for the exploitation, imprisonment, and even murder of those who own nothing.

Nixon wrapped up the broadcast by taking a swipe at black "extremists" while presenting himself as an advocate of black power, in the more "constructive" sense of that term:

> Black extremists are guaranteed headlines when they shout "burn" or "get a gun." But much of the black militant talk these days is actually in terms far closer to the doctrines of free enterprise than to those of the welfarist thirties—terms of "pride," "ownership," "private enterprise," "capital," "self-assurance," "self-respect"— the same qualities, the same characteristics, the same ideals, the same methods, that for two centuries have been at the heart of American success, and that America has been exporting to the world. What most of the militants are asking is not separation, but to be included in—not as supplicants, but as owners, as entrepreneurs— to have a share of the wealth and a piece of the action.
>
> And this is precisely what the federal central target of the new approach ought to be. It ought to be oriented toward more black ownership, for from this can flow the rest—black pride, black jobs, black opportunity and yes, black power, in the best, the constructive sense of that often misapplied term. . . .
>
> It's no longer enough that white-owned enterprises employ greater numbers of Negroes, whether as laborers

[14] Former CORE head Floyd McKissick would apparently agree with this statement. When an official in a big company complained about thievery among black employees, McKissick replied, "Teach them what property rights are. Then they aren't going to have that attitude."

or as middle-management personnel. This is needed, yes —but it has to be accompanied by an expansion of black ownership, of black capitalism.

The next week Nixon spelled out how he planned to implement his program of black capitalism. He urged that tax incentives be granted to corporations which locate branch offices or new plants in the urban ghettos, or which hire and train the unskilled and upgrade the skills of those at the bottom of the employment ladder. He asserted that new capital was needed in the ghettos. He called for expanded SBA loans, reinsurance programs to "reduce the risk of investment in poverty areas," greater use of correspondent relationships between large, white-controlled lending institutions and smaller, black-controlled ones, and he urged that churches, labor unions, and corporations doing business in poverty areas should keep some of their cash deposits in banks that serve those communities. He also called for expanded opportunities for black home ownership on the grounds that "People who own their own homes don't burn their neighborhoods. . . ."

All of this sounds terribly impressive, almost like a new beginning. But close scrutiny reveals it to be only another camouflaged effort to reassert white control over the ghettos, although that control would now be one step removed and sugar-coated with promises that blacks might "get a piece of the action." Nixon's program of black capitalism was enthusiastically endorsed by the white press, including, for example, the *Wall Street Journal* and the *Christian Science Monitor*. Both of these papers also drew attention in editorials to the fact that Nixon's proposals seemed to converge with programs being advocated by CORE. After all, was it not true that CORE had declared in a six-page statement that "We seek to harness the creative energy of private enterprise to achieve a solution to America's crisis"? The *Wall Street Journal* called the political implications of this convergence "fascinating."

The black press was less enthusiastic about Nixon's state-

CORPORATE IMPERIALISM VS. BLACK LIBERATION   231

ments. For instance, the influential Chicago *Daily Defender* voiced suspicion of the presidential aspirant's motives, although, it endorsed the idea of black capitalism. "A marriage of black power to free enterprise is CORE's ultimate objective," the paper asserted, "and the only logical ground on which to build economic independence and self-sufficiency. Without this base, black power takes on the insignificant aspect of a paper tiger." The *Defender* declared that there could be no alliance between black people and the conservatives of the "New South," as Nixon had suggested.

Despite this cautious approach of the black press, at least some of those who regard themselves as black militants found Nixon attractive. In an editorial in *Liberator* magazine, a monthly which appeals to militant black intellectuals, Daniel Watts wrote: "The primary goal of Black people must be economic advancement from which political power and societal equality will result. Therefore, the conservative is the natural ally of the moment for the Black man. Today, as Roy Innis of CORE has attested to, only Richard Nixon is . . . hospitable to Black Power."[15]

While Watts and the *Defender* disagreed over the role of conservatives in relation to black power, the man whom Nixon appointed to head up his newly created Council on Urban Affairs experienced no such conflict. Daniel P. Moynihan believes that the cities cannot be saved by the Washington government. Instead the job will require massive local efforts which, in his view, can be brought about only by an alliance of liberals and conservatives. Moynihan's decentralism probably will work out in practice to mean that more essential social services will be turned over to business, and operated on a profit-making basis.

This privatization of government functions is advocated

[15] Nixon, however, received less than 10 percent of the black vote, thus unsettling the myth that within the two-party system the black vote is crucial. The 1968 election proved that in a situation of increasing polarization, black bloc voting of itself cannot prevent an electoral swing to the right.

on the grounds that it will increase efficiency and reduce waste. While this may be possible, it is also equally likely that corporate inroads into the public sector will result in greater corporate control of ever-widening spheres of public life. The logical extension of this kind of decentralism would reduce the overt function of government to tax collector and subsidizer of corporate "urban development" programs. Put another way, the creation of Max Ways' "public market" would necessarily be accompanied by a reduction in government's ability to intervene in corporate programs and planning as they apply to that market. In the interest of expediency, corporate autonomy would take priority over democratic control. The private sector of the economy normally operates in this fashion, but to extend this mode to the public sector could well culminate in a sort of velvet-fisted corporate dictatorship of American society. However, since corporations already control or heavily influence so many aspects of American life, their open takeover of the public sector probably would be marred by only a ripple of dissent. Americans seem to adjust easily to the role of organization men.

At the apex of the new hierarchical structure being created in the ghettos is to stand the black capitalist and managerial class. This is the class which will have closest contact with corporate America and which is to act as a conduit for its wishes.

But if this new black elite is to perform its role effectively as a surrogate ruling class, then the base of the pyramid class structure being constructed in the ghetto must first be stabilized. It does no good to establish a black governing class if the foundation upon which it is built and which it is destined to rule is shaky and threatens to topple the whole edifice. The "hard-core unemployed" are especially important in this process of stabilization, because it is believed that they are a key factor in contributing to the general unrest in the ghettos. Hence, crash programs were formulated and rushed into operation to absorb at least some of these lumpenproletarians into the work force.

What are these programs to accomplish? A candid answer was given by Professor Herbert R. Northrup, chairman of the Department of Industry at the Wharton School of Finance and Commerce of the University of Pennsylvania, who did research under a Ford Foundation grant into the racial attitudes of American industry. In a magazine interview, Northrup spoke of the value of a job for an alienated black: "A job does wonders. First thing you know, he's got a mortgaged house and a mortgaged car like the rest of us—he's part of the system—and he's got to stay on the job like all the rest of us to meet the payments."[16] These few words, spoken almost casually by an intimate of "the system," nevertheless illuminate one of the many ways by which that system traps people and ties them to it. Northrup would probably term the word "trap" something of an exaggeration. He would prefer the phrase, "integrating the Negro labor force." But this is only a euphemism which obscures a central aim of the "hard-core" programs: creating in black workers a sense of commitment or allegiance to the corporate, capitalist system.[17] Indeed, creating a sense of loyalty or indebtedness to the system appears in some instances to be much more important than actually alleviating black unemployment, the overt and much-publicized goal of these programs.

In fact, one of the criticisms leveled at government-sponsored job training programs is that they frequently tend to be unrealistic, training people for jobs which are not available and thereby unintentionally contributing to black alienation and unrest. The United States Commission on Civil Rights came close to saying precisely this in its annual report for 1967.

From the corporate point of view, a more realistic approach is that currently being taken by many companies.

[16] *U.S. News & World Report,* October 14, 1968.
[17] The participation of employed auto workers in the 1967 Detroit rebellion and now the Revolutionary Union Movement shows, however, that this will not necessarily be the outcome of integration programs.

The Lockheed Corporation, for example, has been actively recruiting minority group workers since 1961. Unlike some companies, Lockheed is especially sensitive about being cooperative in projects that provide jobs for minorities, because it is heavily dependent on federal government contracts, which amounted to 88 percent of all Lockheed's sales between 1961 and 1967. Lockheed, therefore, became one of the first major companies to recruit and train hard-core jobless. Its experiences have become models for other corporations.

Lockheed set up its first hard-core programs at plants in Georgia and California. To qualify, a prospective trainee had to be a school dropout, out of work, with no consistent work record of any sort, and have an annual family income of three thousand dollars or less. At Lockheed-Georgia ninety-eight trainees entered the first twelve-week program. They were paid twenty to thirty dollars a week and given a transportation allowance plus five dollars per dependent. At its Sunnyvale, California plant, 108 trainees signed up for two programs. In one, they were given a training allowance. In the other, they were paid the going wage of $2.40 to $2.80 per hour. Not surprisingly, the company found that those who received the higher wages were less likely to quit than those who got the low training allowance.

More surprising to company officials were other findings. The company discovered that many of the trainees had to be taught "proper standards of dress and decorum." Others had to be impressed with the necessity of reporting to work on time, and still others had to be taught the arts of verbal expression. The Lockheed counselors had to be especially patient during this orientation period.

After completing this phase, the trainees were taught basic factory skills, and then moved on to more specialized operations such as welding, sheet-metal assembly, or keypunch operation. Throughout the training period, counselors had to be adept in dealing with the trainees' personal problems such as habitual lateness, excessive drinking, or occasional jailings. But the effort was worth the trouble. Because of the solicitousness displayed by the company and its training personnel, those trainees who successfully completed the course identified with the company and became loyal employees. Their "quit" rate was substantially lower than that of workers hired normally. In short, they were "integrated" into the system.

Lockheed's experience has been corroborated by other companies which have launched similar programs. Both the Ford Motor Company and General Motors, to name two, have hired and trained hundreds of so-called unemployables and have found them to be among their more loyal employees. The explanation for this phenomenon is relatively simple. The hard-core training programs are far more than mere technical training courses. The trainee's personal habits are carefully and skillfully reshaped, and he is taught socially acceptable methods of resolving ordinary personal problems. In a word, these programs perform the same socializing function as do the public schools —of shaping and programming individuals to fit into slots in the economy and society at large. Since most, if not all, of the hard-core unemployed are school dropouts, their socialization is incomplete, and this goes a long way toward explaining their lack of motivation and inability to find and hold jobs.

If a corporation assumes the burden of completing the socialization process, then, in all likelihood, the trainee will identify with that company. The average ghetto schoolchild does not identify with the school because there is no immediate and positive reason for him to do so. School is a boring or unpleasant experience which the child must endure. But an adult in a training program receives tangible rewards in the form of a training allowance or wages and the expectation of a job at the end of the course. The rewards cannot help but facilitate the individual's identification with the company, especially in view of the low self-esteem such a person is likely to have. Thus, the training programs are the propaganda equivalent of management training courses for budding executives. Both teach requisite skills and build subtle psychological links between individual and corporation. The more sophisticated job trainee, as the more sophisticated junior executive, can be expected to identify with the corporate system as a whole, as well as the individual firm that employs him.

It goes without saying that such time-consuming training programs are expensive. If the companies had to foot the entire bill, these programs probably never would have materialized. But the federal government is picking up most of the tab, including costs for transportation services, health care, and special counseling.

Another innovation in the process of incorporating so-called unemployables into the economy is seen in special on-the-job training programs. For example, an organization known as the Board for Fundamental Education can be hired by a company to teach its low-level workers reading, writing, spelling, arithmetic, and basic English grammar with texts that relate these subjects to the employee's job. B.F.E. officers claim that such on-the-job schooling, followed by upgrading successful pupils, is cheaper for a company than seeking out and screening dozens of applicants for a middle-level job. B.F.E., which was founded in 1948, says that it has trained more than eighty thousand workers. It has been so successful that it has spawned a competitor called MIND, Inc. The latter firm is specifically in the market of training unemployables. In its sales pitch, it tells prospective client companies that it can bring the rejected and disadvantaged up to employment standards for less money than it would cost these companies to advertise for, interview, select, and test the average nonprofessional worker. MIND was set up in 1966 and already has more than fifty customers, including such giants as I.B.M., Procter & Gamble, Crown Zellerbach, and Chrysler. The enterprising company expects to be doing a ten-million-dollar-a-year business by 1971.

In its initial flush of enthusiasm, the business press tended to describe the new job training programs in glowing phrases. But there are long-term problems that mitigate against the eventual success of these programs to find jobs for the hard-core jobless and convince the black working class that it has a stake in the corporate system. To begin with, there is the fact that most of the programs to date are small and have only limited impact. Just to bring the black jobless rate down to the unemployment rate for whites would require finding jobs for some 350,000 unemployed blacks. In an economy which is generating new jobs at the rate of 1,500,000 per year, this may not seem like too difficult a task. But it must be borne in mind that only a very few of these jobs will be open to the average unemployed black for reasons having more to do with technological advancement than racial discrimination. And in the event of a recession, even these openings will disappear.

Assuming that no recession is in the offing, the long-term prospect still favors a critical job shortage in the cities. The Economic Development Administration, a part of the U. S. Commerce Department, said in its 1967 annual report that poverty in rural areas is getting worse. Consequently, more unskilled persons from these areas are flooding into the cities. "By 1975," the EDA reported, "the 25 largest metropolitan areas, excluding those in California, will have a potential shortage of 2.9 million jobs."

To make matters worse, there is a growing trend for industrial concerns and other businesses to move out of the cities to small towns or the suburbs. High taxes and high labor costs in the cities are what motivate this move, but the net effect is to intensify the financial crisis in the urban areas and to add to black unemployment.

Finally, there is the role of the unions. The unions have not been hospitable to training programs for the hard-core jobless as they have not been particularly friendly to black labor in general. The unfriendly attitude toward black workers supposedly stems from the period when the labor movement was in its youth and black workers sometimes were brought in as strike breakers. This occasional scab role played by unorganized blacks fed the racism of the white workers and was used as the excuse for excluding blacks or restricting them to menial jobs. Today, with blue-collar jobs declining in some industries (notably steel) and just barely holding steady in others, the unions have adopted a tacit policy of viewing hard-core jobless, especially members of minority groups, as economic enemies. Labor leaders increasingly stress the need for protecting and preserving the existing jobs held by union members. The unemployed are seen as a great mass of potential strike breakers and scabs, ready on a moment's notice to take the union member's job and upset the wage scales for which the unions have so bitterly fought.

That this narrow-minded policy is ultimately self-destructive seemingly has not occurred to most union leaders and their rank-and-file followers. Their sole concern apparently is to protect what they have and to let the future take care of itself. The labor unions perceive the advance of automation and mechanization as a threat to their interests, but the union leaders, once militant fighters for social change, have no program other than a panicky defensive reaction for meeting this challenge. Pleas to labor leaders to organize the jobless go unheeded as the unions watch their power base eroded; the prospect of their eventual impotence seems ever more certain.

(5)

The growing interest in programs for unemployed black workers has been accompanied by increasing public discussion of various income maintenance schemes. The National Advisory Commission on Civil Disorders in its report recommended that consideration be given to setting up what it called a "national system of income supplementation." Such a system would provide a minimum income for persons who cannot work and also "provide for those who can work or who do work, any necessary supplements in such a way as to develop incentives for fuller employment." The idea of some kind of guaranteed minimum income program has won support from such quarters as former Vice President Hubert Humphrey, Senator Eugene McCarthy, and a business group appointed by New York Governor Nelson Rockefeller. Such a program was one of the original demands of the poor people's campaign, and the general concept has been endorsed by spokesmen for both the political left and the political right. The Office of Economic Opportunity has launched a four-million-dollar pilot project in several New Jersey cities designed to test the feasibility of a guaranteed annual income program.

The guaranteed income proposal fits into the corporate scheme of ghetto pacification in that it would provide a simplified, centrally administered system which could replace the present cumbersome and grossly inefficient welfare bureaucracy. Insofar as this system would make audited payments to those for whom no jobs are available, as well as to those who simply cannot work, it would also constitute a means for exercising a minimum of control over those of the unemployed not enrolled in training programs or otherwise engaged in activities that would subject them to constraints requiring conformity to social norms. These persons would be given a living allowance and, as in the welfare system, the tacit threat of withdrawing this allowance could be used to deter them from engaging in what is deemed antisocial behavior.

Of course, these are not the usual reasons given when advocates of income maintenance programs discuss the subject. Public discussion centers around the contention that a guaranteed income would (1) eliminate the need for the present costly, disorganized, and redundant welfare bureaucracy, and (2) by providing uniform payments it would discourage the indigent from moving from poverty-stricken rural areas to the cities in order to get on the better-paying welfare rolls of the metropolises. The reform-minded will point out that a guaranteed income system would hopefully also remove some of the features of the welfare system that are disruptive of family life. Corporate executives when discussing the matter among themselves may take note of the fact that such a system of money payments would tend to increase aggregate demand throughout the economy.[18] Some political radicals endorse the idea on the grounds that it will yield a more equitable distribution of national income.

However, a look at the proposals being given serious consideration reveals that the latter possibility is not a likely outcome. In 1962 an economics professor at the University of Chicago, Milton Friedman (who became an economics adviser to Barry Goldwater in 1964), proposed a guaranteed income in the form of a negative income tax. Under this proposal individuals whose income falls below a certain line would receive payments from the federal government. The most generous demarcation line widely accepted is the "poverty line" of approximately three thousand dollars for a family of four. In theory, the negative income tax program could simply rebate to every poor family the entire difference between its reported earnings and the demarcation line. A family with an income of two thousand dollars would thus receive a check for one thousand dollars from the government. However, proponents of the plan fear that this procedure would not provide the poor with any incentive for working. They could simply sit at home doing nothing and collect three thousand dollars every year.

To counter the presumed indolent characteristics of the poor and get them out to employment offices, the Friedman plan calls for the government to pay only half the difference between earnings and the poverty line. Hence, a family of four with no income would get only fifteen hundred dollars. If the same family earned two thousand dollars, it would receive a payment of five hundred dollars, making a total of twenty-five hundred dollars. Under this proposal there thus would be a definite incentive

[18] Conservatively oriented businessmen do not approve of this tendency since they believe it will only increase inflation.

for members of the family to find jobs. They would either work, or suffer severe malnutrition while trying to live on fifteen hundred dollars a year.

The Friedman plan would cost from three to five billion dollars a year. At present, nearly eight billion dollars is spent on the welfare system (including almost one billion dollars just for administrative costs). A slightly more generous negative income tax plan proposed in 1965 by James Tobin, a former member of President Kennedy's Council of Economic Advisers, would cost seven to eight billion dollars per year. The Friedman and Tobin plans are apparently the only guaranteed income proposals being given serious consideration. Since neither of them would cost any more than the present welfare system, which they would partially or totally replace, it is evident that their implementation certainly would not be accompanied by any significant redistribution of national income. On the contrary, their primary purpose is to simplify the maintenance *at current income levels* of the underclass of welfare recipients.

If the goal were not simply to maintain the poor in their poverty, but to lift them out of it, then a drastic redistribution of income would be required. The federal "poverty line" is based on the U. S. Department of Agriculture's lowest-cost "economy" diet. But only 23 percent of those who spend no more than the low-cost amount have a nutritionally adequate diet. The USDA has devised a "moderate-cost" plan which would cost something more than eight thousand dollars for a family of four. The Bureau of Labor Statistics calculates that a "modest but adequate" living for an urban family of four, which would allow for more than mere physical survival, but less than the "American standard of living," would require an income of about the same amount. However, a guaranteed income of eight thousand dollars for such families would cost an estimated two hundred billion dollars per year and would necessitate payments to a majority of the people in the country.

Obviously such a proposal is not going to receive very serious attention from public spokesmen or business leaders other than a passing comment to the effect that it is totally infeasible within the present economic framework. But the above does begin to convey some idea of the massive redistribution of income and resources that would be required just to guarantee every American citizen a "modest" standard of living.

(6)

One final point. The great interest in urban problems which was triggered by the black revolts is reminiscent of the newfound interest in Latin America which followed the Cuban Revolution. In both cases the emergence of a revolutionary situation engendered a flurry of concern and activity in the American power structure. In both cases this activity resulted in a glowing program of reforms designed to counter the drift toward revolution. In the case of Latin America these reforms have already proved to be little more than so much verbiage.

The Alliance for Progress, which was to be the vehicle for the new reforms in Latin America, was launched by President Kennedy in 1961. "Let us transform the American continents into a vast crucible of revolutionary ideas and efforts," Kennedy declared. It was certainly true that Latin America was in dire need of a social revolution. Occupying 16 percent of the habitable land mass of the world and containing only 6 percent of the world's population, Latin America is an area richly endowed with natural resources and a generally favorable climate. Yet with an annual per capita income of less than two hundred dollars, it easily qualifies as one of the world's underdeveloped regions.

Presently less than 5 percent of the arable land is under cultivation, and this is largely on one-crop *latifundia* (large landholdings). There is almost a total absence of diversified farming, with vegetables and beef being virtually nonexistent for local consumption (except in Argentina). One-tenth of the population owns 90 percent of the land, and it has been estimated that the highest income group consumes at a rate fifteen times higher than lower income groups. The large landowners constitute a semifeudal oligarchy that totally dominates the economic and political life of the Latin American countries. To the oligarchs reform and revolution amount to the same thing—an assault against their power and property—and both are to be avoided.

But the Alliance was supposed to initiate reforms in order to avert violent revolution. As it developed, the harsh light of political reality exposed this empty rhetoric of reform. A key Alliance program was to be land reform. This was a necessary starting point for further changes. However, both the local rulers and the U. S. Government thwarted this program. Either nothing was done or, as in Venezuela, where one of the most heralded land reform programs was undertaken, it amounted mainly to a re-settlement program, which did not involve the breakup of large estates and did not break the tyrannical political power of the oligarchs.

Any hope of serious land reform was further under-minded by a section of the U. S. Foreign Assistance Act of 1962, which is designed to preclude any radical land or tax reform aimed at U.S. corporations abroad. But since American companies have large landholdings and invest-ments in every important area of Latin America, such an injunction necessarily diminishes any possibility of real reform.

As David Horowitz has commented, the strategic aim of the Alliance was the preservation of vested interests, particularly U.S. private capital, in Latin America. The tactic for achieving this goal was to be reformism, but in the face of a real or imagined social upheaval this tactic was quickly abandoned for more traditional methods. Commenting on the first two years of the Alliance, Horowitz wrote that this period

244 BLACK AWAKENING IN CAPITALIST AMERICA

. . . had revealed that only the most minimal reforms would be tolerated by either the Latin American oligarchies or the U. S. Congress. When any Latin American government attempted to step beyond the bounds of minimal reform, it would find itself toppled by a military *coup*. The United States would then be called upon to provide support for the basically unstable (because unpopular) political replacement. The U.S. could be counted on to provide the necessary support (as seven *coups* in three years testified) because the U.S. elite still had a greater fear of social instability with its promise of far-reaching reform, than the prospect of political dictatorship and the immemorial poverty and suffering of the *status quo*.[19]

There are no oligarchies in black America, but the lesson of the Alliance for Progress in Latin America should be clear. The U.S. corporate elite is more interested in social stability than it is in social reform. It may, on occasion, endorse reforms as a means of subverting revolution, but its commitment to that tactic is at best tenuous. Its one abiding concern is to protect and extend corporate investment and corporate domination. All else, including those blacks who look to corporate America with such hope, must be subservient to that interest.

(7)

To summarize: The black rebellions injected a new sense of urgency into the urban crisis and prompted the corporate elite to reassess its role in handling the problems of the cities. The strategy evolved by the corporatists calls for the establishment of a black elite which can administer the ghettos. Where possible, black workers will be reintegrated into the economy. Those blacks who can't be absorbed into the work force may be pensioned off on some type of income maintenance program. From the

[19] David Horowitz, *The Free World Colossus* (New York: Hill and Wang, 1965), p. 237.

corporate viewpoint, this strategy is more efficient, less costly, and more profitable than either traditional welfare stateism or massive repression. With the federal government (i.e., taxpayers) footing the bill, the corporations have all to gain and little to lose.

This strategy is fraught with difficulties and contradictions, some of which have been discussed in the preceding pages. In essence it devolves into the equivalent of a program of neocolonial manipulation, not unlike what transpires in many underdeveloped countries in the Third World. Whether it will succeed depends partly on the ability of corporate America to overcome the difficulties mentioned, and partly on the black communities themselves. In the long run, this strategy cannot help but intensify class divisions and class conflicts within the black communities. Increasingly, the majority of the black population will find itself dominated by a new oppressor class, black instead of white. But whether this class conflict can be combined with the nationalist sentiments of the black masses to become the motive for social change depends on the ability of black radicals to devise a program which appeals to the popular black masses.

VI. BLACK RADICALS:
RHETORIC AND REALITY

In view of the preceding analysis of the co-optation of the black power moderates, the question naturally arises whether the black power militants, the black radicals, have produced a more penetrating analysis of the problem and constructed a program around which the masses of black people can be organized. Or are they little more than angry voices of anarchistic dissent, the playthings of the mass media? An examination of key figures and organizations in the militant wing of the black power movement should yield valuable insights into this matter.

In an earlier chapter it was contended that the basic ideological foundation of the militant black movement was laid by Malcolm X. He sought to establish an intellectual framework for revolutionary black nationalism by weaving into an integrated whole a series of disjointed ideas. He pointed up the necessity for psychological liberation and black pride. He demanded black control of black organizations and communities, and he was an advocate of self-defense for those communities. Malcolm was an unrelenting opponent of the white, capitalist power structure and its political vehicles, the Democratic and Republican parties. He identified this power structure, rather than the white population as a whole, as the primary agent of black oppression. To counter this power structure he called for independent black political action. Finally, Malcolm identified the condition of black people in the United States as domestic colonialism, explicitly calling for an aggressive internationalism among all colonial peoples if any of them are to be truly liberated.

But Malcolm's ideas were not evenly assimilated throughout the black movement. Some failed to understand him or deliberately misrepresented what he said. Others took one idea, such as cultural nationalism, and inflated it out of all proportion. Still others vacillated, seemingly uncertain of what they were about or where they wanted to go.

Stokely Carmichael, for example, never moved beyond ambiguity. Sometimes his words were those of a reformer, who only wanted to adjust the social system and make it work better. Sometimes he sounded like a committed revolutionary, who sought to topple the whole system. On other occasions, he managed to give the remarkable impression of being at once a reformer and a revolutionary.

His book, *Black Power*, was largely an essay in liberal reformism calling for broadened participation by blacks in the economic and political structures of the country. True, there were vague references to "new structures," but these were not spelled out. The only radical departure in the book was its advocacy of independent politics. Carmichael and Hamilton analyzed the experience of the Mississippi Freedom Democratic party in 1964 and concluded that it was necessary to "build new forms outside the Democratic party." The Lowndes County Freedom party is the model they offer of such a new form.

One reason why Carmichael's book was reformist and not revolutionary was that he and his co-author refused to examine the American capitalist system and to present an analysis of that system within the framework of the larger international context. Yet, at the very moment that this book was coming off the presses, Carmichael was in Cuba, attending a conference of the Organization of Latin American Solidarity. He told the OLAS delegates that the problems of black people in the United States "were an inherent part of the capitalist system and, therefore, could not be alleviated within that system." American capitalism had created a system of domestic colonialism, he said, and

> The struggle for black power in this country [the United States] is the struggle to free these colonies from external domination. But we do not seek to create communities where, in place of white rulers, black rulers control the lives of black masses and where black money goes into the pockets of a few blacks: We want to see it go into the communal pocket. The society we seek to build among black people is not an oppressive capitalist society—for capitalism by its very nature cannot create structures free from exploitation. We are fighting for the redistribution of wealth and for the end of private property inside the United States.

It should be borne in mind that this statement was made at a time when CORE and other groups were drifting toward black capitalism. It was apparently intended to counter this drift and to make explicit the revolutionary implications of black power. However, the substance and meaning of this speech was not widely reported in this country. The speech was later printed and distributed, but still it had only limited impact.

Carmichael linked racism and exploitation, terming them "the horns of the bull that seeks to gore us." A two-pronged counter-strategy was necessary, he continued. "Even if we destroy racism, we would not necessarily destroy exploitation. Thus, we must constantly launch a two-pronged attack; we must constantly keep our eyes on both of the bull's horns." On another occasion in Cuba, Carmichael explained his understanding of the relationship between racism and exploitation; "In order to justify the raping of the countries of the Third World they [the white rulers of the West] developed the ideology of racism, that the peoples of Asia, Africa, and Latin America were subhuman, so that it was okay to exploit them. That is why many Westerners never objected to the brutal oppression of their colonies."

It was in Havana that Carmichael, apparently enamored of the Latin American revolutionaries who had gathered there, first made his now well-known remarks on urban guerrilla warfare. At a press conference he was asked whether black liberation would involve the use of aggressive violence. "Until last year it was a question of self-defense," he answered. "The line between defensive and offensive violence is very thin. We are moving into open guerrilla warfare in the United States. We have no alternative but to use aggressive violence in order to own the land, houses, and stores inside our communities and control the politics of those communities."

This statement was reflective also of a continuing shift in SNCC's orientation. Rap Brown, who succeeded Carmichael as SNCC chairman, soon became the nation's leading advocate of blacks' arming themselves. "We are at war," Brown told a New York crowd. "We are caught behind enemy lines and you better get yourselves some guns!"[1]

When he returned to this country after visiting Cuba, several African countries, North Vietnam, and Europe, Carmichael began organizing black united fronts, the first of which was set up in Washington, D.C. In its structure,

[1] Brown's militant statements soon got him into trouble with the authorities. He was charged with inciting to arson after a riot broke out in Cambridge, Maryland, following a speech he made there. But a special report to the President's Advisory Commission on Civil Disorders concluded that long-standing grievances and police "overreaction," not Brown, caused the troubles. "It may be emotionally satisfying to think that Brown came to Cambridge and that therefore there was a riot," the report said. "But the facts are more complex and quite different." Black grievances over housing, police, education, employment, and antipoverty programs had heightened community tensions, it said. Brown's speech was "unequivocally militant, radical and revolutionary," the report continued, but it was an incident in which Brown was struck by a ricocheting bullet fired by a white sheriff's deputy—not the speech itself—which initiated the violence. Police "overreaction" to the tense situation then triggered the rebellion.

the united front was to include every sector of the black community. Carmichael believed that such united organizations were needed in order to assure black survival in the face of increasing repression. It was only by uniting the entire black community to fight this repression, he believed, that militants, moderates, and apolitical blacks alike could have any hope of surviving. Carmichael also hoped that the united front could serve as a radicalizing agency. "Every Negro is a potential black man," he said repeatedly, and he thought that the black bourgeoisie and other indifferent blacks could be "brought home" and recruited into the liberation struggle.

After he returned to this country, Carmichael dropped the Marxist political ideas which he had been espousing in Cuba.[2] Instead, he adopted a position quite close to that of cultural nationalists. In February 1968, the enemy of blacks was no longer the capitalist system. The prime enemy was the white man, the honky. "We are talking about a certain type of superiority complex that exists in the white man wherever he is," Carmichael told an audience. "We have to recognize who our major enemy is. The major enemy is not your brother, flesh of your flesh and blood of your blood. The major enemy is the honky and his institutions of racism. . . ." It is characteristic of the cultural nationalist to exhibit a simplistic fixation on racism and to be unable (or unwilling) to delve any deeper into the American social structure. Like the Kerner Commission, the black cultural nationalist identifies white racism, originally nothing more than a convenient ideology to justify slavery and exploitation, as the sole cause of black oppression.

Carmichael's new cultural approach ruled out any pos-

[2] In fact, at the black antiwar meeting in April 1968, Carmichael said that Marxism was irrelevant to the black struggle because it dealt only with economic questions, not racism. When challenged on this, he replied that race is more important than class and, speaking of Marx, "we cannot have our people bow down to any white man; I don't care how great he is."

sibility of an alliance with poor whites. ". . . When you talk about alliances you recognize that you form alliances with people who are trying to rebuild their culture, trying to rebuild their history, trying to rebuild their dignity, people who are fighting for their humanity. Poor white people are not fighting for their humanity, they're fighting for more money. There are a lot of poor white people in this country, you ain't seen none of them rebel yet, have you? Why is it that black people are rebelling? Do you think it's just poor jobs? Don't believe that junk the honky is running down. It's not poor jobs—it's a question of people finding their culture, their nature, and fighting for their humanity. . . ."

A few months later Carmichael returned to the formulation he had employed in Cuba. He told a West Coast audience that "black people in this country are fighting against two evil systems: racism and capitalism, or imperialism." (In a speech in Oakland he was even more explicit. "The government of the United States of America is racist and imperialist. Therefore, we are fighting the government of the United States of America.") He castigated the advocates of black capitalism: "All these people want is a piece of the American pie as it is, in which they would impose black capitalists on us and we say the whole rotten system—root and branch—must be changed to wipe out the racist climate in this land."

How did Carmichael propose to restructure the system? This again was not altogether clear. In early 1968, he aligned himself with those black militants who are suspicious of socialism: "The ideologies of communism and socialism speak to class structure. They speak to people who oppress people from the top down to the bottom. We are not just facing exploitation. We are facing something much more important, because we are the victims of racism. Neither communism nor socialism speaks to the problem of racism. And racism, for black people in this country, is far more important than exploitation." But by the summer of that year Carmichael had again decided that racism and exploitation were interlocked and could not be dealt with as separate, unrelated social phenomena. In one speech, he linked ending racism with ending capitalism. The resulting social system, in his view, would be something more than socialist: "Now the question that is uppermost in our minds as black people is whether or not a communist or socialist society will automatically eliminate racism. I tend to think that just because one has socialism or communism does not necessarily mean you get rid of racism. And so I tend to believe that black people will have to move beyond socialism and communism." Unfortunately, he did not elaborate any further.

Carmichael's ambiguities and shifts are in part attributable to the vacillation of the black middle class, the class to which Carmichael belongs. The black bourgeoisie is traditionally torn between militant nationalism and accommodationist integrationism. The black intellectuals, a subclass of the black bourgeoisie, have the additional problem of trying to relate Western left-wing political ideologies to the reality of black life in the United States. The only serious alternate political viewpoint open to the black intellectual is the kind of liberal corporate capitalist reformism which runs through Carmichael's book on black power. Carmichael was certainly affected by these contending social-ideological currents and apparently was unable to resolve the contradictions they presented.

Additionally, one was never fully certain when Carmichael was acting as a spokesman for the groups with which he identified, and when he was speaking from his personal viewpoint. For example, his speech before the OLAS was collectively written by several SNCC staff members, and some of his statements in the summer of 1968 were known to have been influenced by the Black Panthers, with whom he was active at that time. But it has not been possible to ascertain what concrete factors may have influenced the political line articulated by Carmichael at other times. Clearly he was sensitive to the ideological strains and personalities which moved about him, but it must remain for others to unravel the matrix of factors which add up to the enigma of Stokely Carmichael.

(2)

SNCC's most important contribution to the black liberation movement was in the area of education—raising the political awareness of black people. Through speaking tours and the mass media, SNCC spokesmen such as Carmichael, Rap Brown, and James Forman sought to analyze and give political direction to the rebellious ghetto masses. It is true that, as in the case of Carmichael, the content of this analysis of black oppression was not always as clear and consistent as might have been desired. Yet SNCC was able to reach large numbers of black people, particularly the youth, with the message that the "system" or the "white power structure" had to be dismantled and rebuilt if blacks were ever to be truly free.

Another aspect of this educational work was SNCC's efforts to build bridges to the revolutionary forces in the Third World, and to foster among blacks a sense of solidarity with these forces. A SNCC delegation visited Africa in 1964. Then, in January 1967, Carmichael and SNCC staff member Ivanhoe Donaldson visited Puerto Rico at the invitation of the Independence Movement (M.P.I.) and the Federation of University Students for Independence. They issued a joint declaration of solidarity and support with the Puerto Ricans. Then, at its staff meeting in May, SNCC formally declared itself to be

. . . a human rights organization, interested not only in human rights in the United States but throughout the world; that, in the field of international relations, we assert that we encourage and support the liberation struggles of all people against racism, exploitation and oppression.

Former Executive Secretary James Forman was appointed director of a new International Commission, based

in New York, where he sought to establish working contacts with Afro-Asian members of the United Nations.
One of Forman's first acts in his new post was to dispatch an appeal to the Afro-Asian missions to the UN, calling upon them for moral support "in the form of direct or indirect pressure upon that government which loudly proclaims its concern for the freedom of the Vietnamese people, yet will not guarantee basic human rights to black people in this country."

That summer Carmichael, Julius Lester, and George Ware attended the Havana conference of the OLAS, where they articulated the revolutionary aspects of black power. Earlier, Lester and Charlie Cobb traveled to Vietnam as representatives of Bertrand Russell's International War Crimes Tribunal and later served, with Courtland Cox, as SNCC representatives on the tribunal.

In that same summer SNCC took a strong position on the Arab-Israeli conflict. It contended that the basic issue of the conflict was aggressive, expansionist Zionism backed by U.S. imperialism. Although bitterly attacked by former supporters and charged with anti-Semitism, SNCC refused to waver from its stand, arguing that opposition to Zionism does not imply anti-Semitism.

At the time that Carmichael was in Havana, Forman and SNCC's legal officer, Howard Moore, were in Zambia attending a conference on racism, colonialism, and apartheid sponsored by the United Nations. Forman presented a lengthy position paper in which he argued that the fight against racism and colonialism was indivisible; that a defeat for racism and colonialism in southern Africa would hasten the destruction of these institutions in the United States, and vice versa. He pointed out that the Chase Manhattan Bank, which has large-scale investments in South Africa and profits greatly from apartheid, harassed and finally dismissed nine black employees after they sought to challenge the bank's investment policies.

Forman contended that racism in the United States is not merely a domestic issue, and he requested that "the

question of racism and the general condition of Afro-
Americans in the United States [be placed] on the UN
agenda. " A few months later Forman was again involved
with the UN when he made an appearance before its
Fourth Committee. There he made a presentation dealing
with foreign (including American) investments in southern Africa. In general, SNCC was suspicious of the United
Nations because of the heavy influence which the United
States Government wields in that organization, but SNCC
maintained that this world body should be utilized whenever possible as a forum for presenting the viewpoint of
the black liberation movement.

Another way in which SNCC sought to "internationalize" the black liberation struggle was by building an
antiwar movement in black communities. There was a
ready base in black communities for such organizing
efforts. For example, two days before President Johnson
announced that he would not run for re-election, the
Philadelphia *Tribune*, a black community newspaper, completed a seven-week "Vietnam Ballot" in which 84.5 percent of those polled favored a "get out of Vietnam" position. Only 11 percent favored a "stop the bombing—
negotiate" position, and fewer than 5 percent supported
what was then current U.S. war policy.

However, SNCC's effort was only partially successful.[3]
Its most notable achievement was represented by the establishment of the National Anti-War/Anti-Draft Union,
headed by SNCC staffer John Wilson. In April 1968 the
group held an antiwar conference in New York which attracted hundreds of black activists. Workshops discussed
draft resistance techniques and ways of increasing opposition to the Vietnam war among black people. At the
conclusion of the weekend conference, a telegram was dispatched to Vietnamese National Liberation Front representatives in Stockholm. It said in part that the con-

[3] For example, the largest and most important antiwar marches
in Harlem were organized by the Black United Action Front
and the Progressive Labor Party, not SNCC.

ferees "wholeheartedly endorse and support your struggle for national liberation and self-determination." It continued: "We recognize that as you destroy American imperialism, this in turn aids our fight for our national liberation. At the same time our effort to destroy domestic colonization of black people is an aid to your struggle. Our two peoples have a common enemy and a common victory to win. Let us continue to work together toward that goal."

Speeches, statements, and conferences do not, however, constitute a program. SNCC succeeded in gathering together the parts for a revolutionary analysis of American society and the roles of American imperialism abroad and "neocolonialism" at home, but it was not able to transform this analysis into a revolutionary program. Carmichael's book presented a reformist program of ethnic group assimilation, not a radical program of social change. There was talk of building "freedom organizations" around the country on the model of the one which had been constructed under SNCC tutelage in Alabama, but this never materialized. A large part of the reason was that SNCC was constantly caught in time- and money-absorbing legal battles, which severely circumscribed the operations of the organization. Also, SNCC lost considerable financial support because of its espousal of black power and its stand on the Arab-Israeli dispute. And all the while the size of its staff was dwindling. Consequently, it comes as no great surprise that SNCC did not do more. In fact, it is remarkable that the organization had the impact which it did, considering its small size and limited resources.

One area in which SNCC's impact is still being felt is in the black student movement. SNCC was instrumental in organizing the early student sit-in movement, and it, along with groups like the Black Panthers, inspired the current wave of militant protest activity among black high school and college students. The present upsurge of black student activism, which began in 1967, was termed by George Ware, SNCC campus coordinator, the "second phase" of the student movement. The first phase, during the early 1960s, saw students from southern black colleges launch the nonviolent civil rights movement.

This was the period of sit-ins, freedom rides, and hundreds of local protest marches capped by the massive March on Washington, and finally the Mississippi summer of 1964. Then there was a lull followed by the announcement of the death of the civil rights movement. But black power had been incubating in Mississippi and in the thoughts of black militants across the country. The first awakening of the new "black consciousness" among students began as early as 1962, but its significance did not become clear until 1966 with the emergence of Afro-American student groups on many white campuses.

Robert Johnson, then head of a black student group at the University of Indiana, explained the new upsurge this way: "Urban rebellion, the dismal failure of integration as a social, political and economic process, and the inability of the government at all levels to reconcile its rhetoric with its actions have all served to intensify the spirit of self-determination that pervades the entire black community, of which black students are a part."

The manner in which black students should relate to the larger black community was a question that prompted heated discussion in the student movement. Traditionally, black college students have, upon graduation, adopted a bourgeois outlook and often sought to escape from the black community by assimilating into the white. If they returned to their own people, it was frequently in the role of exploitative businessmen, professionals, or politicians who sought to use the black community simply as a means for personal advancement. This provoked much distrust of the black student, professional, and intellectual on the part of less-privileged blacks. It also caused a crisis for the black student, who was slowly awakening to the implications of the fact that he would not always be a student but he *would* always be black.

This identity crisis was particularly acute for black students at Ivy League schools. In the first issue of *The Black*

Student, published in the spring of 1966 by the Students' Afro-American Society at Columbia University, Hilton Clark, then president of the black student group, accused black Ivy Leaguers of seeking to escape their blackness by becoming "white Negroes" and ignoring the black masses. But the Afro student groups that sprang up at Ivy League schools in response to this crisis—and also in response to the sense of isolation felt by many black students on white campuses—were initially only partly successful in their efforts to change student attitudes. In fact, they were criticized as being little more than elitist social clubs.

The Ivy League Afro groups were grappling with a problem which worried black students everywhere. The students questioned the relevance of a typical college education to the growing black liberation struggle. Most of the black student activists adopted the position that higher education in the United States simply served to reinforce the status quo by encouraging "selfish individualism" and promoting the "white line" of the assumed superiority of Western cultural and ethical values.

The student response has been to espouse a kind of communal black nationalism. "What we're trying to do is to convince the brothers who aren't already nationalists that this is the correct goal," said James Carroll, chairman of the Black Allied Students' Association at New York University. "We're trying to unite as a collective person rather than as a mass of individuals."

Courses on black history, culture, literature, and art are proposed by student militants as antidotes to the "Eurocentric" bias of the average university. Many of the student groups have established projects in nearby black communities. These include tutorial programs, liberation schools, community organizing, and draft resistance centers.

The first thrust of the current black student revolt was felt on predominantly black college campuses, many of them in the South. The Orangeburg Massacre, in which three students were killed by police, represents the most violent and bloody attempt to date of local and state authorities to curb student militancy. But severe repressive measures, including the alleged framing of militant student leaders on murder and rioting charges and police and National Guard invasions of black campuses, were reportedly employed at a host of schools, including Texas Southern University, Fisk University, Tennessee State University, Central State College, Miles College, Grambling College, and Howard University, to name just a few.

The situation became so serious that, in the spring of 1968, six presidents of black colleges were prompted to urge President Johnson and other federal officials to "stop these invasions of college and university campuses by the American version of storm troopers."

On the black campuses, students and militant teachers were demanding not only curriculum changes, but a restructuring and reorientation of the colleges themselves. Nathan Hare, formerly a professor at Howard University and later head of the Black Studies program at San Francisco State College, said that present "Negro" colleges must be destroyed and converted into "black" colleges. By this he meant that nationalist-minded students must force the ouster of college officials who continue to advocate integrationist or assimilationist views.

In addition to gaining control of departments and whole administrations, student activists moved to turn college campuses into political bases for organizing the surrounding black communities. To this end they wanted classrooms and other school facilities made available for community use.

The college students are particularly anxious to build bridges to black high school students. Almost all the college groups have programs aimed at motivating and organizing high school students. But in reality the high school kids are even more militant than their collegiate brothers and sisters. "There is no debate in the high schools about black power," commented George Ware. "That's a foregone conclusion, and it's just a matter of 'What can we do? How can we begin to move?' " The high school stu-

dents quickly found their own answers to these questions
—as evidenced by their strikes and demonstrations in cities
such as New York, Philadelphia, Chicago, and the San
Francisco Bay area.

In the spring and fall of 1968, black student rebels carried their revolt to predominantly white campuses in the
North and West. At Columbia University in late April,
a relatively small number of militant students, in a dramatic
but totally spontaneous move, occupied five university
buildings and held them for a week. The students held two
administration officials as hostages for a short time. Both
black and white students were active in the demonstration.

The demonstrators, led by the Students' Afro-American
Society and Students for a Democratic Society, were demanding that the school stop construction of a university
gymnasium in nearby Morningside Park. They argued that
the proposed gym would diminish the utility of one of the
few parks located in the Harlem area, and that it was being
built despite vigorous objections from Harlem community
groups. A second student demand called for the university
to sever its ties with the Institute for Defense Analysis.
IDA does research in counterinsurgency and ghetto repression techniques for the government. A third demand—
amnesty for the protesting students—was added later.

While these demands were important, and enjoyed wide
support among the general student body, they did not
express the basic demands of either SAS or SDS. Both
groups sought far-reaching changes in the practices and
curriculum of the university. But these demands were lost
in the drama of the moment and endless debate over the
propriety of the building-seizure tactics employed by the
militant students. To add to the confusion, by isolating
themselves in five separate buildings (the blacks holding
one and white students the remaining four), the activists
had a difficult problem of maintaining contact with the
student body as a whole and with each other.

Furthermore, the black students, who sparked the demonstration, did not actively lead it. The black students held

the key to the outcome of the protest action. It is probable that the administration hesitated moving against the demonstrators because it feared that any kind of police repression of the black students might provoke a riot in Harlem. Yet, the blacks stood aloof from the protesting white students, who were ready to accept their leadership. It was as though some of the blacks were playing a skin game— that because they were black they were too "revolutionary" to associate with the white kids.

It was a different story at San Francisco State College a few months later. Here the Black Student Union planned, called, and led a strike which involved thousands of black, white, and brown students, and lasted for several months. The immediate issue which prompted the strike was the ouster of Black Panther George Murray from his teaching post. But the Murray issue was largely overshadowed by the BSU's ten basic demands, which were stressed constantly in leaflets and press conferences. The BSU set up a working alliance with Afro-Asian, Latin, and militant white student groups, and five additional demands were added to the list. It chose the tactic of a student strike, rather than seizure of buildings, and this enabled BSU members to circulate freely on the campus, testing student support and keeping the strike moving and under control.

Basically, the BSU demanded the establishment of a degree-granting Black Studies Department, admission of more black students, and no disciplinary action against the strikers. When these demands are examined in detail, it becomes evident that the BSU was calling for nothing short of a campus revolution. The BSU demanded an *autonomous* Black Studies Department, which would have *hiring and firing power*. This was more power than any other college department could claim, but it was what was required if the black studies program was to be relevant to the needs of the black community and the students who hope to serve it. The black students at San Francisco State knew that black studies could not be complacent; that it must be consciously disruptive, always seeking to expose and cut away those aspects of American society that oppress black people; that it could not be modeled after other departments and accept the constraints imposed on them, because one function of these departments is to socialize students into a racist and oppressive society. The function of black studies must be to create enemies of racism, enemies of oppression, enemies of exploitation. This is a revolutionary task which necessarily required that the Black Studies Department be fully autonomous and self-governing.

One further remark on the black student. The black student is crucial to corporate America's neocolonial plans. It is the educated and trained blacks who are slated to become the new managers of the ghetto, the administrators of the black colony. Like the educated, Westernized elites of Africa and Asia, it is assumed that these educated blacks will identify with the values and aspirations of white society, and, therefore, will become the willing (and well-rewarded) agents of the corporate power structure.

The students by their strikes, sit-ins, and what have you, are making known their dissatisfaction with the meaning and content of the average college education, and they are declaring that they will no longer accept the roles usually assigned to educated blacks. The question is, will they consistently follow through with their protest and refuse to become neocolonial administrators of the ghetto also? At this writing (January 1969) the signs are not altogether clear, but certainly the black student revolt is one of the most hopeful indications that black America possesses both the determination and intellectual resources effectively to combat and resist corporate imperialism.

(3)

One of the consistent themes running through the thinking of SNCC activists—and many other black militants—related to the need for an independent, mass-based, black political party. In its southern campaigns, SNCC experimented with "freedom organizations," eventually helping to establish a black political party in Alabama. Subsequent efforts along similar lines in the North were unsuccessful. But the idea was never dropped, and shortly after taking over the leadership of SNCC in 1968, Phil Hutching made a swing across the country, making contacts with local black groups and generally doing groundwork for setting up a national black political party. At one time SNCC thought that the Black Panthers could become such a party. The two groups entered into an "alliance," and SNCC helped the Panthers gain a foothold on the East Coast. But this alliance was short-lived —if it ever really existed—and ended a few months later in angry verbal exchanges and near-violence.

Before this split, the two groups seemed to have convergent political views. Both advocated an anticolonial struggle for self-determination. Spokesmen for both groups stressed that this struggle would, at some point, probably involve widespread violence, and they urged black people to prepare themselves accordingly. Both groups were becoming increasingly revolutionary and anticapitalist, and they called for alliances with other oppressed minorities and potentially revolutionary segments of the white population.

The two organizations differed in that the Panthers were a young and growing organization, whereas SNCC had passed its prime and was in a state of slow decline. They differed further in that the Panthers were a mass-membership group, which appealed to ordinary, untutored black youth, while SNCC was a "band of organizers," which attracted the better-educated, more intellectual blacks.

The Panthers' top official leaders were Bobby Seale and Huey P. Newton—who was sent to prison after a shooting incident in which a white policeman was killed—but their most eloquent and widely known spokesman was Eldridge Cleaver, the organization's minister of information. A gifted writer and orator, Cleaver nevertheless was not a child of the middle class. On the contrary, he spent most of his youth in the Los Angeles ghetto, and he began his working career as a petty thief. After several marijuana convictions, he was sentenced in 1958 to a long prison term on a conviction for assault with intent to rape and kill. Like Malcolm X, it was while in prison that Cleaver became politically conscious and transformed himself into a revolutionary. He became an avid reader and enjoyed debating with other inmates. He joined the Black Muslims and then left them when his hero, Malcolm, was ousted from the Muslims.

By the time he was paroled at the end of 1966, Cleaver was a changed man. He was a committed revolutionary, and shortly after leaving prison he joined the Panthers.

Cleaver took the colonial argument and elaborated it further:

> We start with the basic definition: that black people in America are a colonized people in every sense of the term and that white America is an organized imperialist force holding black people in colonial bondage. From this definition our task becomes clearer: what we need is a revolution in the white mother country and national liberation for the black colony. To achieve these ends we believe that political and military machinery that does not exist now and has never existed must be created. We need functional machinery that is able to deal with these two interrelated sets of political dynamics which, strictly speaking, make up the total political situation on the North American continent.[4]

This new "political machinery" was to take the form of a coalition between the Panthers and California's Peace and Freedom party, a predominantly white, radical organization which was an offshoot of the antiwar movement. The Panthers demanded that the white group aid in defending Huey Newton and in publicizing his case. They also proposed that the antiwar party run Panthers on its ticket. These demands provoked a dispute within the Peace

---

[4] Speech given before founding convention of the California Peace and Freedom party in March 1968.

and Freedom party that eventually was resolved in favor of the Panthers. As it turned out, the Peace and Freedom party experienced a severe decline after the elections, but its vocal support and defense of the Panthers helped make a wide audience of American whites aware of the nature and workings of racism.

For black radicals a long-standing unsolved problem lies in finding the proper relationship between a purely national (or racial) analysis and program on the one hand, and a purely class analysis and program on the other. In the past, radicals have swung from one pole to the other—sometimes espousing simplistic nationalism and at other times advocating simplistic Marxism—but it is becoming ever clearer that at neither extreme can a winning strategy or an effective program for the black liberation movement be found. Cleaver was one of the few of the younger militant spokesmen to acknowledge this consistently:

> We recognize the problem presented to black people by the economic system—the capitalist economic system. We repudiate the capitalist economic system. We recognize the class nature of the capitalist economic system and we recognize the dynamics involved in the capitalist system. At the same time we recognize the national character of our struggle. We recognize the fact that we have been oppressed because we are black people even though we know this oppression was for the purpose of exploitation. We have to deal with both exploitation and racial oppression, and we don't think you can achieve a proper balance by neglecting one or the other.[5]

Because of the stress laid on nationalism, the Panthers possessed the potential for mobilizing a very wide range of the black population. Because they also understood the nature of class exploitation and class conflict in a capitalist society, they were able to work with allies outside the black community and to identify potential enemies within it. "There are classes within the black community," Cleaver

[5] *Guardian*, April 13, 1968.

said, "they're not as elaborate and as stable as the class
division within the white community because they don't
have as strong an economic base, but they do exist. They
have various interests which conflict with the interests of
the black masses and they're going to guard these very
jealously. We call on the black bourgeoisie to come home,
we leave the door open for them to come home, but I
think that we have to assume that a lot of them are not
going to."

Like SNCC, the Panthers also attempted to establish
themselves as an international entity. They sent delegations
to Cuba and other countries, and applied for observer status
at the UN. They also came up with a variation on the
idea of UN intervention first proposed by William Patterson in 1951 and later by Malcolm X. The Panthers called
for a UN-supervised plebiscite in which only black people
would be allowed to participate. The purpose of the
plebiscite was to determine the will of black people concerning their national destiny. Specifically, it was to determine whether blacks wanted integration or a separate,
sovereign nation. The plebiscite idea never got very far, but
it was in trying to gain admission as observers to the UN
that the Panthers and SNCC clashed.

It is not certain who first proposed an alliance or merger
between SNCC and the Panthers, but it is known that
the move was related to a power struggle going on within
SNCC between Stokely Carmichael and James Forman.
In 1967 the Panthers drafted Carmichael as their "prime
minister," and they contend that within SNCC it was
Carmichael who first developed the idea of a close relation
between the two groups. According to the SNCC version,
it was Forman who first came up with the idea. The power
struggle developed at the time Carmichael made his cele-
brated trip abroad. Apparently Forman and other SNCC
people were upset by some of Carmichael's statements
and activities—specifically, his attacks on certain African
heads of state and leaders of liberation movements—and
they sought to discipline him when he returned. But Car-

michael refused to be disciplined and instead allied himself more closely with the Panthers. The anti-Carmichael faction then tried to undercut him by themselves proposing an alliance with the Panthers. The net result of this maneuvering was that the two groups came together in an atmosphere of mutual suspicion and distrust, and with the power struggle in SNCC still unresolved.

Over the next few months Carmichael became more estranged from SNCC. He did not attend an important staff meeting in June at which SNCC affirmed its independence of the Panthers by voting not to adopt the Panther ten-point program. SNCC felt that the Panther program was "more reformist than revolutionary." Clearly, it was only a matter of time before the two groups would break off their shaky alliance.

The rupture was precipitated a few weeks later by an incident in which, according to the Panthers, SNCC tried to "torpedo" their effort to secure observer status at the UN and publicize their call for a UN-supervised plebiscite. SNCC people said it was simply a matter of an unfortunate misunderstanding over the timing of a press conference, not conscious sabotage. In any event, the mold was set. Suspicion and hostility ran too deep, and the breach could not be healed.

Shortly afterward, the SNCC central committee voted to oust Carmichael[6] and to terminate the relationship with the Panthers on the grounds that the alliance had been made by individuals rather than by the organization as a whole. Rap Brown and James Forman, who had been elected to the Panther cabinet, resigned their positions, and Carmichael, to the extent that he was still active at all, identified himself with the Panthers.

The Panthers criticized SNCC for being unable to deal with the problems arising from its basically middle-class nature, and its failure to realize that in 1968 SNCC was

[6] Carmichael was ousted because of his role in the power struggle and, among other reasons, because of his political inconsistency and his espousal at that time of cultural nationalism.

no longer a significant national force. These criticisms are valid, although SNCC made a valiant effort to overcome its middle-class bias. Lerone Bennett took note of this when he wrote: "SNCC workers identify themselves totally with the people—the poor, the despised, the downtrodden, the humiliated. Sharecroppers with eyes, victims with voices, they thrust themselves into the ditches of desperation so they can speak more clearly for the inhabitants thereof."[7]

The Panthers, too, have not been without contradictions. The Panthers represented an effort to mobilize and organize the most alienated and frustrated of the ghetto youth. In this, the organization enjoyed a considerable measure of success. It succeeded in awakening and drawing into its ranks thousands of youths and young adults in cities throughout the country. These were young workers or youths who had dropped out of the system because they saw no hope in established institutions, or they had been forced out because they could find no useful employment. But, because they were young, they were impatient with this fate and refused to accept its finality. They knew from their own experience that alternatives to the establishment existed.

Actually, for those who are not incorporated into the system, for whatever reasons, society provides its own alternative—organized crime. In the ghetto this alternative is legitimized by the fact that so many people are forced to engage in at least petty illegal activity in order to secure a living income. The pervasiveness of the lucrative numbers racket and dope peddling rings further enhances organized criminality in the eyes of ghetto youth. Social scientists have observed that the role of criminal is one model to which such youth can reasonably aspire. It provides a realistic "career objective," certainly more realistic than hoping to become a diplomat or a corporation executive. Consequently, many ghetto youths turn to illegal activity

[7] *Ebony*, July 1965.

—car thievery, pimping, prostitution, housebreaking, gambling, dope pushing, etc.—as a way of earning an income. Those who don't turn to crime still come into contact with and are affected by the mystique of organized crime, a mystique which is widespread in the ghetto. This mystique asserts that it is possible to spit in the face of the major legal and moral imperatives of society and still be a financial success and achieve power and influence.[8]

To the extent that the Panthers were successful in penetrating the hard core of the ghetto and recruiting black youth, it would seem that they would be forced to confront the social implications of organized crime and its meaning for black liberation. They were well equipped to do this, since many of their own activists and leaders —such as Cleaver—were ex-criminals. Cleaver did attempt to present such an analysis shortly before he disappeared from public view last year, but he did not take his analysis far enough and consequently his conclusions only served to confuse the matter further.

Numerous sociological studies have shown that in many respects organized crime is only the reverse side of American business.[9] It provides desirable—though proscribed—goods and services, which are not available to the public through "normal" business channels. And, although there is much public ranting against crime, organized crime—and it must be organized to succeed as a business—enjoys a certain degree of immunity from prosecution due to the collusion of police and public officials. Moreover, organized crime constantly seeks—as would any good cor-

[8] Restated—financial success requires occasional "stretching" of law or morality—this also expresses a favorite maxim of American business.
[9] See for example, Gus Tyler (ed.), *Organized Crime in America* (Ann Arbor: University of Michigan Press, 1962). One could also argue that business is the obverse side of organized crime. A host of studies of "white-collar crime"—beginning with Edwin H. Sutherland's classic, *White Collar Crime* (New York: Dryden Press, 1949)—could be called upon to support this contention.

poration—to expand and even legitimitize its own power, but it has no serious motive to revamp the present social structure because it is that structure, with all its inherent flaws and contradictions, which provides a climate in which organized crime can flourish. Hence, it comes as no surprise that in at least one major riot (in Baltimore), police recruited local criminals to help quell the rebellion. The criminals gladly collaborated with the cops because heavy looting during the riot had seriously depressed prices for stolen goods and otherwise disrupted the illegal business operations upon which the criminals depended for their livelihood.

Cleaver in his analysis, however, misread the social function of organized crime. In speeches and articles, he voiced approval of such underworld notables as Al Capone and Machine Gun Kelly on the grounds that their criminal activities were instrumental in building the present power of ethnic groups such as the Italians and the Irish. He concluded that beneath the public façade there is a history of intense struggle for ethnic group power in the urban centers of America, and that organized criminal activity has played an important part in advancing the status of various groups. But Cleaver failed to note that organized crime has sought to advance itself totally *within* the framework of the established society. It seeks more power for itself, and as a side effect it may bring more money into the hands of this or that ethnic group, but organized crime is far from being a revolutionary force. On the contrary, its social function is to provide an informally sanctioned outlet for impulses that officially are outlawed. It thereby acts to uphold and preserve the present social order.

Cleaver's analysis, to the extent that it reflected Panther thinking, revealed the organization's uncertainty about its objectives. This problem stemmed from an inadequate analysis of the manifold ways in which the American social structure absorbs and neutralizes dissent. However, the purge of criminal elements from the ranks of the or-

ganization in early 1969 and the reassertion of the role
of the party as a *political* vanguard indicated that the
Panther leadership had recognized the flaws in Cleaver's
analysis. This was certainly to be hoped for, because if
they did not, then the organization might well degenerate
into little more than a black version of the Mafia.

The heavy stress that the Panthers laid on arming and
military tactics also had some debilitating repercussions
within the organization. Political work suffered, because
some members viewed the group primarily as a military
organization. Matters grew so serious that the Panther
weekly newspaper ran an article reminding members that
the organization was a political party:

> The purely military viewpoint is highly developed
> among quite a few members.
> a. Some party members regard military affairs and
> politics as opposed to each other and refuse to recog-
> nize that military affairs are only one means of accom-
> plishing political tasks.
> b. They don't understand that the Black Panther Party
> is an armed body for carrying out the political tasks of
> revolution. We should not confine ourselves merely to
> fighting. But we must also shoulder important tasks as
> doing propaganda among the people, organizing the
> people, arming the people, and helping them to establish
> revolutionary political power for Black people.
> Without these objectives fighting loses its meaning and
> the Black Panther Party loses the reason for its existence.

Finally, the usefulness of the electoral campaign which
the Panthers ran in 1968 must be assayed. Several Panther
officials ran for office on the Peace and Freedom ticket
in November. In terms of percentages of the total vote
cast, Bobby Seale fared best, with better than 8 percent of
the fifty-six thousand ballots returned for a State Assembly
seat. Since there obviously could be no hope of winning,
the Panthers justified these campaigns on the grounds
that they were organizational and educational tools. However, since the Panther candidates ran on the Peace and

Freedom ticket, this doubtlessly confused many black people and annoyed others who wanted to cast a vote for the Panther platform rather than for the Peace and Freedom party. On the other hand, this arrangement probably accounted for the fact that, in some racially mixed areas, Panther candidates collected more votes than in all-black communities. But this was hardly an asset to an organization which was trying to organize the black communities.

In terms of educational impact, the Panthers got more mileage out of the Huey Newton defense campaign, the controversy over Eldridge Cleaver's course at the University of California,[10] and the San Francisco State College student strike, because, in all of these affairs, clearly defined issues relevant to the black community were raised within topical contexts, and they were widely reported in the mass media. In the electoral campaign, however, attention was focused on the personalities of the major candidates, and it was exceedingly difficult for minority candidates to raise issues or get serious press coverage. Peace and Freedom candidates (including Panthers) were ignored or dismissed by the media as inconsequential kooks.

For groups like the Panthers, the mass media are usually more of a detriment than a help. True, the media publicized the Panthers, but this was done all too frequently in the context of cheap sensationalizing and outright distortion. The Panther program and the ideas of Panther leaders were conveyed to the public literally *in spite of* the media.

The survival and expansion of the Panthers as a black political organization will depend on intensive local organizing around concrete issues. If it is deemed useful for their purposes to secure a given office or win a certain referendum, and there is a realistic prospect of winning,

[10] Cleaver had been asked to give ten lectures in an experimental course on racism in American society. Governor Reagan and the Board of Regents, in classic displays of open racism, tried to squelch the course on various pretexts, including Cleaver's "lack of qualifications."

then the matter should be pursued on that basis. But dabbling in elections on the pretext of "organizing and educating" is an unnecessary waste of scarce resources. This activity may inflate egos, but it does little to build a mass-based organization.

(4)

SNCC and the Panthers certainly did not speak for all black radicals, but a discussion of these two organizations helps to clarify problems that any radical must be prepared to confront. The two groups sought to give some revolutionary content to the black rebellion, and they helped to fuel the black student movement, but the conclusion remains that revolutionary rhetoric is no substitute for a thorough radical analysis upon which a program can be constructed. Both SNCC and the Panthers tried to provide an analysis, but because of the uncertainties and ambivalences of their own leaders, the basic content varied from month to month, sometimes even contradicting previous formulations. The Panthers produced the beginnings of a full program, and while this was of great importance, it was only incidentally tied in with a specific analysis and strategy. Hence, the continuing main task for the black radical is to construct an interlocked analysis, program, and strategy which offers black people a realistic hope of achieving liberation.

VII. CONCLUSION:
TOWARD A TRANSITIONAL PROGRAM

Since the masses of black people are not going to be integrated into the economy in the foreseeable future, as the
reformers would have one believe, and since there are few
signs of an imminent revolution in this country, contrary
to the hopes of some radicals, it is necessary for the black
liberation movement to devise a transitional program,
which will operate until such time as conditions develop
that will make possible full liberation through social revolution. This program must be aimed at building a mass
revolutionary organization, and it must facilitate community development and offer constructive interim reforms.
  Black people cannot afford the social injustices of capitalism. They cannot afford a system which creates privileged classes within an already superexploited and under-
privileged community. They cannot afford a system which
organizes community resources and then distributes the
resulting wealth in a hierarchal fashion, with those who
need least getting most. Neither can black people afford
some half-hearted compromise which would make the
black community in general, and its educated classes in
particular, subservient to the expansionist needs of corporate capitalism. Of course, capital must be accumulated
to make possible the economic development of the black
community, but this must be done in a way that precludes
the enrichment of one class at the expense of those below
it.
  One program for this sort of economic development
was outlined three decades ago by W. E. B. DuBois. In

his autobiographical essay, *Dusk of Dawn*, DuBois, then over seventy years old, succeeded in modifying and merging black nationalism with radical socialism. The outgrowth was a program for what he termed a "co-operative commonwealth" in black America.

DuBois had come to the realization that while it was necessary to agitate for equality, the struggle would be slow and painful, and genuine equality for blacks in America probably would not be forthcoming for many, many years. Racism, he concluded, was not due simply to ignorance or deliberate maliciousness on the part of whites. These played a part, but more fundamental were the deeply ingrained habits which sprang from (frequently unconscious) economic motives. To white America, black people were a resource to be exploited ruthlessly—and racism facilitated this exploitation by degrading blacks in the eyes of whites, thereby placing the former outside the pale of normal moral or humanistic compunction. DuBois believed that this deeper cause of racism could be changed only slowly, and in the meantime it was necessary to develop the inner economic and social strength of the black community.

At the same time, however, he refused to accept racial separation as the ultimate solution to the race problem. For this reason he opposed "back to Africa" and other emigration schemes. To the degree that segregation is a reality it must be dealt with in the most constructive manner possible, he felt, but this by no means implies that blacks should meekly submit to segregation.

DuBois advocated economic development, but he opposed any program of black capitalism on the grounds that this "will have inserted into the ranks of the Negro race a new cause of division, a new attempt to subject the masses of the race to an exploiting capitalist class of their own people."[1] Instead he insisted that the principle of democracy must be applied to economic relations.

[1] W. E. B. DuBois, *Dusk of Dawn* (New York: Schocken, 1968), p. 208.

I had been brought up with the democratic idea that [the] general welfare was the object of democratic action in the state, of allowing the governed a voice in government. But through the crimson illumination of war [World War I], I realized and, afterward by traveling around the world, saw even more clearly that so-called democracy today was allowing the mass of people to have only limited voice in government; that democratic control of what are at present the most important functions of men: work and earning a living and distributing goods and services; that here we did not have democracy; we had oligarchy, and oligarchy based on monopoly and income; and this oligarchy was determined to deny democracy in industry as it had once been determined to deny democracy in legislation and choice of officials.[2]

What was required, DuBois contended, was careful planning of the inner economy and social structure of the black community so as to promote maximum development of that community *in toto*. Thus he called for "economic planning to insure adequate income" to the members of the community; establishment of consumer unions; elimination of private profit in merchandising operations; a planned system of black hospitals and socialized medicine; cooperative organization of black professionals so that they could provide service to all in need without regard to their own personal profit; and the establishment of a black-controlled educational system.

There were other details in DuBois' plan, but in substance what he proposed was to create a planned, communal social system in black America. Planned, in the sense that all important aspects of this system were to be thought out and analyzed in advance and then carefully guided in order to facilitate community development. Communal, in the sense that property relations would become social rather than private, thereby avoiding economically inspired class division, and making economic exploitation more difficult. Communal, in the sense also

[2] *Ibid.*, p. 285.

of strengthening family and group ties and building a stronger sense of community among black people so that all become dedicated to the welfare of the group rather than personal advancement. The cost of such a program, DuBois maintained, must be borne by the black community itself, rather than by white people or white-dominated institutions. It can be objected, however, that the community does not possess sufficient resources to finance such a program. This objection cannot be ignored, but if neocolonialism is to be avoided, it is essential that control over the use of any outside aid must rest completely in the hands of the black community. This in turn demands thorough political organization of the entire community.

On this latter point DuBois had little to say, and this was a serious flaw in his plan. He did not explain how it was to be implemented. He did not describe a social agency then in existence, or to be created, which could adopt his plan as its program. Perhaps he still cherished hopes that the NAACP could be convinced of the viability of his program, despite the fact that his political thinking diverged dramatically from the politics of the NAACP, and he had split with that organization some years earlier.

Many years later, Harold Cruse, under the influence of DuBois, drafted a similar program for Harlem. Cruse, however, argued that black intellectuals and a new black middle class were to play an important part in implementing this program. There is certainly a role for members of the black middle class, but their past failures and current growing attachment to corporate imperialism raise serious doubts as to their leadership capabilities. The increasing militancy and spirit of independence exhibited among ordinary black workers, as seen in Detroit and other cities, strongly suggests that if the black community is to win real self-determination it must cultivate a militant leadership cadre drawn from its less-privileged classes. The danger of an irresponsible elite arising is far less acute if the leadership of a movement is organically related to the rank and file; that is, if leaders do not come from or otherwise form a social stratum with interests differing from those of their followers.

Implicit in DuBois' program was a vision of a separate and largely self-sufficient black economy. This was not possible in 1940, and it is not possible today. The black community does not have control over all of the essential goods and services which it requires for survival. Moreover, as long as corporate capitalism exists, the black community is not likely to acquire such control. This, however, should not automatically preclude a struggle to create an all-encompassing, planned communal social system on a national scale and with strong international ties. Such a struggle would begin to break down capitalist property relations within the black community, replacing them with more socially useful communal relations. Consequently, any benefits accruing from the planned economy could be distributed throughout the community according to individual or family needs, or income could be reinvested to increase the capital assets of the community. Furthermore, this struggle would aid materially in breaking black dependency on white society. Considerable capital and other white-owned resources within the community could be gradually freed and restored to the community. Many concrete reforms could be won in the course of the struggle and, as long as these reforms did not become ends in themselves and their relation to corporate capitalism were fully understood, this could be immensely helpful. The program of the Black Panther party is a list of some such needed reforms and concessions.

The establishment of close working relationships with revolutionary forces around the world would be of great importance. The experiences of Third World revolutionaries in combating American imperialism could be quite useful to black liberation fighters. For the moment, mutual support between Afro-American and Third World revolutionaries is more verbal than tangible, but the time could come when this situation is reversed, and black people are well advised to begin now to work toward this kind of revolutionary, international solidarity. Imperialism is a worldwide force whose final defeat will require a united effort on the part of its victims, and other anti-imperialist nations.

Finally, the struggle to implement this program should increase the organization, and consequently the fighting ability, of the black community. What is called for is an independent black political party capable of providing militant leadership. To the degree that the proposed party is successful in implementing the program sketched above, it will grow in strength and experience, gradually establishing itself as the effective governing power of black America. This will require many years, but it is not an unreasonable projection, so long as the political party is solidly based upon the masses of ordinary black working people. This means that the popular masses must provide the rank and file and the leadership, and the party must always seek to extend itself among this segment of the black population. Here lies the great majority of black people, and they must lead themselves if self-determination is to be meaningful.

Of course, the party should seek also to encompass, insofar as this is possible, the entire black population. Black intellectuals and members of the black middle class should be encouraged to participate—as individuals. However, because of the inherent ambivalence of these classes, they must not be allowed, *as classes,* to assume leadership of the party. As classes, intellectuals and petty bourgeois blacks are as likely to be reactionary as they are to be revolutionary, and for this reason they must always be somewhat suspect.

The idea of a black political party is not particularly new. In 1904 the National Liberty party was organized and ran George Edwin Taylor as its presidential candidate. The early 1960s witnessed the rise and demise of the Freedom Now party, and currently there exist the Lowndes County Freedom party and the Black Panther party. Both of the latter built solid community bases, and it is within the realm of possibility that one or the other of them will emerge as the kind of political instrument being discussed here.

With respect to encounters with white America, a black party should not rely on exclusively legal campaigns, nor should it restrict itself to all-out street warfare. Instead it must devise a strategy of calculated confrontation, using a mixture of tactics to fit a variety of contingencies. The object of this strategy should be to abolish, by any means possible, the real control of white society over the black community, and to extract needed reforms. Tactical innovation should be the order of the day, and anything workable goes—depending on specific conditions and the relation of forces—from legal struggle, to electoral politics, to direct action campaigns, to force.[3] In short, what is required is a coordinated, multifaceted, multilevel struggle which will enable black America to defeat corporate imperialism and free itself from the shackles of domestic neocolonialism.

Under the aegis of a militant political party—a party which acts not as an occasional vote-getting machine but as a continuously functioning governing instrumentality —diverse activities, from efforts to establish rank-and-file labor union caucuses to struggles for community control of local schools, can assume a cohesiveness and meaning, independent of their immediate success or failure. Within the framework of the party, these activities can become integrated into a unified strategy for winning black self-determination. Over the long run, they could well become

[3] The use of organized force should not be discounted out of hand, nor should it be glorified. This is simply one of a host of tactical questions which will confront a militant party devoted to black liberation. The important thing to bear in mind is that the objectives of the black liberation movement are basically political and economic, rather than military, and every proposed tactic must be appraised according to whether it will bring these objectives nearer to realization.

the individual building blocks of social revolution in America.

Black liberation, however, will not come about solely through the activities of black people. Black America cannot be genuinely liberated until white America is transformed into a humanistic society free of exploitation and class division. The black and white worlds, although separate and distinct, are too closely intertwined—geographically, politically, and economically—for the social maladies of one not to affect the other. Both must change if either is to progress to new and liberating social forms.

It goes without saying that black people should not postpone their freedom struggle until white America rouses itself out of its lethargy. On the contrary, blacks should never desist from struggle and agitation. But neither should black people deceive themselves into thinking that simple separation from oppressive white society will solve the problem. Blacks and whites here have lived in separate worlds for four centuries, but this was hardly an economic or political boon to black people. In the quest for black liberation, white society cannot be ignored or cast aside with a sigh of relief. It must be changed. Otherwise, the racism and exploitative social relations which characterize that society will defeat even the best efforts of black freedom fighters. This is one of the clearest lessons of the black experience in America.

This raises for the nth time the thorny question of domestic allies. The black liberation movement needs allies. It needs allies who are capable both of aiding the black movement and of promoting social change in white America. In recent years a growing sense of unity has developed between Afro-Americans and Puerto Ricans, Mexican-Americans, American Indians, and Orientals. This is good, because all of these communities desire to abolish their present status of semicolonial dependency on white society. As to white allies, they are presently limited largely to militant students and white radicals. The value of these allies should not be underestimated. An advanced industrial society depends ever more heavily on its educated classes for their technical and managerial skills. The student revolt, which has surged across campuses throughout this country, can precipitate a movement to upset the delicate machinery of corporate capitalism. The student militants are demanding greater control over the educational process and, indeed, a redefinition of it. They seek to make education the servant of the best impulses in man rather than the servant of a base and twisted society. White radicals, too, are helpful, despite their small numbers, because they are what might be termed a "leading minority": they are capable of initiating skirmishes, which then mobilize thousands of non-radical whites. Witness the antiwar movement, which started with a handful and grew to include hundreds of thousands.

But black people must assemble a more powerful array of allies than these. Social change requires the active support, or at least benevolent neutrality, of the major part of society. Students, radicals, and minority groups are important, but they are not the majority that is needed. Whether this majority can ever be mustered is problematical. It is currently fashionable among black militants to write off the revolutionary potential of the bulk of the white working population because of its unreconstructed racism. The myopia of the labor unions is adduced as proof.

Two factors, however, may upset this reactionary status quo. First, the advance of mechanization and cybernation promises to undermine the security of even those who believe they are safely ensconced in suburbia. Not only does the industrial system require relatively fewer blue-collar workers, but automation is even making inroads into the ranks of white-collar clerical and middle-level employees.[4] This presents a great challenge to organized labor. The labor movement is in decline. Desperate but short-sighted labor leaders are making concessions to the

[4] See "Automation and the Work Force" by Ben B. Seligman in Robert Theobald (ed.), *The Guaranteed Income.*

rise of automation in a last-ditch effort to preserve their personal power and hold their unions together. This policy is bound to lead to the collapse of organized labor as a social force. The only alternative is for the labor movement to begin organizing the unemployed, white-collar and government employees, and to move beyond traditional union issues and demand that working people as an organized body have greater say in the functioning of the total economy. This program probably transcends both the ability and narrowly perceived self-interest of America's labor bureaucracy, but the rise of rank-and-file militancy since 1966 and widespread organizing committees among white-collar workers point in a more hopeful direction.

The second factor is even more stark. The economic gap between rich and poor nations is widening at an alarming rate. At the same time the world's population is skyrocketing. Already it is estimated that there are 3.5 billion people on this planet, 55 percent of them in Asia alone. It is expected that by the year 2000 this figure could climb well above six billion. Most of these people will be ill-fed, ill-clothed, and angry. The standard solution offered by the American government is more birth control. But, as was suggested in Chapter V, there is, in many underdeveloped areas of the world, an equally pressing need for rational reorganization and redistribution of wealth and resources, which must be done on a national and international basis if a worldwide catastrophe of unprecedented proportions is to be averted. Many population experts agree that the world has the resource capability to support anticipated population growth in the foreseeable future. The question to be decided is whether anachronistic political forms will be allowed to obstruct rational utilization of these resources.

Today's generation of Americans, in the world's richest and most powerful country, have it within their power to make this decision. And some decision must be made soon. Either a fortress America will be established—in which case a bloody and protracted international conflict can be anticipated within fifteen to twenty-five years—or America will take part in building a rational world order in which all men participate, and through which the planet's resources can be intelligently organized and distributed in accordance with need.

The first uncertain steps toward some kind of decision in this urgent matter already are being taken in this country. The Third World, the underdeveloped world, exists just as surely within America as it does across the seas. In the dialectic between black and white America, a preview of what may be in store for the world can be glimpsed. If black liberation is indeed emasculated and equated with corporate imperialism—if this country evinces no better understanding of the necessities of liberation and self-determination—then the hope that the United States will somehow transform itself into a welcome member of the community of humankind is further diminished, even extinguished. The script will have been written, the cast selected, and the stage set for yet another tragedy in man's tortuous ascent toward a just society.

BIBLIOGRAPHY

Aptheker, Herbert A. (ed.), *A Documentary History of the Negro People in the United States* (two vols.) (New York: Citadel, 1968).

The Autobiography of Malcolm X (New York: Grove, 1965).

Baran, Paul A. and Sweezy, Paul M., *Monopoly Capital* (New York: Monthly Review, 1966).

Barbour, Floyd B. (ed.), *The Black Power Revolt* (Boston: Porter Sargent, 1968).

Bennett, Jr., Lerone, *Black Power U.S.A.* (Chicago: Johnson, 1967).

Boggs, James, *Manifesto for a Black Revolutionary Party* (Philadelphia: Pacesetters Publishing House, 1969).

Breitman, George, *The Last Year of Malcolm X* (New York: Merit, 1967).

—— (ed.), *Malcolm X Speaks* (New York: Grove, 1966).

Broderick, Francis L. and Meier, August (eds.), *Negro Protest Thought in the Twentieth Century* (New York: Bobbs-Merrill, 1966).

Broom, Leonard and Glenn, Norval, *Transformation of the Negro American* (New York: Harper & Row, 1965).

Carmichael, Stokely and Hamilton, Charles V., *Black Power: The Politics of Liberation in America* (New York: Random House, 1967).

Cruse, Harold, *The Crisis of the Negro Intellectual* (New York: William Morrow, 1967).

——, *Rebellion or Revolution?* (New York: William Morrow, 1968).

286   BLACK AWAKENING IN CAPITALIST AMERICA

Domhoff, G. William, *Who Rules America?* (Englewood Cliffs, New Jersey: Prentice-Hall, 1967).

DuBois, W. E. B., *Dusk of Dawn* (New York: Schocken, 1968).

Fall, Bernard (ed.), *Ho Chi Minh on Revolution* (New York: Signet, 1967).

Fanon, Frantz, *The Wretched of the Earth* (New York: Grove, 1965).

Fitch, Bob and Oppenheimer, Mary, *Ghana: End of an Illusion* (New York: Monthly Review, 1966).

Foster, William Z., *The Negro People in American History* (New York: International Publishers Company, Inc., 1954).

Frank, Andre Gunder, *Capitalism and Underdevelopment in Latin America* (New York: Monthly Review, 1967).

Frazier, E. Franklin, *Black Bourgeoisie* (New York: Collier, 1962).

Galbraith, John Kenneth, *The New Industrial State* (Boston: Houghton Mifflin, 1967).

Grant, Joanne (ed.), *Black Protest: History, Documents, and Analyses; 1619 to the Present* (Greenwich, Connecticut: Fawcett, 1968).

Hayden, Tom, *Rebellion in Newark* (New York: Vintage, 1967).

Horowitz, David, *The Free World Colossus* (New York: Hill and Wang, 1965).

Karenga, Ron, *The Quotable Karenga* (pamphlet) (Los Angeles, US Organization, 1967).

Kinzer, Robert H. and Sagarin, Edward, *The Negro in American Business: The Conflict between Separatism and Integration* (New York: Greenberg, 1950).

Lasch, Christopher, *The Agony of the American Left* (New York: Alfred A. Knopf, 1969).

Leggett, John C., *Class, Race, and Labor* (New York: Oxford University Press, 1968).

Lenin, V. I., *The Right of Nations to Self-Determination*

(New York: International Publishers Company, Inc., 1951).

Lester, Julius, *Look Out, Whitey! Black Power's Gon' Get Your Mama* (New York: Dial, 1968).

Lundberg, Ferdinand, *The Rich and the Super-Rich* (New York: Lyle Stuart, 1968).

The Negro and the City (New York: Time-Life Books, 1968).

Nelson, Truman, *The Right of Revolution* (Boston: Beacon, 1968).

Nkrumah, Kwame, *Neo-Colonialism: The Last Stage of Imperialism* (New York: International Publishers Company, Inc., 1966).

Stalin, Joseph, *Marxism and the National Question* (Moscow: Foreign Languages Publishing House, 1954).

Theobald, Robert (ed.), *The Guaranteed Income* (New York: Doubleday, 1966).

Williams, Eric, *Capitalism and Slavery* (New York: Capricorn, 1966).

Woddis, Jack, *Introduction to Neo-Colonialism* (New York: International Publishers Company, Inc., 1967).

INDEX

Addonizio, Hugh, 130, 134
Aden, 16
Africa, 35, 36, 37, 38, 253, 254; colonialism in, 7–8, 11, 13, 14–16, 60–65, 171; colonization of, 91, 117; culture of, 167–68, 171; nationalism in, 60–65, 97; pan-Africanism, 97
African Union Company, 94
"Afro-American," use of term, 180
Afro-American student groups, 257–62
Algeria, 60–65, 171
Allen, Charles R., 203–5
Allenwood, Pa., detention camp, 204
Alliance for Progress, 77, 242–43
Allies, whites as, 35, 36, 54ff., 251, 281–82
American Colonization Society, 91
American Indians, 7, 281
American Negro Labor Congress (ANLC), 102–3
Anti-black riots, 93, 100
Anti-poverty programs, 26, 75, 144, 153, 164
Antiwar movement, 49, 112–13, 255, 282. See also Vietnam war
Aptheker, Herbert, 90n, 96n, 99n
Arab-Israeli conflict, 254, 256
Army (armed forces), U.S., 9,
10, 56; antiriot measures, 201–2, 207; blacks in, 99–100, 104–5; Reconstruction era, 93
Art, black, 165, 168, 172, 174–79
Assassinations, 30, 31, 39
Assimilationalism, 89, 256
Atlanta, Ga., 224; B. T. Washington's Exposition Address, 98
Atlantic City (N.J.) national convention (1964), 25
Autobiography of Malcolm X, 31n
Automation, 3, 105, 116, 226, 282
Avon Park, Fla., detention camp, 204

B&H Enterprises antiriot equipment, 198
Baltimore, Md., CORE meeting (1966), 65
Banking industry, 154, 155, 218, 224
Bank of America, 224
Banks, black-owned, 224
Baran, Paul A., 212
Bedford-Stuyvesant area, Brooklyn, N.Y.C., 186n
Bennett, Lerone, Jr., 9n, 92, 268
Berle, A. A., 18n
Birth control, 169–71
"Black," replacement of "Negro" by, 180

Brown, H. Rap, 171n, 181, 196, 202, 249; elected to Black Panther cabinet, 267; program of, 249, 253
Browne, Robert, 44
Bundy, McGeorge, 22, 71–77, 146, 149–51, 212
Burrell, Berkeley G., 220n
Buses, segregation on, 106, 110–11
Businesses, black, 52–53, 149–50, 153–56, 185–91, 210–45. See also under "Buy black" campaign, 159, 167

California, black business in, 222, 224; Panthers' political activity, 264, 271–72
Cambodia, 40, 42
Camp, Abraham, 91
Camus, Albert, 128
Capitalism, U.S., 37, 57–58 (see also Corporate capitalism); black, 19, 52–54, 149, 153–56, 158ff., 182–83, 186–91, 210–45, 274–78; and black liberation and nationalism, 48, 91–95, 100–1, 114–20, 149, 151n, 153ff., 161ff., 176ff., 193–245, 246–73, 274–78, 281–84; black radicals and, 251–52; and colonialism, 7, 10–20; and racism, 185
Cargo Cults, Melanesian, 122–24
Carmichael, Stokely, 6, 21, 22, 46–60, 78, 136, 145, 196, 202, 211n, 247–53; and Forman, 266–67; Gould on TV exposure of, 181–82; ousted from SNCC, 267; and SNCC, 247–53, 254, 256, 266–67
Carroll, James, 258

Carson, Robert, 183n
Carter, Philip, 148
Castro, Fidel, 43, 77
Chambers, Ernest W., 3
Chase Manhattan Bank, 254
Chauvinism, black male, 168–71
Chemical Mace, 198
Chicago, Ill., national convention (1968), 25n; open-housing campaign, 113; poverty areas, 27; riots, 196, 201; sit-ins, 65
Chicago (Ill.) Daily Defender, 231
Christianity, 12, 107. See also White Anglo-Saxon Protestants
Christian Science Monitor, 230
Church (religion), black, 12–13
Cities, 51, 129–30, 137–44 (see also specific aspects, cities, organizations); black self-government, 187–88; crisis and revolts in, 27–28, 193–245 (see also Urban revolts); ghettos, 7 (see also Ghettos)
Civilian review boards, 130
Civil Rights Act of 1875, 93
Civil Rights Congress, 38n, 66
Civil Rights Law (1964), 24–26
Civil rights legislation, 14, 21, 24–26. See also specific areas, legislation
Civil rights movement, 19, 23, 51, 110–13, 144ff. (see also specific aspects, individuals, organizations, etc.); black power and, 21ff. (see also Black power movement); failure of, 70, 110, 178

United Nations, 38–39, 86,
104; Black Panthers and,
266; SNCC and, 254–55
United States Commission on
Civil Rights, 233
Universal Negro Improvement
Association (UNIA), 100–1
Urban Coalition, 17
Urban Development Corp.,
189
Urban League. *See* National
Urban League
Urban rebellions (urban crises), 27–28, 58, 70–78ff.,
113, 126–43ff., 152, 207
(*see also* Riots; specific aspects, individuals, organizations, places); corporate
capitalism and, 193–245; violence in, 136ff., 152, 195ff.
(*see also* Violence)
US organization, 165

Venezuela, 243
Vietminh (guerrilla) forces,
42
Vietnamese women, role of,
170
Vietnam war, 3, 23, 40–45, 68,
73, 77, 113, 208, 254, 255
Vigilante groups, 200
Violence, 47–48, 58–59, 61–
64, 69, 76, 153 (*see also*
Riots); black radicals and
use of, 248–49; ghetto rebellions and, 136ff., 195ff.
(*see also* Urban rebellions);
government policy and,
207–11; "law and order"
and, 195ff.; measures
against, 195–245
Voting, blacks and, 25, 33, 79,
143, 147–48, 231n. *See also*
Political activity
Voting Rights Act (1965), 25

Woddis, Jack, 11n
Wall Street Journal, 114, 165,
225, 230
Ware, George, 254, 256
Washington, Booker T., 93–
96, 98–99, 100; Atlanta Ex-
position Address, 98–99
Washington, D.C., 52; Black
United Front, 136, 142;
riots, 207
Washington Post, 78, 137, 203
Watts, Daniel, 231
Watts district, Los Angeles,
Calif., 27, 28, 82, 165, 223
Watts Manufacturing Co., 223
Ways, Max, 216, 232
Weapons, antiriot, 197–200,
207, 208
We Charge Genocide, 104
Welfare payments, 228, 239
Welfare programs, 70, 194–
95, 214, 228
White Anglo-Saxon Protes-
tants, 174
White Citizens Council, 110
White Collar Crime, 269n
White House Conference on
Civil Rights (1966), 194–95
White militants (white radi-
cals), as allies, 35, 36, 54ff.,
251, 281–82. *See also* spe-
cific organizations
Who Rules America? (Dom-
hoff), 17n
Wickenburg, Ariz., detention
camp, 204
Wilkins, Roy, 145, 152
Williams, Robert, 23, 28–30,
40, 48
Wills, Garry, 198–99
Wilmington, Del., 196
Wilson, John, 255
Wilson, Woodrow, 99
Women: black, role of, 168–
71; Vietnamese, 170
Woods, Joseph I., 201